Celebrity Society

On television, in magazines and books, on the Internet and in films, celebrities of all sorts seem to monopolize our attention. *Celebrity Society* brings new dimensions to our understanding of celebrity, capturing the way in which the figure of 'the celebrity' is bound up with the emergence of modernity. It outlines how the 'celebrification of society' is not just the twentieth-century product of Hollywood and television, but a long-term historical process, beginning with the printing press, theatre and art.

By looking beyond the accounts of celebrity 'culture', Robert van Krieken develops an analysis of 'celebrity society', with its own constantly changing social practices and structures, moral grammar, construction of self and identity, legal order and political economy organized around the distribution of visibility, attention and recognition. Drawing on the work of Norbert Elias, the book explains how contemporary celebrity society is the heir (or heiress) of court society, taking on but also democratizing many of the functions of the aristocracy. The book also develops the idea of celebrity as driven by the 'economics of attention', because attention has become a vital and increasingly valuable resource in the information age.

This engaging new book will be a valuable resource for students and scholars in sociology, politics, history, celebrity studies, cultural studies, the sociology of media and cultural theory.

Robert van Krieken is Professor of Sociology at the University of Sydney, and Visiting Professor at University College Dublin. His research interests include the sociology of law, criminology, the sociology of childhood, processes of civilization and decivilization, cultural genocide, as well as contributing to the theoretical debates around the work of Elias, Foucault, Luhmann and Latour. Previous books include *Norbert Elias* (1998), *Celebrity and the Law* (2010, co-authored) and *Sociology* 4th edition (2009, co-authored).

Celebrity Society

Robert van Krieken

Routledge
Taylor & Francis Group

LONDON AND NEW YORK

First published 2012 by Routledge
2 Park Square, Milton Park, Abingdon, Oxon, OX14 4RN

Simultaneously published in the USA and Canada
by Routledge

711 Third Avenue, New York, NY 10017

*Routledge is an imprint of the Taylor & Francis Group, an informa
business*

© 2012 Robert van Krieken

The right of Robert van Krieken to be identified as author of this work has
been asserted by him in accordance with sections 77 and 78 of the
Copyright, Designs and Patents Act 1988.

British Library Cataloguing in Publication Data
A catalogue record for this book is available from the British Library

Library of Congress Cataloging in Publication Data
Van Krieken, Robert.
  Celebrity society / Robert van Krieken.
    p. cm.
  Includes bibliographical references and index.
  1. Fame—Social aspects. 2. Celebrities. 3. Media—Social aspects.
  I. Title.
  BJ1470.5.V36 2012
  306.4—dc23

                                           2011048934

ISBN: 978-0-415-58149-3 (hbk)
ISBN: 978-0-415-58150-9 (pbk)
ISBN: 978-0-203-11634-0 (ebk)

Typeset in Times New Roman
by RefineCatch Limited, Bungay, Suffolk

MIX
Paper from
responsible sources
FSC® C004839
www.fsc.org

Printed and bound in Great Britain by
CPI Group (UK) Ltd, Croydon, CR0 4YY

It is a principal end of government to regulate this passion [for the esteem of others], which in its turn becomes a principal means of government. It is the only adequate instrument of order and subordination in society, and alone commands effectual obedience to laws, since without it neither human reason, nor standing armies, would ever produce that great effect. Every personal quality, and every blessing of fortune, is cherished in proportion to its capacity of gratifying this universal affection for the esteem, the sympathy, admiration and congratulations of the public. Beauty in the face, elegance of figure, grace of attitude and motion, riches, honors, every thing is weighed in the scale, and desired, not so much for the pleasure they afford, as the attention they command.

John Adams (*Discourses on Davilia*, 1805: 28–29)

Contents

List of illustrations   viii
Preface   ix
Acknowledgements   xii

Introduction: understanding celebrity society   1

1 From fame to celebrity: the celebritization of society   15

2 Producing celebrity and the economics of attention   40

3 Celebrity as a social form: status, charisma and power   62

4 Imagined community and long-distance intimacy   81

5 Celebrity in politics, diplomacy and development   98

6 Business and management celebrity   119

7 Celebrity's futures: 15 minutes of fame, or fame in 15 minutes 132

Notes   145
Bibliography   149
Index   180

Illustrations

Figures

4.1   'I'-Ideal diagram by Sigmund Freud.   87
5.1   Four-fold typology of the positions that politicians can adopt
        in relation to celebrity   111

Table

6.1   Institutional ownership in the 26 largest US corporations   123

Preface

Although I would obviously like this book to be of interest to everyone that has already spent more or less time thinking about celebrity, in many respects its primary concern is to address those readers who would not normally think of celebrity as a particularly serious topic. For myself, when I was first asked to contribute a chapter to a book on celebrity and the law by two colleagues in law at the University of Sydney, Patricia Loughlan and Barbara McDonald, I didn't quite know what to make of the idea. I normally write about, well, *weightier* subjects – cultural genocide, state formation, the historical sociology of childhood, Norbert Elias's theory of civilizing processes, the formation of the modern self. But then I read the sociologist Dick Pels' (2003b) book on the Dutch politician, Pim Fortuyn, who was assassinated in 2002 by an animal-rights activist, Volker van der Graaf, and this changed my mind.

Pels explained how Fortuyn was introducing a new, romantic and emotional style into Dutch political life, organized around a skilful approach to concentrating attention on himself and essentially constructing himself as a celebrity. Fortuyn – interestingly, a sociologist who left university life to become a politician – had turned himself into an easily recognizable brand, fusing together a particular mode of address, speech, appearance and behaviour (Pels 2003b: 39). His trademark catchphrase, which he would often utter as a sound-bite, was 'at your service', which suggests that he clearly understood, in ways that no other Dutch politician did, a central feature of celebrity: the particular kind of power relationship between the celebrity and their audience in which the recognition accorded to the prominent individual is in exchange for their acknowledgement that it can always be withdrawn.

The 1930s American actress Myrna Loy also used the phrase 'at your service' to describe her relationship with her audience and admirers, and she said she would like to tell aspiring movie stars that her 'boss' was 'the Public' (Service 1970: 142). As Pels has observed, 'on his own he made it clear that a new celebrity-politician was busily emerging which, via public visibility delivered by the media, can become a significant factor outside the established party-political order' (2011: 120). Together with more recent examples of similar approaches to politics such as that of Geert Wilders in the Netherlands, it seemed clear that there was potentially an important shift taking place in how politicians related to their voters, and that this had to be approached in terms of an understanding of the logic of celebrity.

A second stimulus to rethinking the place of celebrity in sociological theory and research more broadly was re-reading C. Wright Mills's (1957) *The Power Elite*. Everyone who has read the book will have had their own particular concerns filtering how they engaged with it. When I read it, a long time ago now, the issue was the affinity of his portrayal of the operation of power, as organized in terms of a set of interlocking elites, to that of Ralph Miliband in *The State in Capitalist Society*, and how to relate this construction of the state under capitalism as the instrument of capitalists to structuralist accounts such as that of Nicos Poulantzas (1975) and his conception of the 'relative autonomy' of the capitalist state. The focus was not on the details of the power elite, but on whether one should think in terms of an elite at all. Not surprisingly, and I don't think I was alone in this, I skipped over the chapter on 'The Celebrities', considering it not especially relevant to the more important question of what kind of structural constraints a capitalist economy imposed on state action.

To the extent that this is what many other readers of Mills's book did in disciplines such as sociology and politics, this is, with the wisdom of hindsight, very much a pity, as is the relative neglect of that chapter in the scholarship on celebrity. Mills in fact developed a very substantial analysis of celebrity that any analysis of society should take into account, and which one has to work hard to improve upon. Whether one pays attention to Mills's analysis also marks the borderline between being inclined towards the concept of 'celebrity culture', the more prevalent understanding in media and cultural studies, or that of 'celebrity society', since Mills takes us a long way towards understanding the structure and inner logic of celebrity as a particular social form that is centrally interwoven with the other core features of modern social life, and especially the operation of power.

Having become reasonably familiar with the work of Norbert Elias, and especially his account of 'court society', I also found I could recognize some clear lines of continuity between the kind of 'performative habitus' generated in court society and the dynamics of celebrity–fan relationships. Looking at celebrity through the lens of Elias's analysis suggested the possibility that much of what constitutes the social construction of celebrity today can be understood as a development of the dynamics of court society, and that it was necessary to identity the institutional and structural underpinnings of celebrity along similar lines to court society, making it possible to speak of 'celebrity society' as the contemporary heir (or heiress) of court society.

In many respects the book remains unfinished, abandoned to publication rather than completed, to a large extent because the development of celebrity society keeps throwing up surprises about how much more complex, nuanced and extensive it is than one would first anticipate. New actors, actresses, politicians, musicians and artists in a variety of historical periods are constantly being unearthed, or old ones being reinterpreted in the light of their identities as celebrities, and new relationships between them as celebrities being discovered and rethought. There are many leads that I've only been able to follow a short distance.

Shifting one's cognitive frame from merely noticing the superficiality of celebrity identity – which is not the end of the analysis, but only the beginning – towards thinking in terms of celebrity society as 'court society in a mass media age', and in terms of *attention* as the commodity being traded, of which celebrities themselves are largely the expression – the 'mighty secret' of celebrity, as John Adams put it – opens the door to a enormous range of possibilities for social research and analysis, drawing out an important dimension of the way in which contemporary social and political life operates. The place of celebrity in social science is the process of shifting significantly, and hopefully this book will have made its own contribution to that evolving conversation.

Dublin and Sydney, 2011

Acknowledgements

An earlier and shorter version of some of the discussion in this book was part of my contribution to the book *Celebrity and the Law* by Patricia Loughlan, Barbara McDonald and myself, published by Federation Press in 2010. I would like to express my thanks to Patricia and Barbara for asking me to be part of that project in the first place – it's highly unlikely I would ever have thought of writing about celebrity if they hadn't introduced me to the idea – as well as to Federation Press for their kind permission to include parts of that material here.

Both the University of Sydney and University College Dublin have been very supportive in providing a congenial research environment enabling me to undertake the research for the book and its writing, for which I'm also grateful. I've given talks about the book in a number of arenas, including the students in my Celebrity Society module at UCD and the postgraduate students at the University of Vienna and the Free University, Amsterdam, and I want to thank everyone who has provided me with support and feedback on the earlier versions of these ideas.

Writing always makes life more difficult for one's nearest and dearest, so I am grateful to everyone I've given less time to than I should have for putting up with me, especially my partner, Virginia Watson. Thanks also to Matty, our Labrador, for taking me away from the computer every so often and getting me some exercise.

Introduction

Understanding celebrity society

> Well, you know, it's interesting to see who we choose as our celebrities . . . And why, what makes them tick. You can learn a lot about a society by who it chooses to celebrate.
>
> (Woody Allen, *Celebrity*, 1998, delivered by Judy Davis as 'Robin Simon')

In Stephen Poliakoff's television film *Shooting the Past*, a team of curators is attempting to save a collection of 10 million photographs from destruction in the face of the take-over of the building by the 'Management School of the 21st Century'. The storyline is a reference to the Hulton Picture Collection, and its incorporation within Getty Images in 1996. One of the junior curators, a young woman, Stig, proposes that celebrity may be a useful tool. 'Celebrity', she suggests, 'You have to have a bit of celebrity around somewhere. Nothing much happens any more without it.' This is an observation that often comes to mind today, and it is clear that today we all live in a world of celebrities who increasingly play significant roles in society, economics and politics.

Celebrities have strong emotional resonance, negative as well as positive, both in life and in death – John Lennon, Princess Diana and Michael Jackson are just among the more obvious and recent examples. The economic significance of celebrity is enormous, and the cross-over between the realm of supposedly superficial celebrity and politics appears only to be intensifying, with actors and pop stars becoming politicians, politicians needing to function in the same way as celebrities and increasingly relying on their association with celebrities for their political effectiveness. The more one looks around the world today, the more one sees social, economic and political life being organized around celebrities.

However, we still understand very little about what different celebrities have in common with each other, what celebrity actually means, how its role has changed over time, and what its future development is likely to look like. It is frequently treated as a frothy and insubstantial issue, perhaps a guilty pleasure, and we often 'love to hate' particular celebrities – Paris Hilton is only one more recent example. The focus is mostly on an endless parade of individuals at the expense of seeing what binds them together, what makes celebrity a historically specific social form. In this book, my aim is to reflect on the deeper significance of celebrity for our everyday life, our sense of self, and relations of status, recognition and power. Others have examined celebrity from this general perspective before, and to a large extent I will be merely standing on the shoulders of giants. But there are a number of aspects of my approach that will make the book different from what has gone before, beginning with the title.

Why 'celebrity society'?

The book has been called *Celebrity Society* for two reasons underpinning what I hope will be its distinctive contribution. First, when there is any attempt to understand celebrity in more systematic and analytical terms, the overwhelming inclination has been to turn to the concept 'celebrity culture' (Cashmore 2006; Couldry & Markham 2007; Epstein 2005; Gitlin 1998; Jaffe 2005; Nayar 2008; Rojek 2001; Schickel 1985; Turner 2004; Friedman 1999: 27–43). No doubt this has a lot to do with the fact that, as Graeme Turner notes, 'the heartland of celebrity studies remains within media and cultural studies' (2010: 12), as opposed to the social and political sciences more broadly.

Although the concept 'culture' has its virtues, unless it is given a very particular and rather unusual definition, it is generally not very adept at capturing issues or concerns that go beyond values, mores, attitudes, forms of behaviour, cognitive orientations and ways of life, to understand the social, political and economic structures as well as the institutional foundations of what we experience as 'celebrity'. Thinking in terms of 'celebrity culture' tends to encourage a certain cultural pessimism, where one does little more than bemoan the 'cult' of celebrity and the popular 'obsession' with celebrities. The concept of 'celebrity society' is intended to be something of an antidote to that inclination since, as Anthony Elliott has stressed, it is important to approach celebrity as 'a political, institutionalized phenomenon ' (1998: 834). My argument in this book parallels Elliott's: that it is equally important to pay attention to the *social structuring* of celebrity, by which I mean the ways in which celebrity is assigned, distributed, organized and responded to as a part of a particular form of institutionalized social life.

A useful way to capture this book's approach relates to the account where one begins the analysis. Writers working with the concept 'celebrity culture' will very often start with Daniel Boorstin's (1962) critique of the public relations manufacture of the 'pseudo-event', and his definition of a celebrity as someone 'known for their well-knownness'. Although this captures one aspect of celebrity, it misses a lot, too, and I would much rather begin with two specifically sociological accounts – C. Wright Mills's (1957) analysis of the role of celebrities in the structure and dynamics of power in *The Power Elite*, as well as Robert's Merton's (1968; 1988) discussion of the practices of scientists, and what he called the 'Matthew effect': the way in which scientific reputation can itself generate further rewards and resources. Both of these writers provide, I will be arguing, much more useful foundations for the sociological analysis of celebrity.

Elliott has proposed that 'the task of a theoretically reflective social and political analysis of celebrity' is 'to place the phenomenon within the context of societies, cultures, and polities of the transnational global system of late modernity' (1998: 836). Much of the writing on celebrity does already approach celebrity as an important and meaningful aspect of changing modes of ordering both social relationships and the individual sense of self, as an expression of a particular structured distribution of visibility, recognition and esteem. However, a central part of my argument is that this kind of understanding will be far better served when it is organized around the concept of 'celebrity society' than it is currently with 'celebrity culture'.

Second, the title is also a reference to Norbert Elias's study of what he called 'court society', the particular structuring of social relationships characteristic of the royal and princely courts which emerged in Western Europe from the Middle Ages onwards. Elias saw the aristocracy and their modes of social interaction as far more than just a relic of tradition and feudalism, left behind in the transition to modernity. He argued that court society should be seen as a historically significant form of social organization, with a dual relationship to the bourgeois society which followed it. As Elias put it, 'aristocratic court society developed a civilising and cultural physiognomy which was taken over by professional and commercial bourgeois society partly as a heritage and particular as an antithesis and, preserved in this way, was further developed' (2006: 44). On the one hand, bourgeois morality and forms of life were developed precisely in opposition to those of the courts, particularly the distinction between public and private life, the organization of life around criteria of instrumental, economic rationality, and the placement of a dedication to work at the centre of human existence. On the other hand, bourgeois rationality never actually won the battle with court rationality, and many features of the forms of social relations in court society continued into the modern world.

Whereas Marx looked for the formation of modern social relations and a corresponding personality structure in the logic of the capitalist production process, Weber in Protestantism and bureaucracy, and Foucault in a range of social institutions and systems of knowledge about human beings, Elias argued that the extension of the familial households of French kings and their dependents into a larger 'court society' was a crucial foundation-stone of contemporary psychic structure, or *habitus*, and social relations. Just as there is a connection between aristocracy and celebrity, which is why we can say that celebrities are today's nobility, there is also a connection between court society as a specific social form and 'celebrity society' as its modern heir. Taking a closer look at court society is a counterweight to the tendency to see the history of subjectivity through the lens of the bourgeoisie. The bourgeois conception of the boundary between the public and the private self (Sennett 2002) is only one possible perspective, and needs to be seen alongside that of its main competitor, the aristocracy, which has in many ways found the means, thanks to a large extent to the mass media, to reassert its conception of the self and social relations in ever-expanding forms and contexts.

To understand the basic principles and logic driving and underpinning celebrity as a social, political and economic phenomenon, then, a central argument in this book is that it is useful to identify the ways in which we can see the world we live in today as a 'celebrity society' with its own distinctive, constantly changing social practices and structures, moral grammar, construction of self and identity, legal order and political economy organized around the distribution of visibility, attention and recognition.

From Rousseau to Diana – the celebritization process

A useful example here would be a comparison between Jean-Jacques Rousseau and Princess Diana. At first glance one would not expect to be able to say that the philosopher and the princess had very much in common. But in fact Rousseau was the European celebrity of his day, constantly being gossiped about in newspapers and cafés, as recognized a face on the streets of Paris as Diana was globally two centuries later. Rousseau complained about the visitors plaguing him:

> They were officers and other people who had absolutely no taste in literature. In fact the majority of them had never read my work. And yet this did not prevent them, based on what they told me, from trekking thirty, forty, even sixty leagues to come and admire an 'illustrious man, a celebrity, quite cele- brated, a great gentleman, and so forth.'

> (in Lilti 2008: 69)

It was not Rousseau's philosophy which was attracting this kind of attention, but his celebrity, the fact that it had become fashionable to know about and talk about Rousseau.

The characteristics of celebrity which Rousseau and Diana shared included the capacity to communicate with comparatively large audiences relatively quickly, a fascination with social mobility, meritocracy and the possibilities of 'democratic aristocracy', a split between the private and the public self and a need to manage the relation between the two (Lilti 2008: 53; Ward 2001). For Rousseau as well as for Diana, the public interest in who they 'really' were, the human being behind the public image, was both a benefit and an unwelcome intrusion into their private lives. In both the eighteenth and twentieth centuries, 'being well known' was an autonomous form of capital or surplus-value, independent of whatever achieve- ment or social position one was well known for, capable of being exchanged for, and transformed into, other kinds of capital: power, wealth, esteem, status. The power relation between them and their audiences was entirely symbolic, as opposed to political, military or economic power. Of course, the differences are also important. Diana could reach a much larger audience much more rapidly, Rousseau's network of peer-celebrities was tiny compared to Diana's, she could draw on much more sophisticated forms of visual representation that generated new types of relationship between celebrities and their audiences, which were far more intimate than was possible in the eighteenth century. Rousseau's public- relations technology was in its infancy, whereas Diana was bound up with a highly complex and independent industry of celebrity-production.

Alongside all the differences between them, then, Rousseau and Diana also shared the experience of celebrity: of being highly visible to a broader public and possessing the capacity to attract relatively large amounts of attention. Attention which can in turn be transformed into other kinds of 'capital' – esteem, status, wealth, influence, perhaps even power. Celebrity, like its older half-sister, fame, is essentially about relatively high public *visibility* and *recognition*. Rousseau and Diana both had 'fame' in the sense of being well known, just as large numbers of people knew of Alexander the Great, Abelard and Heloise, and Henry VIII. But their fame also had other characteristics, not shared by earlier generations of the famous, which made it particularly modern and deserving of a distinct concept: celebrity, by which I mean fame – being visible, recognized and well known – plugged into networks of mass communication, themselves circuits of desire and commerce.

Rousseau and Diana can then be seen as occupying different positions in a process which can be called, rather clumsily I admit, the 'celebritization of society' (Gabler 2001: 15). By this I mean, at the most general level, the ongoing historical process by which social institutions, social interaction, and the individual sense of self are increasingly organized – negatively as well as positively – around an ever-more differentiated network of more highly visible and recognized individuals. It also refers, as Milner has suggested, using the term 'celebrification', to the related questions of whether 'relationships between ordinary people become similar to the relationship of celebrities to their audiences', as well as the extent to which identity is increasingly organized around selected celebrities, 'resulting in many people attempting to become diminutive versions of a celebrity' (Milner 2005: 74).[1] At other times, celebrities can be precisely a *negative* reference point for self-formation, establishing identity by embodying its opposite.

The comparison between Rousseau and Diana leads on to a number of central issues running through the way I will be approaching the analysis of celebrity and how it can be understood as part and parcel of modern society (Elliott 1998: 836–7), as well as providing an 'index' to the character, and also the underlying logic, of contemporary social life. They include rejecting the distinction between hero and celebrity, the need to go beyond looking at celebrities as individuals, to see them as part of broader 'celebrity networks', the relationship between the analysis of celebrity and the concern in social theory with recognition and respect, the question of how to define celebrity, and an explanation of how I have divided up my account of celebrity society.

Hero vs celebrity

Thinking about celebrity tends to be dominated by an opposition between the 'hero' and the 'celebrity' (Bauman 2005: 47–51), between deep and shallow achievement. This contrast is usually bundled up with a moral critique of contemporary social life as being overly 'obsessed' with the 'cult' of celebrity, an obsession which is by definition a distraction from more 'real' and virtuous concerns. Paris Hilton is a frequently used reference for this kind of approach, and this is why the McCain campaign in the 2008 US presidential election sought to undermine Barack Obama's political authority by drawing a comparison with her. By the eighteenth century, the word had already come to be accompanied by a critique of the possible, indeed often probable, 'falseness' of the attention generated by celebrity, and this idea is central to what is possibly the most frequently cited definition of celebrity, Daniel Boorstin's observation that '[t]he celebrity is a person who is known for his well-knownness' (1962: 67). Today one would say 'famous for being famous', the circularity of the formulation indicating the superficiality of celebrity.

The broader framework of Boorstin's book was a critique of the illusory character of contemporary American social and cultural life, or more specifically of the role of the mass media in the construction of everyday consciousness. 'We suffer', he wrote, 'primarily not from our vices or our weaknesses, but from our illusions. We are haunted, not by reality, but by those images we have put in place of reality' (Boorstin 1962: 18). His analysis was organized around a distinction between the real and the illusory, the authentic and the synthetic, the actual events and the 'pseudo-events' – 'publicity stunts' – that had become so widely used by the mass media to manipulate public opinion in the course of the twentieth century. Celebrities were 'human pseudo-events', entirely manufactured creations to be contrasted with genuine 'heroes' – someone (apparently always a man) who did 'great' things or displayed 'great' qualities. 'The hero', wrote Boorstin, 'was distinguished by his achievement; the celebrity by his image or trademark. The hero created himself; the celebrity is created by the media. The hero was a big man; the celebrity is a big name' (1962: 61). The logic is one of historical decline, where authentic fame and greatness has been replaced by synthetic and empty celebrity – well-knownness – with no basis in accomplishment, talent, moral capacity, or skill.

One of his many examples is that of Carl Laemmle (1867–1939, founder of Universal Pictures in 1914), promoting the Canadian silent film actress (and inventor of the first automobile turn signal) Florence Lawrence by publicly 'denying' a story that Lawrence had been killed by a street car, a story he had planted himself in the St Louis newspapers (pp. 160–1). Another is the concept of the 'best-seller' in publishing, which he describes as the 'celebrity among books' – a book 'known primarily (sometimes exclusively) for its well knownness' (p. 168). The decision to purchase and (perhaps) read any book becomes increasingly determined, observed Boorstin, not by its content, its intrinsic worth, the author's literary skill, but by the knowledge that it seems to have been purchased by a relatively large number of other people.

This account does help us understand the dynamics of Oprah Winfrey's Book Club, but beyond that it leaves us with not much more than a sense of moral outrage and pessimism about cultural decline. It is important, I will argue, to reject this opposition between authentic heroes and synthetic celebrities. As Neal Gabler has emphasized, Boorstin's definition 'is simply not true for the vast majority of celebrities' (2001: 2). It is in the nature of 'heroism' that it be communicated to a public, and there will always be some technique to how the available media are used to that effect. As Lance Strate points out, people only get to know about heroes through the circulation of information, and in that sense 'there are no such things as heroes, only communication about heroes. Without communication, there would be no hero' (1994: 16). It simply is not true that a real hero requires no public relations; there is no such thing as an 'unsung hero', only anonymous individuals who have done unrecognized heroic things. Integral to heroism is precisely its 'celebration' – achievement and merit need to be communicated to exist as social realities.

One can take any of the heroes that Boorstin celebrates(!) and identify the public-relations machinery that was associated with the achievement of their status *as* heroes. Abraham Lincoln was adept at using the new technology of photography to imprint his image on the public mind, Benjamin Franklin was expert at manipulating the public's perception of him, and Samuel Johnson was similarly concerned with how his reputation could be systematically enhanced. Indeed, it is precisely an element of the hero's 'presentation of self' to deny that there is any strategy, that *their* heroism is entirely 'natural' and requires no synthetic support from the organization of their public perception. 'All the world's a stage', wrote Shakespeare, 'and all the men and women merely players': this is as true of heroes as it is of movie stars and television chat-show hosts.

Problems also emerge on the other side of the distinction – Charles Lindbergh made various deliberate efforts to establish his celebrity status, but he did also actually fly across the Atlantic for the first time; Michael Jordan might be attached to the most sophisticated public relations and marketing machinery known to human history, but his basketball skills are also pretty impressive. Was Einstein a hero or a celebrity (Missner 1985)? Darwin (Browne 2003)? Rousseau (Lilti 2008)? Babe Ruth? Churchill? John F. Kennedy? The strategic communication of one's claims to attention and visibility is an aspect of every public figure, varying only according to the technology available, and Boorstin mistakes this part of public identity for the whole, seeing celebrities as *nothing more* than their public relations. In reality, celebrity consists of varying combinations of some contribution to human existence, which can be either negative or positive, and the communication and marketing of that contribution in the public sphere, organized around various techniques of attracting public attention.

Celebrity should not be understood as distinct from 'real' achievement, so that one is *either* a hero *or* a celebrity. In reality, the two are combined in some way, so that every celebrity lies somewhere on a spectrum of combining achievement or talent, and what can be called the 'surplus value' of celebrity, or the 'celebrity effect' – that is, the independent value of 'well-knownness'. Some celebrities, it is true, are shooting stars, lying more at the marketing end of the spectrum, with very little to give to the world beyond youth or novelty, others somewhere in the middle with their basically mediocre skills being inflated by the wonders of public relations, others will be making significant contributions to human existence almost despite their marketing, and still others have a constitutional dislike of the publicity apparatus and will make some, generally feeble, attempts to hide their genuine talents under a bushel. To the extent that individuals such as Paris Hilton constitute key examples of particular social types and social forms, it is important to go beyond dismissing them as merely 'famous for being famous' and take them more seriously as embodying central aspects of modern social life which they share with many others, including presidents.

Celebrity beyond celebrities

Celebrity is also by definition about individuals, and this poses a particular problem for analysis. It makes it difficult to look beyond an endless string of particular examples – Monroe, Elvis, Madonna, Diana and so on – to see what social position all these individuals occupy, how they are constituted as a group and what underpins celebrity as a changing social, political, economic and legal phenomenon. For that purpose, we need to couple our account to another set of concepts: visibility, attention, status, recognition, but also power, symbolic capital, the constitution of the self, social networks and to see celebrity as a central aspect of a range of features of modern social life, such as democracy, individualism, state-formation, long-distance intimacy, imagined community, the public sphere and of course the changing technologies of the mass media.[2]

It is possible, then, to look beyond celebrities as unique individuals and see the circuits of power which produce celebrity as a social phenomenon, one which has its roots in aristocracy, but which had become democratized in two senses: increasing numbers and categories of people gain the capacity to become celebrities, and the power-balance in the relationship between celebrities and their audience shifts increasingly towards the latter, so that celebrity is to a large extent controlled by the audience, effectively supplying the audience's demand. Celebrities are in many respects *democratized aristocrats*, both the subjects and the objects of power relations.

This orientation in turn enables us to tease out the various aspects of the logic underpinning the production of celebrity, a certain kind of 'celebrity function' or role, independently from the specific individuals who become celebrities at any particular time and place (Turner 2004). The identification of a relatively small group of people as celebrities helps to reduce social complexity, and provides dense bundles of symbolic and cultural capital around which social life can be organized. Celebrities also provide a means of cognitive orientation, as 'expressive elites' (Keller 1963), and constitute the embodiment and reference points for both social stability and processes of social change, representing emerging as well as established social 'characters'. As P. David Marshall put it, 'the celebrity system presents a structure for the organization of public personalities as well as a structure for the models of modern subjectivity' (1997: 185). As a stimulus and focus for celebrity gossip, they make a significant contribution to social integration, establishing and reproducing a particular moral grammar of recognition and esteem.

Recognition

The fact that celebrities are the focus of the attention of large numbers of people and are inherently the product of mass *recognition* raises the question of how celebrity relates to the question of how recognition in contemporary social life has been understood in social theory more broadly. For example, the German social philosopher Axel Honneth (1995) has emphasized how what he calls 'struggles for recognition' – the pursuit, not of wealth, status or power, but simply of self-confidence, self-respect and self-esteem through being acknowledged as unique, particular individuals – is in fact a central element of all social movements and political activity. The word 'recognition' can mean 'acknowledging as true, valid, or entitled to consideration', which is the sense that Honneth works with. However, it can also mean 'The action or fact of perceiving that some thing, person, etc., is the same as one previously known; the mental process of identifying what has been known before' (OED 1989), which is the 'recognition' central to celebrity.

These two senses of the concept 'recognition' mean that there are at least two dimensions to 'struggles for recognition'. The first, Honneth's concern, is related to acknowledgement as a worthwhile, unique individual with 'a felt confidence that one's achievements or abilities will be recognized as worthwhile by other members of society' (Honneth 1995: 128), and that one's life is free of disrespect. He argues that 'social relations of symmetrical esteem between individualized (and autonomous) subjects' constitute a prerequisite of social solidarity (p. 129), and that 'symmetrical esteem' means not that we all esteem each other to the same degree, but 'that every subject is free from being collectively denigrated, so that one is given the chance to experience oneself to be recognized, in the light of one's own accomplishments and abilities, as valuable for society', so that social esteem takes 'a form not marred by experiences of disrespect' (p. 130). Honneth's normative aim of social solidarity is that of a form of social life characterized by a horizontal and symmetrical relationship between members of society, with as few individuals as possible falling below a particular threshold of respect, acknowledgement and recognition.

The second concerns the projection of that acknowledgement into the public sphere, for the larger-scale, mass-media based recognition ('haven't I seen you somewhere before?') characterizing celebrity, constituting a vertical and asymmetrical relationship between celebrities and their audiences. The focus here is not on identifying the social conditions that make it possible for people to avoid disrespect, to achieve a socially valued minimum of recognition, but on the mechanics of particular individuals rising far above the basic threshold of recognition, in a sense becoming super-rich in their possession of recognition-capital. As Kerry Ferris has emphasized, a fundamental aspect of celebrity is the *asymmetry* of the relationship between a celebrity and their fans or their audience, 'the experience of being recognized by far more people than one can recognize back' (2010: 393).

In a sense, Honneth is primarily concerned with eliminating *poverty* (of recognition), but there is the additional issue of the enormous disparities in the distribution of recognition wealth and income 'above the poverty line', so to speak. The intriguing question then becomes that of the structure and dynamics of the relationship between these two dimensions of struggles for recognition, the horizontal and symmetrical, and the vertical and asymmetrical, and their implications for the inherently unequal distribution of recognition. What I will be arguing in Chapter 2 is that once one looks at the accumulation of recognition 'above the poverty' line, it becomes another kind of capital, 'attention', and that understanding the economics of attention – the accumulation, distribution and circulation of the abstract form of capital that is attention – is central to understanding how celebrity and celebrity society works.

Defining celebrity

There are many definitions of celebrity: Boorstin's widely circulated 'known for being well-known', Rein, Kotler & Stoller's 'a person whose name has attention-getting, interest-riveting and profit-generating value' (1997: 15), Joseph Roach's an idolized person or the exalted state of being one, a kind of apotheosis marked by a persona that circulates even when the person does not (2003: 213), Chris Rojek's 'the attribution of glamorous or notorious status to an individual within the public sphere', or 'nothing more than cultural impact on a public' (2001: 10). Perhaps a good-enough rule of thumb would be that a celebrity is a person whose image or life story has any commercial value. One Chinese term for celebrity, *mingliu*, translates as 'name-flowing' (Jeffreys & Edwards 2011: 20). But it is difficult to reduce it to a single line, so I would prefer to offer the following, admittedly more convoluted definition:

* Celebrity is a quality or status characterized by a capacity to attract attention, generating some 'surplus value' or benefit derived from the fact of being well known (highly visible) in itself in at least one public arena. It can be either positive or negative, including notoriety.
* It is always accentuated by some degree of 'ordinariness' – a movement from humble origins to higher status, some similarities with the experiences of a significant proportion of their audience, allowing for some degree of identification by non-celebrities. Celebrities need not be powerful, although it helps, but their status as celebrities is enhanced if they have a distinctive narrative, allowing themselves to be subjected to constant scrutiny and a demand for perpetual performance, encompassing their private life and personality as well as their public roles.

'Celebrity society' can be understood, then, as the assembled social practices and structures, formations of the self, legal order and political economy which systematically attaches this quality or status to selected individuals.

Core themes

The book's argument is composed of a number of different components, beginning with the history. It is important, I believe, to take the longer-term development of celebrity seriously and not equate it with the Hollywood film industry. There is an increasing awareness of this in the writing on celebrity (Rojek 2001; Gamson 1994; Ponce de Leon 2002; Morgan 2011a, b; Tillyard 2005a, b; Postle

2005a, b; Riall 2007a, b; Parry-Giles 2008; Evans 2005; Inglis 2010), but despite how widely Leo Braudy's (1986) *The Frenzy of Renown* is read, the level of historical literacy in the field remains less than it could be. To be frank, it is often woeful – there is a strong tendency towards mistaking intensification or acceleration of a phenomenon for its invention or creation, and it will be said that something started in a particular period not as the result of a careful comparative analysis of what came before, but because no effort has been made even to consider any earlier period. The development of celebrity society is certainly bound up with that of modernity itself, especially with the development of modes of communication, but this does not mean, as some observers believe, that 'there was no such thing as celebrity prior to the beginning of the 20th century' (Schickel 1985: 23).

Contemporary celebrity is firmly anchored in the world of the theatre, and in the theatrical dimensions of social life more generally, both of which have a much longer history. The basic elements of the dynamics of celebrity–audience relationships that we see around us today can be seen clearly in earlier periods – the eighteenth century was an especially important period, but in England it was the return of Charles II to the throne and the granting of access to the stage for women which had an enormously important effect on the promotion of celebrity dynamics. Painting was as important in its time as photography and film became later, so that Joshua Reynolds has to be seen as a key early figure. But the roots go back even further – Elizabeth I embodied many of the features of modern celebrity in her relationship with her subjects, both powerful as a monarch and acutely conscious of how dependent her power was on how she was represented and how she was perceived by the English public. Henry VIII before her was also excellent at stage-managing his public persona, and this was not a merely superficial aspect of his power and authority. I explain what Norbert Elias meant by 'court society', and how we should understand the ways in which the structure of celebrity society emerged from, and remains continuous with, the social and interpersonal world of the aristocracy in early modernity.

Having established the historical foundations, I go on to look at what is specific about the trajectory of celebrity when it became industrialized in the nineteenth century, to later become 'the Josephine machine' that all current celebrity production is modelled on, including the importance of pioneers such as PT Barnum, Buffalo Bill, Lola Montez and the Civil War actresses, and Giuseppe Garibaldi as perhaps the world's first movie actor as well as the creator of a unified Italian nation-state. This leads on to the need to see celebrity as a differentiated field, with many different sub-industries and different types of celebrity with larger or smaller audiences. We are then able to think through what underpins all celebrity – the management of attention – and how important attention has become in an information or knowledge society. Economics is about the management of scarce resources; when there is a surplus of information, data and knowledge, the scarce resource becomes attention, and it is the capacity of celebrities to function as 'bundles of attention-capital' that is the key to understanding how all forms of celebrity operate.

The social sciences have tended to overlook celebrity as a 'serious' topic. It would not be a bad wager to bet that most people who have read C. Wright Mills's book *The Power Elite* (1957) have either skipped or quickly skim-read his second chapter on 'The Celebrities', because surely that wasn't what 'real' power was about. I certainly did myself, and the paucity of references to Mills in the celebrity literature seems to suggest that he tends to be passed over. I go on, then, to take a closer look at Mills's characterization of celebrity and its roots in café society, and the importance of New York columnist and radio journalist Walter Winchell in the emerging networks of 'attention capital'.

The discussion of power by Mills leads on to an important distinction that needs to be made between the different forms that power can take, and what is distinctive about celebrity. The form most often discussed in the social sciences, what Michel Foucault called 'panoptic' power, is about ordinary people being observed by those wanting to control them, the few watching the many, working with concepts such as the 'surveillance society'. But there is also, as Norwegian criminologist Thomas Mathieson has pointed out, 'synoptic' power, the form that emerges when the many watch the few, or what Richard Lanham calls the 'centripetal gaze'. Although its roots lie in the exercise of direct coercive power by monarchs and the aristocracy, modern celebrities constitute the embodiment of the current, in many respects democratized forms of synoptic power, making up the framework for the structuring of attention capital.

In order to understand how celebrity is anchored in our social relationships, it is important to see how our interactions with each other are mediated by relations with celebrities, so we need to look at what gets called 'para-social interaction' and 'long-distance intimacy', the various ways in which we connect with the many virtual characters in our social world, as a reference point for our self-formation as well as our relationships in the 'real' world. This leads onto reflecting on the role of gossip generally as a social lubricant and what is specific about celebrity gossip in structuring our relationships with each other.

It is impossible not to notice the role that celebrity plays in the world of politics and diplomacy today; the 2008 McCain presidential campaign, for example, tried to delegitimate Barack Obama by characterizing him as a celebrity. Unsuccessfully, of course – it was always going to be a tough sell with Sarah Palin, celebrity politician extraordinaire herself, on board. Here I draw out particular aspects of the history of celebrity in politics, linking the strategies of Henry VIII and Elizabeth I in the fifteenth and sixteenth centuries, the Duchess of Devonshire in the eighteenth and Garibaldi in the nineteenth centuries, Queen Victoria as the first global 'media monarch' and the utilization of celebrities in political campaigning from the late nineteenth century onwards, accelerating enormously with technological innovations such as photography, radio and, of course, motion pictures. It is at this point that the celebrity production process takes a giant leap forward with the appearance of 'experts' in public relations, publicity and image-management, men such as Albert Lasker and Edward Bernays who sold oranges, cigarettes and presidents according to more or less the same logic. The world of democratic politics is inherently divided between what is actually going on and what can be conveyed to the broader public, and the increasingly significant role of 'spin' and politicians who function as celebrities is part and parcel of how that split in the politics of democracies is managed.

To bring home a bit further the extent to which celebrity is a dimension of all aspects of modern life, it is useful to look at its role in fields that appear to be most distant from the world of entertainment, glitz and glamour – business and management. In fact, the construction of entrepreneurs and CEOs as celebrities has been central to the development of capitalist enterprise in all of its stages, and the dimension of celebrity has become only more important as a means of attracting investment and securing the firm's image in the marketplace. Celebrity CEOs do not need to be real, they can be virtual characters such as Ronald McDonald, and they need not still be alive, or have anything to do with the firm, such as Colonel Sanders. Celebrity is now one of any firm's intangible assets, and its management requires increasing levels of sophistication.

The question that then remains is how to identify the most probable future trends in the operation of celebrity society – having developed a more detailed sense of where it has come from, it helps to get a sense of the direction it is now taking. Again technological shifts are having an important impact. The stimulation to the speed and reach of the distribution of information provided by the Internet and by social media has had a powerful impact on the sheer diversity and proliferation of characters able to gather enormous amounts of attention to become global celebrities within very short periods of time. As always improbably ahead of his time, in 1979 Andy Warhol changed his most well-known aphorism to 'In fifteen minutes everyone will be famous.' I develop some ideas, then, on how the field of celebrity is likely to become increasingly finely differentiated, generating new, in some respects more democratic forms of celebrity, and shifting the rules governing the operation of celebrity society. Just as Rousseau and Diana had much in common, but also important differences between them, so too tomorrow's celebrity society will be familiar and recognizable in many respects, but also driven by a new combination of technological, social, political and economic forces.

The book ends with some reflections on a question it has tended to avoid – what could a *critical* account of celebrity society look like? The problem with starting off with a critical stance is that it often impedes analysis, to the extent that one has already arrived at the position one wants to take up – celebrity is silly, a cult, an obsession, a sign of our being deluded by advertisers, and so on. I am perhaps a bit old-fashioned in that I still believe that understanding the world around us helps us to be less at its mercy, and is the first step towards improving our capacity to steer it in one direction rather than another – leaving aside the problem of how a highly diverse 'we' can come to agree on what that direction should be. The question of the power dimensions of our relationships with differing forms of celebrity, together with the idea that celebrity is primarily about the management of attention capital in a world awash with information and knowledge, are probably the most useful places to start in establishing how we might approach celebrity society more reflexively, in a way that comprehends its inner logic. Once the various aspects of celebrity society are clearer, it might then be possible to experience celebrity as less of a mysterious neurosis of the media age, and more as a manageable feature of contemporary social life, with which we can engage in an active, creative and thoughtful way.

1 From fame to celebrity

The celebritization of society

One useful place to start in thinking about celebrity is to look at how the word itself first emerged. The Oxford English Dictionary identifies Richard Hooker's reference in 1600 to 'the dignity and celebrity of mother cities' as the earliest use of the word, but 'celebretie' first appears in English in 1565, in the commentary by the leading Protestant reformer John Jewel (1522–71), Bishop of Salisbury,[1] on the baptism practices of the Apostles. Bishop Jewel remarked that 'whereas he [Jesus] commanded them to baptize in the name of the Father, and of the Sonne, and of the Holy Ghost, they [the Apostles] baptized in the name of Iesus Chiste Onely, intending thereby to make that be of more fame and celebritie'.[2] A little later, in 1587, John Bridges, Dean of Sarum, explained that the Apostle John preached at the Church of Ephesus, which he saw as a key site, 'because for the multitude of beleeuers, and the celebritie of the place'.[3] It was used, then, to refer to the condition of being well known, in forms such as 'the celebrity of his name' or 'the celebrity of his writings'.

Although celebrity was often defined in dictionaries as simply equivalent to 'famousness', in practice it was used alongside or instead of fame to capture something additional, a degree of *currency* and *activity*. The derivation from the Latin *celebritus* is usually described as 'famous or thronged',[4] but a more accurate rendition would be to say 'famous *and* thronged'. The Latin word also means 'much spoken of', and this is an important slant on the meaning – one can be famous without being 'thronged' or very much spoken of. Celebrity was attributed to individuals who were famous for particular reasons, and with specific effects, linked to its original meaning as a noun, indicating a celebration, or festivity. One could be respectably and quietly 'famous', whereas to have 'celebrity' had different quality, a certain buzz in everyday social life. Alexander the Great, Charlemagne and King Arthur were famous, to be sure, but not exactly exciting topics of everyday conversation, unlike what Nell Gwynn – the seventeenth-century English actress and Charles II's mistress – got up to with the king. Fame was something stored safely in a display cabinet, framed, or cast in stone, marble or bronze – and thus tending to be posthumous, although not exclusively – whereas celebrity was a current topic passed around the table, inspected, fondled, turned over and tapped – which also meant a more fragile lifespan.

The first use of the word as a noun to refer to individuals appears to be in the mid-nineteenth century, in Ralph Waldo Emerson's commentary on the English aristocracy, where he notes that the English nobility included 'the celebrities of wealth and fashion' among those to be kept firmly in their place (Emerson 19–: 56). It is probably only in the early twentieth century that the word starts to be used with a frequency and breadth that approximates its contemporary meaning, with the spread of film and radio. However, the word was lagging behind its referent, the history of which is more complex, and which does not lend itself easily to neat categorizations, identifications of 'origins', or sequences.

In every human group, at the point where power, status and wealth is unevenly distributed, certain individuals will become more publicly visible than others – emperors, kings, queens, princes, aristocrats, prophets, popes, saints, martyrs, philosophers, warriors and heroes – become eligible to be considered as worthy of distinctive attention. Given its family connection to 'fame', one obvious place to begin any history is with Alexander the Great, who made sure that the populations of the enormous swaths of Europe and Asia Minor he conquered kept him at the forefront of their minds by having his image imprinted on the coinage used in those territories. As Leo Braudy observes, Alexander 'remains the earliest example of that paradoxical fame in which the spiritual authority of the hero is yet a model for a support of ordinary human nature' (1986: 43).

But Alexander's fame is not yet Rousseau's celebrity, and like the concept 'modernity' itself, from the European Middle Ages onwards, there are various turning points, watersheds and revolutions that one could choose to identify the beginnings of a specifically 'modern' form of fame which constitutes the core of celebrity. In the history of the West, the increasing value placed on individualism, rise of the public sphere and then the mass media, democratization, increasing social differentiation and social density have all turned fame into something requiring another word – celebrity – to capture its distinctive and ever-changing features. The 'landscape of renown' changed along with society itself (Braudy 1986: 588), and in many respects the history of celebrity runs alongside that of whatever we choose to conceive of as 'modernity'.

The best way to grasp the modernization and democratization of fame, and the corresponding production of celebrity, is to see it as lying at the intersection of a number of different historical developments, with changing configurations of those distinct transformations producing differing kinds of celebrity. Chris Rojek, for example, focuses on the combination of democratization, the declining role of organized religion and the commodification of everyday life (Rojek 2001: 13). My own preference is to highlight the three lines of historical transformation, all integral to the emergence of modern society itself, overlapping with each other and themselves the products of intersecting processes of structural change.

First, the formation and evolution of a 'court society' characterized by theatricality, performativity and the competitive organization of power and social mobility around the strategic projection of symbolically constituted identity. Court society was given its particular form, as Norbert Elias has argued, by the concentration of political and military power in the state within the context of urbanization and the development of capitalist economic activity, beginning with Absolutist monarchies and then developing into the modern, democratic nation-state.

Second, the changing social and political construction of human beings as *individuals* with particular rights, possibilities and opportunities. Modern celebrity is by definition individualistic and meritocratic: it attaches to individuals not to collectivities. Even celebrity couples need each to be celebrities in their own right. It presumes the possibility of the attainment of higher visibility and greater recognition through individual attributes and talents, and there are meant to be no ascribed restrictions to the possible movement from obscurity to celebrity. The idea that celebrities are 'ordinary folk, just like us' has become a central if contradictory theme in contemporary celebrity society. Thus, photographs of celebrities in modes other than the carefully posed and glamorous both serve to situate their celebrity in its ordinariness while marking out that their ordinariness is unlike ours – the spectators – for they are celebrities who are capable of transcending the mundane in which we are rooted. Such a meritocratic conception of human beings as distinct individuals has its own important history, linked to the rise of capital and property as forces loosening social structures and permitting new levels of social mobility – enabling the concept of self as *property*, to be done with what one will, with particular rights attached – and has a central bearing on the nature of modern celebrity. Celebrity is a central aspect of *the social production of individuality* – the ceaseless generation of personality in an impersonal world, expressing particularity in the face of ever-more powerful universalizing societal processes, and a particular resolution of the social dialectic between the universal and the particular.

Third, the evolution of what has been called 'the public sphere' (Habermas 1974, 1989), driven by urbanization and capitalism but also by evolving modes of mass communication, beginning with the emergence of the printing press in the late fifteenth and sixteenth centuries, its expansion in the eighteenth century and industrialization in the nineteenth century, followed by successive additions of photography, radio, film, television and the Internet. This development in turn needs to be seen against the background of the public sphere's secularization; that is, the break-up of the Catholic Church's more or less complete monopoly over the symbolic realm of representation, to be taken over by a combination of the State, literature, theatre and the later developments in the modes of communication. Although both celebrity and fame are about being well known, celebrity establishes a particular kind of relationship between the modern aristocracy and its increasingly 'mass' public. By celebrity I mean, then, fame – as 'well knownness' – plugged into networks of human communication which are at the same time circuits of desire and commerce.

Court society and state-formation

When the period in European history very roughly between the fourteenth and seventeenth centuries is described as the 'Renaissance', the focus tends to be on the history of ideas and culture, the emergence of humanist philosophy, new forms of artistic expression, painting and architecture, and new approaches to knowledge. However, it was also a period of the consolidation of political and military power in absolutist national monarchies, fuelled by European colonization of Africa, the Americas, the Middle East, India and East Asia, as well as increased extraction from the population. As Hugh Trevor-Roper wrote,

> It is a fascinating spectacle, the rise of the princes in sixteenth century Europe. One after another they spring up, first in Italy and Burgundy, then all over Europe. Their dynasties may be old, and yet their character is new: they are more exotic, more highly coloured than their predecessors. They are versatile, cultivated men, sometimes bizarre, even outrageous: they bewilder us by their lavish tastes, their incredible energy, their ruthlessness and panache . . . Undoubtedly, in the sixteenth century, the princes are everything. They are tyrants over past and future; they change religion and divine truth by their nod, even in their teens; they are priests and popes, they call themselves gods, as well as kings.
>
> (1967: 52–3)

In England, for example, the structures of power shifted significantly as the Tudor monarchs managed to play off opposing interests among the nobility against each other and diminish the wealth and authority of the Catholic Church, concentrating power and the means of violence in their own court, so that it is possible to speak of a 'de-militarization of the nobility' (Corrigan & Sayer 1985: 63). As Penry Williams observes: 'Most of the landowning class was, during the Tudor epoch, turning away from its traditional training in arms to an education at the universities or the Inns of Court' (1979: 241; see also Stone 1966).

Political power and authority became concentrated in court society, heavily dependent on lines of patronage flowing around the monarch which were both volatile and relatively 'open' and competitive, given the ever-present need for sources of income to finance the expanding needs, some legitimate and some merely profligate, of the sixteenth-century courts. Increasing wealth among the merchant class made it possible for them to purchase noble titles, which the Crown was happy to supply in order to meet its own financial requirements (Stone 1958), as well the education required to serve in the state's administration. The European absolutist monarchies of the sixteenth century can usefully be seen as 'theatre states, in which the dramatic effect of ceremonial actions was at least as important as the reality of power' (Asch 2003: 93), with Henry VIII, Elizabeth I and Louis XIV only among the more prominent examples of such anchorage of power in its performative, charismatic projection on the realm of symbol and ceremony (Sharpe 2009; Burke 1992).

Norbert Elias speaks of this period as one of the 'courtization of warriors' (2000), a shift in status, prestige and patronage away from troublesome warrior knights unable to resolve their disputes without constantly dragging the population into warfare (Hobbes's 'state of nature') towards 'gentlemen' with different skills of eloquence and communication, diplomacy, political prudence, wit and charm. By 1576, only a quarter of the English peerage had seen active service (Corrigan & Sayer 1985: 63). 'It was for this reason', writes Trevor-Roper, 'that the Renaissance princes and their great ministers founded all those schools and colleges'. Their aim was 'to satisfy the royal demand for officers—officers to man the new royal bureaucracies—and, at the same time, the public demand for office: office which was the means to wealth and power and the gratification of lavish, competitive tastes' (Trevor-Roper 1967: 56–7).[5] It was the royal and princely courts, suggested Elias, which had come to constitute the social nucleus of sixteenth- and seventeenth-century European societies, with the town largely modelling itself on the court (Elias 2006: 40). Court society constituted the vital arena of interaction between the monarch and courtiers consisting of the nobility and aspiring nobility, and through them the towns and countryside.

It should be clarified here that a court society is any type of social formation and structuring of power relations, not necessarily restricted to any specific historical period, which concentrates on a central actor – the monarch or prince – and their relations with a network of only slightly weaker actors (courtiers) with their own greater or lesser economic, military and political resources, related to each other hierarchically. As a system of power relations, it is characterized by a field of unstable and volatile norms and rules of conduct across which the prince deploys a range of strategies to ensure that courtiers are constantly competing with each other rather than with the prince, and giving the prince maximum flexibility to promote or suppress those who suit their particular ends, or to draw in outsiders as required. As Gabriel Herman notes in his study of Hellenistic court society, successful princes were those who enhanced the power of 'the managerial sectors of their courts at the expense of the military, carefully keeping alive (and preferably exploiting) the rivalries and tensions between the two' (Herman 1997: 215). Individuals who combine both sets of skills are, of course, the most dangerous to a prince.

In contrast to the bourgeois orientation towards the acquisition of *economic* capital, court rationality revolves around the acquisition of *symbolic* capital, status and prestige, no matter what the financial cost, often – obviously – with disastrous economic consequences. As Elias put it,

> Bourgeois-industrial rationality is generated by the constraint of the economic mesh; by it power opportunities founded on private or public capital are made calculable. Court rationality is generated by the constraint of the elite social mesh; by it people and prestige are made calculable as instruments of power.

> (2006: 121)

In court society, individual existence and identity is profoundly *representational* – they consist of how one exhibits one's position and status, and this process of exhibition and performance is highly competitive and constantly fluctuating.

There was, as Asch observes, 'no longer a unified system of criteria which could be relied upon to determine the status of each individual, so that one continually had to reassert one's rank' (2003: 87). 'For established and mobile Elizabethans alike', notes Frank Whigham, 'public life at court had come under a new and rhetorical imperative of performance. Esse sequitur operare: identity was to be derived from behavior' (1983: 625). The king was both the expression of an existing order of social esteem and prestige *and* the creator, or rather re-creator, of that order according to his grace and pleasure (Revel 1997: 93). The main vehicle for the representation of social identity was the practices of etiquette and manners, because the rituals of etiquette both *demonstrated* each individual's position within the social network (where was one entitled to sit at the dinner table, in what order were people served, etc.), and were the *means* by which individuals could negotiate and manoeuvre that position. The management of emotions is crucial to these manoeuvres, and advantage accrues to those who could control their emotions most effectively (Elias 2006: 121).

In court society there is only a weak division between public and private life – one's public position is heavily dependent on all aspects of one's relation with others. Behaviour at any time and place can 'decide a person's place in society, could mean social success or failure', and 'society encompassed the whole being of its members' (Elias 2006: 125–6). The operation of this type of power relationship demanded continuous *observation* both of others and of oneself, and the constantly fluctuating relations between various members of court society. Because the pool of resources was closed, as Revel observes, 'the only way to know where one stood was to know where everyone else stood: there was no necessary relation between apparent rank and actual standing' (1997: 96). Elias refers to the mechanisms of court society as a 'perpetual motion' machine, 'fed by the need for prestige and by the tensions which, once in place, endlessly renewed the competitive process' (2006: 97). This made information perhaps the most strategically important type of capital in court society, since only with accurate information could one assess one's situation, threats and risks, and plan future alliances and strategies.

'We princes, I tell you', declared Elizabeth I, 'are set on stages, in sight and view of all the world' (Ward 2001; Levin 2002), and she had a very clear sense of the centrality to her power, legitimacy and authority of her self-presentation and public performance in public. Carol Levin notes her on-going interest in drama, the centrality of theatre to her court, and observes for Elizabeth herself, 'Even in her most casual, seemingly spontaneous remarks, Elizabeth was playing a role, aware of how her audience – whether foreign ambassadors, Parliament, her council, or her people – would respond' (2002: 114). How she was viewed mattered enough for Elizabeth to attempt to control her portraiture, issuing a draft proclamation 'Prohibiting Portraits of the Queen' (1563) which:

> commandeth all manner of persons . . . to forbear from painting, graving, printing, or making of any portrait of her majesty until some special person, that shall be by her allowed, shall have first finished a portraiture thereof;

after which finished, her majesty will be content that all other painters of gravers ... shall and may at their pleasures follow that said patron or first portrayer.

(Hughes & Larkin 1969: 241)

This principle applied to all members of court society, and this form of observation in the court, its 'gaze', does not 'consider the individual person in isolation, as a being deriving his essential regularities and characteristics from within. Rather, the individual is always observed in court society in his social context, as a *person in relation to others*' (Elias 2006: 114). Elias argued that court society promoted a 'specific form of self-observation', one with 'a view to self-discipline in social life' (2006: 114), essentially complementary to the observation of others.

The other side of the coin to the requirement for observation was, of course, an insistence on perpetual exposure to public view, beginning with the king himself. As Revel observes, 'in the palace everything was to be seen, and therefore one saw everything, from the king's waking in the morning to his going to bed at night, from his work and play to his love affairs and even his final agony' (1997: 101).[6] This also meant that the king was perfectly turned-out and publically observable at all time. Saint-Simon commented on how 'unbelievable' it was, the extent to which Louis XIV's punctiliousness in relation to his appearance, deportment and conduct 'contributed to his service, to the luster of his court, and to the convenience of paying him court and speaking to him' (p. 101). The king's own subjection to a strict regime of self-discipline then in turn became the nucleus for the imposition of a similar regulation of the self on everyone around him, beginning with courtiers and then extending to the rest of society – this is the essence of what Elias calls the 'civilizing process'.

The point of observing others is to ascertain their true motives and desires, but also, more importantly, to search for any point of leverage to gain some advantage over them. The superiority of one's position is heavily dependent on how one displays that superiority to subordinates. There is a permanent tension between 'prudence' and 'authenticity', between the management of one's emotions in the calculated pursuit of long-term ends, such as the maximization of power and prestige, and the expression of one's 'real' self, which is usually 'punished by social downfall or at least degradation' (Elias 2006: 123) in court society. Authenticity is to be avoided at all costs, for it simply gives competitors advantages in the constant struggle for psychological dominance. Elias cites Jean de La Bruyère in this regard: 'A man who knows the court is master of his gestures, of his eyes and of his face; he is deep, impenetrable; he pretends not to notice injuries done to him, he smiles to his enemies, controls his temper, disguises his passions, belies his heart, speaks and acts against his real opinions' (2006: 114). More than that, as Whigham suggests, 'not only does reputation articulate the frame in which virtue is judged, it is epistemologically necessary for its public reception' (1983: 636). Although authentic moral status does not entirely disappear, it is subordinated to 'the judgment of the human audience, visible in the form of reputation. One is to act as if reputation were true, whatever one knows to the contrary. Public opinion takes precedence over one's own moral perception' (p. 635).

The driving forces for Elias are *competition*, and the *opportunities for advantage* which competitive success offered to its participants. Court society is 'shot through with the countless rivalries of people trying to preserve their position by marking it off from those below while at the same time improving it by reducing the demarcation from those above' (2006: 84):

> Life in court society was not peaceful. The number of people permanently and inescapably bound to one circle was large. They pressed on each other, struggled for prestige, for their place in the hierarchy. The affairs, intrigues, conflicts over rank and favour knew no end . . . There was no security.
>
> (p. 113)

The combativeness of court society, observes Whigham, is 'almost paranoid, and invades and dominates even those private moments most unperformed. The ideal courtier is never offstage' (1983: 634). It is the competition between various social groups for advantage over others which generates both the willingness to submit to the demands of etiquette and the process of 'courtization', where the body, emotions and desires are increasingly subjected to stringent controls and ever more demanding forms of self-discipline.[7] As Elias wrote, 'the competition of court life enforces a curbing of the affects in favour of a calculated and finely shaded behaviour in dealing with people' (2006: 121).

These basic elements of court rationality together constitute, I would argue, the core of a nascent 'celebrity rationality'. Court society established a particular psychological disposition, a certain *habitus*, organized around a constitutive theatricality and heightened visibility both upwards, to one's superiors, and downwards, to one's inferiors. The court self was perpetually performative and subject to intense and constant competition according to ever-shifting rules and norms, leading to a blurring of the boundary between public and private life, and the production of every-changing 'favourites' surrounded by their own networks of patronage and favouritism, but also constantly renewed patterns of competition. As Baldassare Castiglione (1478–1529) formulated it in *The Book of the Courtier* (1528), court rationality compelled members of court society to mobilize their public image to their best advantage, so that whenever the courtier goes anywhere he has not been before, 'he must send there first, before his own person, a good image of himself, making it known that in other places, at the courts of other lords, ladies, and knights, he enjoys good esteem' (in Scaglione 1991: 280). The figure of the sixteenth/seventeenth-century courtier then became differentiated into a number of different social types – the public servant, the politician's advisor, the manager, but also the celebrity, the witty, beautiful and talented focus of public scrutiny and attention with access to power, constituting a living lesson in how to achieve such access.

In 1662, Louis XIV was pleased to have created a 'society of pleasure, which gives the persons of the court an honest familiarity with us, touches them and charms more than one can say. The peoples, meanwhile, are pleased by the spectacle, whose goal is basically always to please them. And all our subjects, in general, are delighted to see that we love what they love and what they are most successful at. In this way we would hold their minds and hearts, in some cases more firmly perhaps than through rewards and benefits' (Revel 1997: 86).

A central vehicle for court society's establishment of an architecture of social relations and a moral grammar of esteem and recognition organized around celebrity, that remained standing even when under different occupation, was the French salon, which constituted the interface between the court and aspiring nobility as well as leading intellectuals and highly placed members of the bourgeoisie. Conceived by Catherine de Vivonne, Marquise de Rambouillet (1588–1665), precisely as an alternative to the intense ferocity of the power struggles at court, salons were 'an architectural framework for a new kind of sociability' (Kale 2004: 4) ranging across literary, philosophical, political, moral and aesthetic events, discussions and social interactions which created novel social spaces for women to participate in public life, as well as constituting vehicle for the transmission, stabilization and transformation of particular psychological dispositions and cultural orientations. Above all, salons were:

> a historically specific expression of the aristocracy's determination to regulate and control the transition from a hereditary to an open elite. They emerged at a time when the justification of noble privilege in terms of a traditional military function was under attack, when circumstances promoted a more modern view of nobility based on a combination of birth, education, manners, and sociability, and when an increasingly wealthy bourgeoisie was gaining entry into an expanding service nobility and aspired to 'live nobly'.
>
> (p. 9)

As Antoine Lilti insists, French salons 'belonged to court society in the extensive sense that Norbert Elias gave to the phrase: a society strongly shaped by the values and the practices of the court. Salons were not venues cut off and isolated from the constraints of court society, but on the contrary they were part of it' (2009: 5). They were a social and cultural 'technology' central to what Arno Mayer (1981) has called the 'persistence of the Old Regime', a 'kind of interface between court society, elite networks, and the literary sphere' (Lilti 2009: 11), giving the French nobility the means to sustain their values, beliefs and psychological orientations through mechanisms of adaptation and habituation to new social conditions (see also Goodman 1989).

A central feature of the salon's 'social technology' was the fluidity of its relationship to its audience or 'market' – people could choose whether to attend or not, which constitute a large part of the attraction of the social form, but also made it volatile and dependent on shifting fashions and tastes. Celebrity had the effect of stabilizing those tastes and preferences – philosophers, artists, musicians, poets, writers, politicians, prominent courtiers and aristocrats, sometimes actors and actresses who already had some public visibility and reputation could draw a crowd and enhance the attractiveness of the salon, but would also increase their own visibility in the process, making the relationship a mutually beneficial one (Kale 2004: 28). As Lenard Berlanstein argues more generally, 'celebrity culture, far from being a revolt against elite good taste, already existed—in one of its historically contingent forms—before mass culture arose and, in effect, "trickled down" to the masses from media that first reached primarily the bourgeoisie' (2004: 82). In this way, an ever-changing 'celebrity rationality' jumped the walls of court society, much as discipline escaped the confines of the monastery and the army barracks (Weber), to spread throughout society, carried along by social forms such as the French salon, the German reading clubs, and the English Restoration theatre. Between the seventeenth century and the First World War, then, one can see the 'migration' of the logic of court society – competitive self- and mutual-observation and performativity organized around more highly visible 'favourites' (celebrities) – from its original location in princely courts, via a range of intermediary social institutions, throughout the rest of social life. As Bernard Giesen (1998) has argued, in many respects the French Enlightenment can be understood not as a rejection, but as an extension of court culture.

Individualism and meritocracy

The idea of celebrity is by definition individualistic – the more communal the sense of self is, the less response there will be attaching recognition and esteem to particular individuals, and the more individualistic social and cultural life is, the more likely it is that it will generate a more expansive network of celebrities. Celebrity and individualism are joined at the hip, and process of individualization and celebritization can be seen as interdependent, mutual indexes of each other. The origins, nature and development of the idea of 'the individual' as a self-actualizing entity constituting the foundational principle for the allocation and distribution of esteem and regard, then, have important implications for the structure and dynamics of celebrity society itself.

To a large extent the construction of this issue has been bound up with a parallel contrast between tradition and modernity, which is seen as overlapping with a distinction between the binding of identity to its communal location – in kinship and family relations, geographic locality, and language – and a recognition of the distinctiveness of individual experience and action. The first model produces a hierarchical, immobile society in which everyone has their place and stays in it, at least until they arrive at either the gates of Heaven or Hades, whereas the second produces a fluid structuring of social relations which is both democratic and meritocratic – there are no pre-ordained limitations to social mobility, and, correspondingly, social status mobility, esteem and recognition are determined by the individual's talent and effort.

The most influential account of the historical emergence of an individualistic consciousness is Jacob Burckhardt's *The Civilization of the Renaissance in Italy* (2004 [1860]). Burckhardt drew attention to the significance of the Italian Renaissance as a transformation of society, culture and experience that was itself anchored in the specifics of northern Italian political conditions, in releasing people from the medieval conception of the self as a communally defined entity to allow for a recognition of identity and self-interest apart from the collectivities to which people belonged. He argued that, in the Middle Ages, both the way in which people regarded each other and the way they observed their interior life 'lay dreaming or half awake beneath a common veil', a veil 'woven of faith, illusion, and childish prepossession, through which the world and history were seen clad in strange hues'. Individuals were only conscious of themselves as members of 'a race, people, party, family, or corporation—only through some general category' (p. 98). But towards the end of the thirteenth century, observed Burckhardt, 'Italy began to swarm with individuality', with Dante only the most prominent example. 'The Italians of the fourteenth century', wrote Burckhardt, 'knew little of false modesty or of hypocrisy in any shape; not one of them was afraid of singularity, of being and seeming unlike his neighbours' (p. 99).

For Burckhardt, Renaissance individualism was associated from the beginning with the idea of celebrity – one achieved and sustained one's individuality precisely through distinction, prominence and public recognition. This was why Burckhardt went on to argue that the new forms of individuality were accompanied by 'a new sort of outward distinction – the modern form of glory' (p. 104). Again Dante was exemplary – although he also had his reservations about the transience of this-worldly fame, Burckhard felt that 'he laid stress on the fact that what he did was new, and that he wished not only to be, but to be esteemed the first in his own walks' (p. 104). Individuality was expressed through the constant production of novelty and innovation, and the organization of individual striving around the high points, the landmarks and reference points of these creative production processes. He highlighted the 'cultus' of the birthplace, death and burial sites of famous men such as Dante, Petrarch and Boccaccio. It became 'a point of honour for the different cities to possess the bones of their own and foreign celebrities' (p. 106), so that '[h]istory and the new topography were now careful to leave no local celebrity unnoticed' (p. 107).

The 'boundless ambition and thirst after greatness' (p. 109) in this 'age of overstrained and despairing passions and forces' (p. 110) in northern Italy was indeed powerful enough for people commit murder in order to achieve celebrity; he quoted Machievelli's critique, in his *History of Florence*, of his predecessors, who had 'erred greatly and showed that they understood little the ambition of men and the desire to perpetuate a name. How many who could distinguish themselves by nothing praiseworthy, strove to do so by infamous deeds!' (p. 109). These crimes included, for example, the assassination of Alessandro de' Medici, Duke of Florence, by Lorenzino de' Medici in 1537, which the historian Paolo Giovio attributed to Lorenzino's desire, after a public disgrace, for 'a deed whose novelty shall make his disgrace forgotten' (p. 110).

Thinking in terms of an 'emergence' or 'discovery' of 'the individual' is not without its problems. Peter Burke, for example, argues that Burckhardt's contrast with the Middle Ages was too sharply drawn, underestimating the significance of individuality in the Middle Ages, particularly from the twelfth century onwards (Morris 1987), and exaggerating the concern with the self in the fifteenth and sixteenth centuries, with people continuing to identify with 'family, guild, faction or city' (Burke 1997: 18). The Renaissance concern with celebrity was not a universal passion, there were equally strong countervailing currents, and the evidence on portraiture is contradictory, showing a concern for *both* the collective and institutional aspects of identity *as well as* individual distinctiveness. Although Burke agrees that one can observe 'a changing sense of self between Petrarch and Descartes, both more unified than before and more sharply distinguished from the outside world of family and community' (Burke 1997: 27), his own preferred account is a multi-layered one, drawing attention to the effects of increased travel, the spread of print, urbanization, Protestantism, and the return to classical Greek and Roman thought.

Burke does mention an alternative to thinking in terms of a change in 'spirit', but only in passing, noting that '[T]he parallel between these developments and the rise of the centralized nation state is an intriguing one' (1997: 27). This idea is developed in more detail by Aaron Gurevich, who suggests that it is important to see shifts in individual self-awareness as interdependent with changing structure and dynamics of the social groups of which individuals were part, and more generally 'the emergence of the individual' as interlinked with broader social transformations (Gurevich 1995: 10–14). In other words, to understand the nature of individualism, one has to look simultaneously at the social forms and institutions within which people are able to express or manifest their individuality. As soon as one looks beyond the worlds of art, literature and philosophy, there is no shortage of evidence concerning the institutional dimensions of early modern European society, politics, administration and law, which probably did more than the emergence of a 'spirit' of individualism to systematically turn 'peasants into Frenchmen' (E. Weber 1976) and to make all levels of social life an ensemble of factories of individualism.

Max Weber (1930), for example, saw the individualizing discipline associated with ascetic Protestantism as playing a crucial role in the development of Western capitalism, and for the German historian Gerhard Oestreich, the kind of psychology and world-view promoted by the Reformation was in turn the product of a more general, non-confessional cultural and ideological change related to the regulatory interventions of the state at all its levels in everyday life. We can only answer 'the troublesome question of how it was possible for constitutional ideas emanating from the Calvinist Netherlands to exercise so much influence in Lutheran and Catholic countries', he wrote, by 'simultaneously considering political Neostoicism (which was essentially unconfessional) and the philosophy of natural law' (Oestreich 1982: 69).

The princes had their own problems of power and control at court, but there were more than enough issues at the local level as well: the population movements from country to towns produced a variety of problems of social order and discipline as people used to the intense daily gaze of village life had to adjust to the 'freedom' of town air. As Oestreich observes, the newcomers 'all had to adapt to new lifestyles for which rural customs and traditions were an inadequate preparation' (1982: 156). Vagrancy, poverty, work discipline, social order generally were all ongoing issue for local and regional authorities, and it did not take long for those authorities to understand that the normalization of conduct was most effective when it was individualized – the whole point was to break down communal identities resistant to the demands of changing social conditions.

Existing forms of social organization, particularly the Church, were sluggish in managing to maintain social order in the face of the turbulence of life in the late Middle Ages. Town councils were acting within an atmosphere of crisis, of 'something has to be done', as the moral authority of the Church and – more importantly – its organizational means of policing that authority, appeared inadequate to the task of dealing with the new problems of social order, especially vagrancy and the establishment of a work discipline appropriate to the developing forms of urban production. By the end of the sixteenth century, wrote Oestreich, one can speak of 'regulation mania' in Western European towns, with police ordinances laying down rules and regulations for 'every conceivable area' of private life – Sunday observance, blasphemy, expenditure on weddings, christenings and funerals, as well as the time spent on them, the upbringing of children, hygiene, patterns of consumption, breaches of the peace, begging and alms-giving, and so on (1982: 157). Workhouses and welfare systems needed to be established to satisfy Christian consciences about the welfare of fellow human beings, while also managing the potentially endless drain of the poor and unemployed on town finances and inculcating new habits of work discipline.

This surge of policing activity during the sixteenth century accompanied the transformation of medieval Christianity by the new conceptual and philosophical framework provided by the renewed study of Roman philosophers and lawyers by humanist intellectuals, generating a neo-Stoicist philosophical orientation to the world which aimed to generate a reading of ancient Stoic ideas which was consistent with Christianity, stressing the construction of 'good order' based on obedience to a central, secular authority – the state – and a rational self-discipline. Oestreich sees this intellectual shift as revolving around the person and work of Justus Lipsius (1547–1606), a Flemish professor of history and law at Leiden University, as well as the transmission of his ideas throughout Europe – Germany, France, England, Scandinavia, Spain, Italy and Switzerland – through the 'Netherlands movement'. Lipsius wrote prolifically on army reform, the conduct of politics and administration, and the law, and whose object was work 'to educate a new kind of man, the individual with a civic sense who would go beyond the Christianity of the Middle Ages, embrace the old Roman values, and demonstrate the importance of rationality in character, action and thought' (1982: 28).

The starting point for the spread of Lipsius's ideas and the Netherlands movement was their role in the reform of the House of Orange's army and its subsequent military successes against the occupying Spanish army. Lipsius's work on military ethics provided an answer to the question exercising the minds of Europe's military commanders – 'how to establish and maintain good order and military discipline in the unruly armies of the day'. The actual means by which social discipline was meant to be imposed was a disciplined ordering of individuals' external environment – drill, routine, regime – which would then in turn impose order on their internal psychic life. An increasing proportion of Europe's scholars and administrators came to be educated either by Lipsius himself or by teachers of ethics, philosophy and law who shared his views on rationality and self- discipline, to spread the neo-Stoicist argument for rationality in everyday life among Europe's university-trained elite and court society.

Neo-Stoicism was far more this-worldly and practically oriented than Calvinism, and had a discernable effect on the thought processes and conceptual apparatuses of early modern European bureaucrats and lawyers, as neo-Stoicist thinkers encouraged the European aristocracy and upper bourgeoisie 'to assume an educative role and to bring many areas of public life under the control of the state for the first time' (Oestreich 1982: 7). Although a concern with interior psychological life and the self as a distinct individual was not especially new, in the sixteenth century, driven by these broader social and political changes, it became more pervasive and more intense in the work of Petrarch, Montaigne, Shakespeare, Erasmus and Luther, and reached an ever-expanding audience in the greatly expanded 'public sphere' of the printed word.

There were two central element of the intensified concern with the self which are useful to highlight in relation to the question of celebrity. The first was an increase in attention to an obvious corollary question, that of authenticity and sincerity, of what distinctions could or should be made between the 'real' self as opposed to its theatrical presentation. This was a question which was possibly most acute in court society given its stress on performativity, but it had also become a more general issue throughout sixteenth-century social life. A useful illustration of the problem of sincerity is the story of French peasant Martin Guerre, who disappeared in 1548, and the capacity of impostor Arnaud du Tilh to appear in 1556 and come close to persuading a sufficient number of people, including Martin's wife, of his authenticity, finally foiled only by the real Martin's reappearance at Arnaud's trial in 1560 (Davis 1983). The opposition which emerged was between 'prudence' – the conscious tailoring of the presentation of self to particular ends divorced from any particular relationship to ethics (Machiavelli) – and 'sincerity' – the insistence that exterior presentation and interior psychic life should more or less correspond. Montaigne expressed the second position when he wrote 'It is enough to make up our face, without making up our heart' (1958: 773–4). This contrast between 'political prudence' and 'beautiful souls' (Vowinckel 1983) often took the form of a tension between aristocratic and bourgeois or republican rationality, as well as a bourgeois critique in the name of authenticity, of aristocratic deceitfulness, and this can be explained in terms of the distinct structures of their differing situations (Vowinckel 1987: 490).

However, in practice there was never any final victory to the model of authenticity, and the psychological logic of court society remained salient. Later in the French Revolution, as Lynn Hunt points out, dissimulation was an important question:

> The ability to conceal one's true emotions, to act one way in public and another in private, was repeatedly denounced as the chief characteristic of court life and aristocratic manners in general. These relied above all on appearances, that is, on the disciplined and self-conscious use of the body as a mask. The republicans, consequently, valued transparency – the unmediated expression of the heart – above all other personal qualities. Transparency was the perfect fit between public and private; transparency was a body that told no lies and kept no secrets. It was the definition of virtue, and as such it was imagined to be critical to the future of the republic.
>
> (1992: 96–7)

There is no better illustration of the persistence of court society, then, than the continuation of the tension between prudence and sincerity as a live issue in all aspects of modern life to this day, with being 'true to oneself' remaining an aspiration never entirely realizable, a problem to be constantly wrestled with and meditated upon rather than one lending itself to definitive solution. This is one of the constitutive reasons for the acute interest in the question of how sincerity and prudence, private and public lives relate to each other, which in turn underpins the fascination with the management of these issues by those prominent individuals socially constituted as exemplary.

The second important aspect of the logic of early modern individualism worth pausing beside, itself tied to the expansion of court society and state administration, was the close association with the related ideas of democracy and meritocracy. If one allowed for some degree of detachment of individual identity from its social origins and context, it followed that social status was increasingly to be understood in terms of individual attributes, talent and effort rather than social location, as *achieved* rather than *ascribed*. Individualistic cognitive structures, institutional forms and social practices opened the doors to the idea of the distribution of esteem and recognition becoming increasingly democratic – accessible to everyone regardless of their lineage or social location – and meritocratic – its outcomes explainable in terms of individual merit – skill, aptitude, expertise, knowledgeability, effort, application, stamina, wisdom, charisma, and so on – rather than characteristics such as background, class, racial or ethnic identity. Such a distribution of recognition need be no less hierarchical and no less productive of elites and aristocracies, it was simply that its logic and foundations had shifted to questions of merit.

The idea that the king had two bodies, a public persona or office as well as his physical body, had characterized theories of politics since the twelfth century. In *Willion v Berkley*,[8] the court argued as follows:

[T]he King has two Capacities, for he has two Bodies, the one whereof is a Body natural, consisting of natural Members as every other Man has, and in this he is subject to Passions and to Death as other Men are: the other is a Body politic, and the Members thereof are his Subjects, and he and his Subjects together compose the corporation, as Southcote said, and he is incorporated with them, and they with him, and he is the Head, and they are the Members, and he has sole Government of them: and this Body is not subject to Passions as the other is, nor to Death, for as to this Body the King never dies, and his natural Death is not called in our Law (as Harper said) the Death of the King, but the Demise of the King, not signifying by the Word (Demise) that the Body politic of the King is dead, but that there is a Separation of the two Bodies, and that the Body politic is transferred and conveyed over from the Body natural now dead, or now removed from the Dignity royal, to another Body natural.[9]

However, in the course of the sixteenth and seventeenth centuries, as court society and absolutist state administration expanded, the king's 'Body politic' became an increasingly complex beast, and under influences such as the utilitarian concerns of neo-Stoicist approaches to politics and society, kings such as Louis XIV expanded the conception of personal service by the nobility to include and become consistent with more impersonal conceptions of service to state and society driven by more pragmatic and goal-directed criteria of value, worth and nobility. By the late eighteenth century, the shift had run most of its course and Chaussinand-Nogaret goes as far as to argue that 'there was no longer any significant difference between the nobility and the bourgeoisie' (1985: 53).

Transformations of communication: print and theatre

Celebrity depends on its communication. This means that the nature of the means of communication has a defining impact on the structure and dynamics of celebrity, and the communication revolution that took place with the advent of the printing press in the fifteenth and sixteenth centuries was a key element of the foundations of modern celebrity. In a sense, every age produces its celebrities, its famous and prominent individuals, but the nature of the modes of communication supporting celebrity in the ancient and medieval worlds were slow and cumbersome, and as soon as information was to flow beyond their immediate context, it was delayed in time and tended to be about events and personalities in the past, rather than in the present. This was to change with the invention of movable type and the printing press, many say by Gutenberg in the German town of Mainz around 1450, and the spread of printing workshops and presses from that point onwards. The large-scale utilization of the printing press could be said to have been more or less in place throughout Europe by the beginning of the sixteenth century.

The impact of printing on European culture, society, politics and law is difficult to overestimate. Elizabeth Eisenstein, for example, argues that we might as well dispense with concepts such as the Renaissance which are difficult to pin down and define, and simply speak of the transition from a scribal to a typographical culture and society. It is hard to imagine the transformations wrought by the Reformation, for example, without print – A.G. Dickens estimates that Luther's 30 publications sold more than 300,000 copies between 1517 and 1520, and Protestant reformers were keenly aware of the power of the printed work in liberating them, as they saw it, from the Roman bondage. As Dickens observes:

> Unlike the Wycliffite and Waldensian heresies, Lutheranism was from the first the child of the printed book, and through this vehicle Luther was able to make exact, standardized and ineradicable impressions on the mind of Europe. For the first time in human history a great reading public judged the validity of revolutionary ideas through a mass-medium which used the vernacular language together with the arts of the journalist and the cartoonist.
>
> (1966: 51)

The spread of the printed word and the creation of a reading public contributed to an increasing individualism, because every reader had their own, individual and anonymous, relationship to the imagined community created by books, newspapers and pamphlets. Printed text became a tool of the powerful and those who resisted them alike, an arena which struggles over power had henceforth to enter sooner or later. From this point onwards, the mobilization of any effective number of people was organized around printed materials. The bourgeoisie was by definition a republic composed of 'men of letters', their ideas spread as effectively and widely as they were only by virtue of the printing press. Even if literacy was slower to spread, up until the end of the nineteenth century, hearing publics were listening to written materials (Eisenstein 1968: 30). Everything that ordinary people knew about themselves, their lives and their social roles was transformed, henceforth informed to a far greater extent than was even possible before printing, whether directly or indirectly, by the thoughts of Erasmus, Luther, Calvin, Dante, Shakespeare, Castiglione, even Aristotle, Plato and the neo-Stoicists.

The emergence of 'typographical man' was to open up an enormous new, and infinitely expandable, social space in which a growing number of individuals could use the greater circulation of stories and images to carve out novel ways of attracting attention, recognition and esteem – novelists, philosophers, diarists, playwrights, biographers and autobiographers, and then actors and actresses, through the publicity which surrounded their performance. A public sphere organized around the printed word created both new foundations and a new vehicle for celebrity. As Eisenstein pointed out, print made literature hugely more attractive and effective as a means of achieving celebrity, and Juvenal's *insanabile scribendi cacoethes* – incurable passion for writing – was transformed into something quite different when it became an 'itch to publish' (Merton 1965: 83–5, 1968: 61):

The wish to see one's work in print (fixed forever with one's name, in card files and anthologies) is different from the urge to pen lines that could never get fixed in a permanent form, might be lost forever, altered by copying, or – if truly memorable – carried by oral transmission and assigned ultimately to 'anon'.

(Eisenstein 1968: 23)

One of the many ways in which the nature of the radical transformation of social life in the eighteenth century has been captured has been to speak of the emergence of a 'public sphere', a realm of ongoing debate of current political and social issues which the German sociologist Jurgen Habermas defines as 'a forum in which private people, come together to form a public, readied themselves to compel public authority to legitimate itself before public opinion' (1989: 25–6). He sees this emerging public sphere as consisting of books, pamphlets, newspapers, journals as well as locations and events such as literary salons, coffee houses, meeting halls, reading clubs, public assemblies. For Habermas, the bourgeois public sphere is that space between private life and the state, where 'something approaching public opinion can be formed', a form of public opinion that was a counter to the projection of royal authority, built on 'the remains of a collapsing form of publicity (the courtly one)' (1989: 30) and increasingly subject to critical contestation by every individual conducting themselves as rational and responsible citizens.

Although he often refers to 'the' public sphere, Habermas also sees it as internally differentiated into distinct 'public spheres' – he distinguishes, for example, between the political public sphere dealing with public policy and the state, and its precursor, the literary public sphere, engaging with culture, literature and art. But in both arenas, for Habermas, the public sphere is something sober, serious and deeply meaningful, where public opinion is formed about weighty political and philosophical questions, where profound intellectual issues generate intense and consequential debate.[10] But as John B. Thompson observes, this characterization of the public sphere is to a large extent a result of Habermas's focus on the periodical press, and if he had examined the full range of printed material available at the time, a different picture of early modern public life would have emerged:

one which placed less emphasis on the idea of gentlemen engaged in coffeehouse debate and highlighted more sharply the commercial character of the early press and the somewhat scurrilous and sensationalist content of many of its products.

(Thompson 1995: 72)

Equally important, both in general terms and for our purposes of analysing celebrity, was the world of the theatre – another central aspect of the revival of the thoughts and practices of antiquity – the arena where critical perspectives on public authority were also aired, often with greater effect because of the immediacy and physicality of the theatre experience. As Braudy emphasizes, the 17th century thus marks the increasing importance of theatre not only for the self-presentation of public men, but also for the way in which all individuals contemplate the nature of their rules and themselves as social beings. Without Elizabethan and Jacobean theatre, the theories of personality pioneered by writers like Hobbes and Locke are impossible to understand.

(1986: 319)

The public intimacy accompanying Restoration theatre life was, as Roach observes, 'the sexy version of the worthy but stolid bourgeois public sphere described by Jürgen Habermas' (2003: 216). It was the theatre that provided people with 'equipment for living' (Burke 1941) in period of dramatic social change and, alongside the symbolism of the Tudor and Elizabethan state, contributing significantly to the displacement of the Church's hold over popular as well as elite culture.

Medieval theatre had in many respects been dominated by religious concerns, consisting of liturgical dramas, mystery/miracle plays (Bible stories) and morality plays, although in practice the Christian concerns often functioned primarily as a 'shell' for secular, sometimes pre-Christian pagan themes.[11] During the sixteenth century, the combination of Protestant reform, expanding capitalist enterprise, and the spread of printing underpinned both Protestants and Catholics attacking religious theatre for the rival faith's content, the revival of Greek and Roman drama, and 'a proliferation in the publication and circulation of vernacular texts, including works of fiction and play texts'. As Louis Montrose outlines,

Not only writers but also printers, booksellers, editors, translators, redactors, commentators – and, of course, readers and audiences – shared in this increasingly dispersed and diversified process of formulating, glossing, disputing, and revising cultural meanings. The momentous consequence of this decentering of control over the signifying process was a decentering of the sources of cultural authority.

(1996: 22)

The Elizabethan aristocracy saw the theatre as a crucial strategic field for a number of reasons. In the first place, they did not much like or enjoy what was on offer. Armed with their new-found literacy, education and cosmopolitan tastes, endless repetition of religious themes was not very interesting any more, and they had no desire to be preached at. Second, they wanted to promote a professional, secular and national theatre largely to break down the medieval theatre's Catholic symbolism, rooted in local traditions, to make way for a representation of social order, authority and community organized around the absolutist state.

Absolutist monarchs and nobilities thus began patronizing new forms of theatre for their own entertainment, first at court itself, evolving out of the earlier forms of 'playing' – juggling, acrobatics, jesting – and then in permanent theatres also open to a wider public, to help defray costs, enhance their own experience and also to project their own symbolic power more widely and effectively. 'It is very clear', wrote Frank Wilson, 'that if the court had not been addicted to drama, or had been powerless to protect the players, there would have been no Elizabethan drama' (1955: 41). 'Players' still had no legal status in sixteenth-century society,[12] defined as vagabonds and beggars unless they were attached to a noble, so the movement away from medieval theatre emerged from an alliance between court society providing legitimation on the one hand, and commercial enterprise on the other, with theatre companies often taking the form of joint-stock companies owned by the leading actors and financiers. Shakespeare's company, Lord Chamberlain's Men, was established in 1594, becoming the King's Men in 1603, and the other companies included Lord Strange's Men (1560s), becoming Lord Derby's Men in 1593 and Lord Howard's Men (1570s). By the 1570s, there were a number of enormously popular and generally commercially successful professional theatre companies operating in London, stimulated by the building of permanent theatres, but all under the patronage of powerful nobles. Actors such as Edward Alleyn (1566–1626), Augustine Phillips (d. 1605), Richard Burbage (1568–1619) and William Shakespeare (1564–1616) became wealthy, although as theatrical producers and entrepreneurs, not as actors or playwrights.

However, the court's patronage of secular, professional theatre proved quickly to be a double-edged sword, because the skilled actor demonstrated how all of life can be 'acted' with greater or lesser talent, including the role of the monarch. 'I am Richard II, know ye not that?' Elizabeth I is reported to have said when attempting to censor Shakespeare's play, and bad performers such as Charles I who paid too little attention to their audience's expectations would end up losing their heads. In attempting to use the theatre to project state power, the absolutist state had created a new legitimation problem, because actors could outperform actual kings, and the theatre changed people's perception of authority and social order, making problematic the distinction between the social role and the real human occupying it. As Erasmus wrote in 1516, 'if a necklace, a scepter, royal purple robes, a train of attendants are all that make a king, what is to prevent the actors who come on the stage decked with all the pomp of state from being called king?' Perhaps Charles II understood this when, after theatre was released from Puritan bondage with the Restoration of the monarchy in 1660 and actresses began appearing on the public stage, he frequented the theatre and included actresses Moll Davis and then Nell Gwynn (1650–87) among his many mistresses – he dissipated the dangers of the new form of attracting and holding public attention by becoming resolutely part of it.

The appearance of women on the public stage after 1660 with the ascension of Charles II to the throne was particularly electrifying in England. There had been a convention of female parts being played by pubescent boys, the general public had been hostile to women on stage, and theatre had been banned between 1642 and 1660 under the Puritans. 'Imagine the frisson', writes Amanda Vickery in *The Guardian*, about an exhibition at London's National Portrait Gallery – *The First Actresses: Nell Gwynn to Sarah Siddons* – 'when Nell Gwynn first showed herself aged 14 to a packed house at the Theatre Royal, Covent Garden, in 1664' (2011).

The re-opening of theatres quickly produced a new relationship between audiences and male but especially female actors in the theatrical public sphere. Women on stage challenged deeply rooted conceptions of femininity as confined to the private realm of family life, and an important aspect of the way this challenge was dealt with was the eroticization of women's public presence as well as developing intimate and personal relationships between actresses and their audiences. An important device here was the intimate prologue and epilogue (Howe 1992: 91–8), where actresses would step out of character and address the audience directly, making suggestive linkages between their private lives and their characters.

By the late seventeenth century the character of individual actors and actresses had come to play a central role, and plays came to be written around the leading players – actresses such as Anne Bracegirdle, Moll Davis, Elizabeth Barry, Anne Oldfield and Nell Gwynn on her own and as part of a very popular 'gay couple' with Charles Hart. As John Wilson observed:

> Shakespeare's women were the creation of a teeming imagination; his poetic pen gave to airy nothing a local habitation and a name, and its only limitation was the number of competent, well-trained boys available at a given time . . . But the Restoration playwright, working in an age when the speaker had become more important than the word, confined by the necessity of writing not just for actresses but for a specific Nell, Anne, or Betty, and influenced during the creative process by the acting styles of those women, had to suit his roles to their abilities, their types, and, worst of all, to their personal reputations.
>
> (1958: 107–8)

Audiences took a keen interest in the backstage private lives of actresses in particular, circulated and kept alive through personal connections and gossip, but also, importantly, through printed satires, biographies and memoirs, making Restoration actresses of more interest than the roles they played. As Felicity Nussbaum observes, the creation of public intimacy 'involved performing within the public realm with the express intent to expose private matters and to generate affect around their own persons in order to kindle celebrity' (Nussbaum 2005: 150).

Elizabeth Barry (1658–1713) is particularly interesting as a seventeenth-century Pygmalion story – in her first attempts at acting with Sir William's company, 'she showed so little promise that she was dismissed . . . as hopeless stage material' (Lanier 1930: 63). She was not a particular beauty, and she had no ear for music. John Wilmot, the Earl of Rochester, took a liking to the 16 year old and took her under his wing, becoming her lover. There is a story told by Edmund Curll, perhaps unreliable, that he made a bet that he could turn her into a fine actress in six months. Regardless of whether he did coach her, she was indeed a triumph at her first subsequent performance, before Charles II, the queen, and the Duke and Duchess of York – as Isabella, queen of Hungary, in the earl of Orrery's *Mustapha*. She went on not only to become a star of the English stage, but, alongside a number of other talented actresses and actors, also to exercise a 'return effect' on the aristocracy she was mimicking as an actress, who quickly realized they had much to learn about the grace, elegance and conviction of their own performances. A star system which linked the world of the theatre to the world of the court and the aristocracy was firmly in place by the beginning of the eighteenth century and, as Felicity Nussbaum observes, '[t]he new celebrity of actresses made many of them, if not equivalent to royalty, the sought-after imitation of it' (2005: 152).

The alliance between theatre and the printed word was an important vehicle for the spread of ideas, practices and psychological dispositions from court society through the rest of the social body, to gradually become 'society'. The celebrity produced in the theatrical public sphere starts off within and under the control of the court, gradually straddles court, town and countryside, and then cuts loose from court society altogether to generate its own autonomous forms, and the circulation of books, newspapers, journals and magazines such as *The Tatler* and *The Spectator* eagerly seeking their readers' attention was central to this expansion of the world of celebrity. Cheryl Wanko points out that people 'spoke more frequently about figures with whom they had little or no contact, as newspapers and magazines worked to fill their pages, stoking and feeding readers' growing desire for information about their contemporaries' (Wanko 2003: 211).

By the middle of the eighteenth century, playwrights such as Colley Cibber (1671–1757) and actors such as David Garrick (1717–79) were perfecting the production of celebrity, encouraged an illusion of familiarity with the private lives of those entirely distant from, but nonetheless apparently intimately well known to, an ever-expanding domestic and international audience (Glover 2002: 523). Court society and its psychological disposition had gained still more ground, with celebrities such as Cibber and Garrick embodying the principle that one was never offstage.

In addition to print becoming cheaper and the audience larger, wealthier and increasingly hungry for books and printed materials of various sorts, an important shift in the production process of all aspects of the public sphere was the expiry of the Licensing Act in 1694. Up until then, the two 'players' in relation to the control of the expanding market for printed materials were printers and publishers on the one hand, and the Crown on the other, seeking 'to prevent printing seditious and treasonable Book, Pamphlets, and Papers' (Licensing of the Press Act 1662), which was achieved by granting a monopoly over printing to the Company of Stationers. The House of Commons refused to renew the Licensing Act in 1694 – they felt it was bad legislation for a number of reasons, including that it gave the Company of Stationers disproportionate monopoly rights, placed too many restrictions on the importation of books, and its penalties were far too draconian for the offences it identified (Auchter 2001: 389–90). In response to lobbying from both authors (seeking another form of protection) and publishers (who shielded their own interests behind those of authors in relation to the Crown), the *Statute of Anne* (1710)[13] granted copyright to authors (for 28 years). The growing audience for books, magazine, journals and newspapers – there were 60 weekly newspapers being printed in London by 1770 (Tillyard 2005b: 63) – meant that authors joined their publishers in having a greater financial interest in all types of literary production, and private patronage had given way to the public market as the primary source of economic support for authors. The effect of this was to give the public even greater control over what was to constitute celebrity, and weak libel laws meant that scandal, gossip and innuendo dominated the public sphere. As Stella Tillyard observes, 'by the 1750s, all sorts of people who wanted notoriety were leaking to or placing in the press intimate or scandalous details of their own lives. Celebrity was born at the moment private life became a tradeable public commodity' (2005b: 64).

The proliferation of the means by which celebrity could be generated, in newspapers, coffee-houses, salons and reading clubs, meant that it became possible for celebrity producers to become celebrities themselves at the same time. It had been possible for historians and philosophers to become celebrated themselves by writing about other famous people, but projected into the past, hardly ever while they were still alive. It was after the production of printed materials had reached a certain degree of efficiency and range of distribution that it was possible for celebrity producers to become contemporaneous with their celebrities, and for individuals seeking celebrity to work with increasing efficiency on the production of their own celebrity. Peter Lely (1618–80), both the portrait painter of Oliver Cromwell 'warts and all' and Charles II's court painter, stimulated the field of celebrity portraiture in the seventeenth century, producing images of the leading figures of the aristocracy as well as of Charles II's mistresses, and introducing the practice of making prints of his portraits for circulation in England and on the continent. Lely's portraits of women were clearly eroticized, observes Joseph Roach, and he argues that Samuel Pepys's commentaries on the new approach to portraits suggest that he regarded them as constituting the 'appropriation of the religious aura of celebrity by an erotic one' (Roach 2003: 215). Pepys himself was mesmerized by the image of one of Charles II's mistresses in particular, Barbara Villiers, Countess of Castlemaine, obtaining three copies of one of Lely's portraits, as Roach emphasies, 'the modern effigy, a mesmerizing image of unobtainable yet wholly portable celebrity' (2003: 223).

The next important figure in this expanding generation of celebrity in England was Joshua Reynolds (1723–92), with Thomas Gainsborough the dominant portrait artist of the eighteenth century. Reynolds pursued a very active social life, both attending whatever social events and clubs he could get to, and founding his own very selective 'Literary Club', at first with nine members including Samuel Johnson, Edmund Burke, Oliver Goldsmith and Reynolds, and later admitting David Garrick, Edward Gibbon, Charles James Fox, Adam Smith and Richard Brinsley Sheridan, 'a coterie that eclipsed even the most exclusive aristocratic and courtly enclaves' (Tillyard 2005b: 23).

Reynolds used his position as the first president of the Royal Academy relentlessly for 'the promotion of his personal status, through friends, patrons, his own writings on art, and his astute manipulation of the media' (Postle 2005: 22). He also realized that having the favour of the court was not all there was to success in eighteenth-century London, that the city was also important, but especially the aristocrats opposing the king in the Whig party. In his choice of portraits to paint, Reynolds 'openly identified with fashionable Whig society; the Georgian 'glitterati' – liberal in their politics, liberated in their social attitudes, and libidinous in their sexual behaviour' (Tillyard 2005b: 23), including alongside his powerful lords, dukes, princes and admirals, their courtesans and mistresses as well as their wives and daughters. As Reynolds, put it, '[d]istinction is what we all seek after . . . and I go with the great stream of life' (cited in Postle 2005b: 32). An important aspect of his achievement of distinction was his astute use of print – he made sure his portraits were engraved, printed and widely distributed throughout the British Isles and Europe, greatly enhancing the celebrity status of both Reynolds himself and his sitters – including the Prince of Wales, the future Charles IV, William Blackstone, Edmund Burke, Samuel Johnson, Adam Ferguson, but also prominent aristocratic women such as Georgina Cavendish, Duchess of Devonshire, and courtesans such as Kitty Fisher and Emma Hart (Clayton 2005).

The mechanics of celebrity production and its particularly modern, democratic logic establish an intimate relationship of identification with the audience that is now clearly visible, as Braudy notes, in the figures of Rousseau and Benjamin Franklin, a 'living emblem of the self-created and self-described for the 18th century' (Braudy 1986: 366). What Braudy refers to as 'modern' fame is by now distinctive enough to be understood as 'celebrity':

> Both Franklin and Rousseau practice an assertiveness, a willingness to take the stage, that is justified not by blood or money but by a paradoxical uniqueness: Praise me because I am unique, but praise me as well because my uniqueness is only a more intense and more public version of your own . . . Rousseau strikes a wholly modern note in the history of fame by his preoccupation with the expectation of being recognized for what he 'really' is. He seeks a fame for naturalness, a fame for inner qualities, for what one is without the overlay of social forms. It is a fame of feeling, a 'natural fame' that is held personally, without forebears or tradition, and rejects any honor or virtue that must be validated by social position and social visibility.
>
> (1986: 371–2; for Rousseau, see Lilti 2008 and Brock 2006)

John Adams also provides interesting commentary on George Washington as a celebrity, his status and recognition as much a product of talents such as a handsome face, tall stature, graceful movement, self-command in public, and being a Virginian – 'this is equivalent to five talents. Virginian geese are all swans' (Parry-Giles 2008: 95). The concept of 'puffing' – 'the giving of extravagant or unwarranted praise or commendation; promotion or advertisement through the writing or publication of puffs' (OED 1989) – had emerged to capture what would today be called public relations or publicity, a manufacturing of public opinion, the systematic and goal-directed organization of the presentation of self in public which was increasingly to become the norm. Authors, for example, would arrange for their friends to write favourable reviews; when the Scottish writer James

Beattie asked a colleague to write a favourable review of his forthcoming book, he observed that '[p]uffing is so constantly used on these occasions that the omission of it would seem to bespeak either total unconcern about public approbation or that the production is altogether unsupported or friendless' (cited in Sher 2006: 138).

These three intersecting trajectories of historical transformation – the emergence and evolution of court society, the growth of individualism, and the development of printing as a means of mass communication, especially in relation to theatre and art – together established the basic principles and logic of celebrity society, but they were to be taken to new levels with the industrialization of celebrity, the expansion of mass society as well as mass markets and, above all, the emergence of new forms of representation and communication – photography, film, radio, television and most recently the Internet. Let us now turn in the next chapter to a closer examination of the industrialization of celebrity, the economic logic underlying the production of the 'attention-traps' that constitute celebrity.

2 Producing celebrity and the economics of attention

In fact, the mass of the English people yield a deference rather to something else than to their rulers. They defer to what we may call the theatrical show of society. A certain state passes before them; a certain pomp of great men; a certain spectacle of beautiful women; a wonderful scene of wealth and enjoyment is displayed, and they are coerced by it. Their imagination is bowed down; they feel they are not equal to the life which is revealed to them. Courts and aristocracies have the great quality which rules the multitude, though philosophers can see nothing in it – visibility.

(Walter Bagehot 1867: 51)

As New Yorkers have learnt, nurses and firemen are real heroes. Celebrity is a bit silly, but it is a currency of a kind.

(Paul Hewson (aka Bono), in Mueller 2001)

The 'Josephine Machine' – producing celebrity

During the course of the nineteenth century, celebrity society was industrialized along with the rest of social life. Populations grew and urbanized enormously; in the United States, the population grew from 5 to 76 million between 1800 and 1900; in England, it went from 10 to 38 million. The growth was especially marked in the cities – Berlin, for example, doubled in size from one to two million between 1875 and 1905. As populations grew and towns and cities expanded, so too did audiences for all forms of entertainment – advances in stage technology and better costuming made theatre more spectacular, guided in Britain by a new generation of highly successful actor–managers including Stephen Kemble (1758–1822), Elizabeth Satchell (1763–1841), Eliza Vestris (1797–1856), Charles Kean (1811–68), Henry Irving (1838–1905) and Herbert Beerbohm Tree (1852–1917). The development of railways, steamships and the telegraph made the rapid transfer of information and news possible, and the demand for news was insatiable. Printing presses became faster and more productive to match the growing size of the readership. *The Times* was first printed with steam-driven printing presses in 1814, and, in 1833, the rotary printing press was introduced in the United States, capable of printing millions of copies of newspapers per day. The growth of newspapers was spectacular: the *New York Sun* was founded in 1833 and sold 3000 copies that year; by 1838 it was selling 30,000.

The introduction and spread of photography from 1840 onwards made an enormous difference to the democratization of the production of celebrity, taking, as Braudy puts it, 'the art of imaging out of the hands of those skilled enough to paint or engrave as well as those rich enough to and placing it at the disposal of virtually everyone' (1986: 492). To get a sense of how quickly photography spread, in 1851 there were around 51 photographers in Britain; in 1861, there were 2800 (Mathews 1974: 18). The photograph made it possible for the aspiring celebrity to establish a far more intimate relationship with their audience, spontaneous, adaptable and with the aura of 'reality'. By the 1860s, it had become virtually compulsory for anyone wishing to have a public profile – royalty, aristocracy, politicians, writers, poets, painters, sculptors, musicians, actors and actresses, scientists, social reformers, explorers, and generals (Mathews 1974: 52–60) – to have their photos taken and distributed as their *carte-de-visite* (McCauley 1985). Karl Marx had one produced around 1870, taken by John Mayall. The *carte-de-visite* was created by a French photographer, André Adolphe Eugéne Disdéri, in 1854. Disdéri's clever innovation was to use cameras with multiple lens so as to produce eight images on every photographic plate, dramatically reducing the cost of individual *cartes*, and putting them within reach of a mass audience.

The *carte's* format – originally a 9x6cm visiting or calling card, but rarely used as such – made them, observes John Plunkett, a more appealing way to insert one's image into public circulation (2003: 151). Taken at a distance, they did not exaggerate prominent features, signs of ageing, or other imperfections, and by the late 1850s the *cartes* were the latest fashion throughout Europe and North America from 1859, a central focus of domestic sociability, increasingly assembled into the first photo albums, the proliferation of which rivalled that of the *cartes* themselves (Linkman 1993: 69–72). Albums would contain *cartes* of 'aunts in costly looking clothes, uncles in responsible and learned looking pose, and children' but they would lie alongside:

> the writers, the artists, the actors, the politicians (Gladstone in a Liberal home; Disraeli for the Tories), the clergy, the American generals, the assassinated Presidents Lincoln and Garfield, native, Aborigines, Maoris, European and British royalty . . . the famous in juxtaposition with the infamous, the well known with the little known, for admiration, for interest, for love.
>
> (Mathews 1974: 9–10)

The very idea of being able to see what a celebrity *really* looked like, and at a much lower price than a painting, print or drawing, was intoxicating. The firm of Marion & Co, distributed an enormous number and variety of celebrity images – Plunkett reports that 'their manager claimed that 50,000 *cartes* passed through the firm's hands every month', and they had difficulty keeping up with demand (Plunkett 2003: 153). They were really the precursors to *Hello* and *heat* magazines, generating a mass circulation of celebrity images which were incorporated into everyday life as soon as it became technologically and economically feasible. The most frequently photographed personalities copyrighted – and thus of some commercial value – in nineteenth-century England were the Prince and Princess of Wales, followed by the actress Ellen Terry (1847–1928), Queen Victoria, the actor–manager George Alexander (1858–1918), William Gladstone (1809–98), and another actress, Lille Langtrey (1853–1929) (Plunkett 2003: 157–9). But the field of celebrity also expanded, with photographers also able to make a reasonable living from *cartes* of local celebrities in provincial towns (Linkman 1993: 67).

'Cardomania' – 'cartomania' in France – spread to the US, and in 1863 Oliver Wendell Holmes wrote that 'card-portraits . . . as everybody knows, have become the social currency, the sentimental green-backs of civilization, within a very recent period' (1863: 8). The American Civil War simulated their popularity, as soldiers and their families captured each other's images as consolation for separation, either temporary or permanent.[1] Braudy notes few Americans would have known what Adams or Jefferson looked like, but by Lincoln's day 'the photograph had made the dissemination of the face even easier than that of the reputation or the ideas' (1986: 497). Lincoln accordingly attributed his election to both his New York Cooper Union address, which put him in contact with Eastern politicians and publishers, and the *carte-de-visite* that Mathew Brady – the American Joshua Reynolds in the age of photography – made for him in New York (Braudy 1986: 494). Even John Wilkes Booth, Lincoln's assassin, had a *carte* made (Mathews 1974: 26). Around the turn of the century, photography became even more convenient and widespread with the Brownie camera, as well as focusing and motorized film advance.

Alongside the technology of mass communication, the organizational technology of celebrity-production was also developing. Reynolds and Brady were still what Rein et al. (1997) call a cottage industry as public relations outfits, and Rein et al. do not see the industry as industrializing until Hollywood in the 1920s, but entrepreneurial characters such as the father of Irish child actor William Betty (1791–1874) and publicity entrepreneurs such as P.T. Barnum (1810–91) were to push the boundaries of that cottage industry to its outer limits, and pioneer techniques and strategies which laid the foundations for the expansion of the celebrity industry in the twentieth century. As Leo Braudy notes, musicians such as Franz Liszt, Frederic Chopin, Hector Berlioz and Niccoló Paganini constructed 'performing personas' which 'mingled aspects of the great artist with backstage tales of private life'. Liszt's enamoured audiences were entranced by any details about his private life, and pursued physical traces such as cigar butts and gloves with the same enthusiasm that the relics of saints and martyrs were sought. What Heinrich Heine called 'Lisztomania' was 'one of the earliest examples of the audience's desire to know more and more about the private life of the charismatic figure in an effort to ground his overwhelming appeal in some kind of common human nature' (Braudy 2010: 174; Gooley 2010). Celebrity in all its forms had become, suggests Lenard Berlanstein, 'an important prism through which the world was captured, explored, and explained' (2004: 79).

William Henry Best Betty, born in Shrewsbury and raised in Belfast, fell in love with the theatre and the idea of becoming an actor at the age of ten on seeing

Sarah Siddons perform in *Pizarro* at the Theatre Royal, and he had sufficient talent to secure roles in Belfast and then in Dublin, which generated sufficient audience interest to launch a tour of Edinburgh, Liverpool, Birmingham and then London during 1804, when he was 13. His performances generated a new form of popular frenzy, driven by a number of factors including the astute public relations strategies of his father, the appeal of his youth to Romantic culture, a desire for escapism in the shadow of impending conflict with Napoleon. David Garrick had been referred to as the English Roscius in the late eighteenth century, and Betty was billed as the 'Young' or 'Infant' Roscius to draw on Garrick's established place in popular memory. William Betty Sr built up audience interest in Ireland, Scotland and the English cities by tailoring Betty's performance to local concerns and interests – in Belfast and Dublin to loyalist pre-occupations, in Edinburgh to Scottish nationalists, and in England to the concern to sustain Britishness in the face of French aggression. Betty Sr pioneered a more intimate form of merchandising – smaller items designed to adorn the body or take up little space in the pocket. Jeffrey Kahan observes that the Betty merchandise, 'allowed buyers to pick and to choose the object that fit best their standard of living and their routine of daily existence' (Kahan 2010: 20), and helped underpin an 'illusion of a relationship' between Betty and his fans (p. 22).

Betty Sr had a talent for the construction of the artificial 'event' or act of heroism which would attract still more attention to Betty and make him the sole topic of conversation. An intense public interest was generated, recognizable as an early form of fan frenzy, described by Kahan as follows:

> Like the groupies who would a century and half later mob Elvis or the Beatles, fans raved and regularly fainted when near 'the divine Master Betty'. The *Caledonian Mercury* reported that on Betty's first London appearance, the 'screams of the females were very distressing, and several fainted away'; the *Morning Chronicle* reported that during a performance of Betty's Romeo, 'nearly thirty persons were pulled from the pit, in fainting fits.' One emboldened woman stood up in the theatre and promptly stripped down to her underwear. Even older, sophisticated men were strangely overcome by emotion; when watching the boy perform, Drury Lane's manager R.B. Sheridan sheds sighs, tears, and sobs; a similarly affected William Pitt, the prime minister, wept openly and controllably.

(2010: 14)

His youth, beauty and sexual ambiguity (there were some calls to investigate whether he was biologically male or female), combined with reasonable acting talent, were central objects of attention. Together with the claim to be the reincarnation of Roscius – both the original Roman actor and David Garrick – this meant that, as George Taylor has noted, 'The images he performed were thus of classical perfection, while his personal image was of innocence and inspiration' (2000: 153). At that particular point in British history, it was an ideal combination for the manufacture of public obsession:

What better distraction from the new-fangled armed ideology of France? What better validation for the naturalness of cultural nostalgia and for the innate creativity of the British? Beauty, nature and tradition were the icons of aristocracy and the cornerstones of Burkean conservatism. The court of Napoleon was artificial, a fantasy construction on bourgeois pretension and the force of arms, hypocritically eliding professions of liberty with national-istic aggrandisement, but in Britain we had the real thing – the purity of the child and the genius of nature.

(p. 153)

As powerful as Betty's celebrity was, it burned too brightly to last very long – by 1806 audiences were losing interest, there was increasing criticism of his acting talent, and of course as time went on he lost the novelty of his youth, suffering the fate of many a child prodigy to become a merely average actor, never quite succeeding in repeating the success for his own son's acting career. But Betty Sr had established many of the public relations techniques which were to be further developed in the course of the nineteenth and twentieth centuries – repackaging for particular local markets, the artificial creation of 'events' to stimulate public interest, the utilization of sexual ambiguity, the promotion of a particular novelty feature (here, Betty's youth), drawing on positive historical connections (Roscius, Garrick), and intimate forms of merchandising to establish an emotional connection with the audience.

For Queen Victoria, there was no need to generate artificial events, there were enough that were a normal part of her role as monarch – the coronation, wedding, visits, tours of just about every part of her domain (Plunkett 2003: 43), but like Betty, the public crowds attending Victoria's appearances were so enthusiastic and displayed such unrestrained intense emotion as to attract description in terms of madness and obsession (p. 135). The monarchy was under constant attack from radical and republican critics, making it a genuine achievement to sustain popular support and legitimacy, one that was realized in large part by Victoria and Prince Albert through the pursuit of a continuing affective bond with their audience, in large part through the utilization of the rapidly expanding print and visual media. They constructed a relationship with their subjects that displayed many of the core characteristics of celebrity – constant and frequent public exposure, access to their private lives, thoughts and feelings, inclusion in the domestic lives, gossip and everyday concerns of her 'audience', and in many respects a certain kind of powerlessness in relation to that audience in terms of its capacity to define their role (see Armstrong 2001). In this respect, they were key examples of the broader shift in political culture during the nineteenth century which Richard Sennett (2002) identified as the intrusion of 'personality' into politics, in which political figures come to be 'judged as believable by whether or not they aroused the same belief in their personalities which actors did when on stage', and the content of 'what the politician believes has become less and less important in deciding whether or not to believe in him' (p. 196).

As John Plunkett emphasizes, the representation and reception of Victoria displayed 'a strikingly comparable mixture of identification, intimacy, and performance' to that of Hollywood stars. In the imagined conversation between Victoria and her mother from the satirical magazine the *Penny Satirist*, Victoria complains of the constant surveillance of her every move and gesture, and yearns for the privacy of ordinary life. 'Every lady in the country has a private home but myself. The palace is a public house in which everyone claims a right to peep, and whose domestic arrangements everyone claims a right to judge' (cited in Plunkett 2003: 125). Like for all celebrities, as Plunkett observes, '[t]he degree of collective imaginative investment in Victoria promoted a sense of intimate connection and empathy. Yet the greater the degree of investment, the greater the risk of Victoria being turned into a wholly fabricated figure' (p. 120). This was a core element of the critic of monarchy by radicals such as Thomas Paine, who saw the *ancien regime*, as John Barrell points out, as 'an entirely fictive system of government; entirely without substance, because entirely the creature of the imagination' (2000: 20)

Lewis Carroll's reference to Victoria in her later years as the bad tempered and authoritarian Queen of Hearts in *Alice in Wonderland* has stood in the way of appreciating the original meaning of the epitaph – it was first intended to refer to her genuine affective bond with her subjects, the strong positive emotions generated in the early years of her reign (Lacey 2003: 19–30). William Harvey's (1796–1873) portrayal of 'England' as Britannia has on the reverse of the card:

Beautiful England-on her Island throne, –
Grandly she rules, – with half the world her own;
From her vast empire, the sun ne'er departs:
She reigns a Queen-Victoria, Queen of Hearts.

Princess Diana's celebrity and status as the 'Queen of Hearts' a century and a half later was thus a reworking of a style of specifically female royal celebrity, organized around an intimate, highly personalized and emotional relationship between the queen or princess and her audience pioneered by Elizabeth of York (1466–1503), Henry VIII's mother and the first Queen of Hearts, and Elizabeth I (Richards 1999; Ward 2001), but made more recognizable modern by Victoria in the context of the enormous and rapid expansion of print and visual media in the course of the nineteenth century. Ian Ward suggests that there is an essential and enduring 'Englishness' in

the imagined affinity fashioned by a political aesthetic that presents heroes and heroines, Fairy kings and Fairy queens, soap stars and media icons; fantasy figures who appear to 'touch' England, bless it and in so doing reaffirm an historical sense of national destiny which excuses its citizenry from taking any further responsibility for fashioning its own future.

(2001: 17)

He is no doubt exaggerating the extent to which it is a uniquely English phenomenon, but the identification of the centrality of a celebrity logic to the construction of political authority hits home precisely.

These mechanisms of celebrity production were democratized and further developed in the United States. P.T. Barnum's genius as a promoter of events and shows that captured the public's attention was not that he was good at fakery, fraud, and hyperbolic invention, it was that he tricked his audiences but also revealed the nature of the trick. As Braudy remarks:

> Barnum not only revealed his tricks, but also made the audiences love it and come back for more – because they had been given the privilege of being let in on the processes by which the illusion of reality had been created. He put his audience on their mettle as people of sophistication and insight into what was true and what wasn't – and charged them admission for the chance to prove it.
>
> (1986: 501)

What Barnum was good at was attracting public attention, and the value he and his entourage possessed because of this was recognized by the English aristocracy, including Victoria and Albert, when he toured England with General Tom Thumb (Charles Stratton) in 1844 (Carlson 2009). Abraham Lincoln interrupted a Cabinet meeting to receive the recently married General and Mrs Tom Thumb, and Braudy remarks that this was more than just light diversion, Lincoln was 'entertaining American celebrities whose faces and names were beginning to become at least as recognizable as his own' (1986: 503). Barnum was particularly adept at projecting the 'natural talent' of those he made celebrities, able to 'make capital of what Lincoln exemplified: An interest turned into disinterest by a straightforward, unbuttoned, demystified presentation of one's public self' (p. 504).

The nineteenth and early twentieth century is populated by an expanding network of celebrities in a variety of fields – politics, theatre, literature – who draw on increasingly sophisticated techniques of celebrity production. I look at Giuseppe Garibaldi (1807–82), in more detail in Chapter 5, but it is worth highlighting here how his status as a radical hero, as Lucy Riall (2007a) observes, was orchestrated and managed by the nationalist leader and political organizer Giuseppe Mazzini, together with a team of publicists. Imagery and the printed word were used to build on Garibaldi's real achievements as a military commander and political leader, establishing a consistency between Garibaldi's life and the basic tropes and plotlines of Italian romantic literature, combined with concerted efforts to establish an intimacy with his audiences. In the process, something much larger and more politically effective than an able (and, admittedly implausibly handsome and charming) soldier and politician emerged: a radical hero of mythic, Arthurian proportions capable of the monumental symbolic effort required to unite – indeed, to create – a unified political entity from the fragmented cultural and ideological landscape that became 'Italy'. Garibaldi was a master of the capacity to generate intimacy in public setting, a skill also possessed by contemporary politicians such as Bill Clinton, and his publicity apparatus made astute use of controlled revelation of his private life to sustain his celebrity status. Riall emphasizes that Garibaldi's status as a political celebrity 'was a symptom of the democratization of the public sphere in the mid-nineteenth century and of the creation of a new relationship between public figures and their audiences in which feelings of awe and hero-worship mingled with a sense of immediacy and familiarity' (Riall 2007b: 46).

William 'Buffalo Bill' Cody (1846–1917) was another important example, responding to the demand for tales and representations of the Wild West, first with the reporting of actual exploits as a buffalo hunter and Indian scout, but then, with the frontier more or less conquered, and with more significant impact, as a showman endlessly portraying and re-creating the frontier world and the ideal American carving out the New World in an image of his own choosing. As Robert Cathcart observes:

> On a daily basis, with the help of publicists and the press, he recreated his own image as a frontier hero. He was now performing on stage the deeds that first brought him to public attention. Throngs eagerly awaited his arrival. They rose and shouted hearty hurrahs as he rode into the ring in glittering attire, carrying high a huge American flag. They bought their tickets and cheered mightily with each reenactment of his gallant defense of the wagon train against the heathen Indians. It was no longer necessary to recall the original deed of heroism. The celebrity performed the role of hero every day, and the press celebrated the performer rather than the deed.
>
> (1994: 41)

Buffalo Bill was the perfect example of the hero turned celebrity, in which heroic deeds take on an extended symbolic life as they are endlessly mimicked, and the skill of the representation becomes as important as the heroic act itself; indeed, it becomes more important, and reality turns into hyperreality and a simulacrum of itself.

There were numerous women in public life achieving celebrity status, as singers, poets, lecturers and of course as actresses and dancers (Sentilles 2003). The word 'star' was first used in England in 1824 to refer to an actress who could sell out a theatre by virtue of her name alone (Roberts 2010: 108). A number of women found that eccentricity as a strategy of public exposure worked very successfully (Roberts 2010) – the examples include George Sand, Sarah Bernhardt, Rosa Bonheur, and Lola Montez (Seymour 1996). Lola Montez (1821–61; identified in London's National Portrait Gallery as 'adventuress') was an important early pioneer of the eccentric female celebrity identity, the contemporary heiress of which is Lady Gaga. Born Eliza Rosanna Gilbert in 1821 in Grange, County Sligo, Ireland, the daughter of a British soldier and a 15-year-old Irish shop assistant, she spent her early childhood in India where her father had been sent and died of cholera shortly after her arrival. Lola's mother remarried. She was sent back Britain, to Scotland when she was six, and she quickly got a reputation as a wild and mischievous child. She married another soldier when she was 16, and after they had separated five years later, she decided to strike out on her own, adopting the persona of a 'Spanish' dancer, Lola Montez, and carving out a striking career for herself as a dancer, courtesan and actress, more because of her beauty, eccentricity and capacity to generate gossip than talent. In London, she had been recognized as the former wife of an English soldier, and she had to move to the continent to continue her career. She quickly became part of the continental celebrity circle, including George Sand and Alexandre Dumas, and had an affair with Franz Liszt. Montez became the mistress of Ludwig I of Bavaria, who abdicated in 1848 partly because of her influence over him and her unpopularity – Montez ended up in California, toured Australia in 1855, and died in New York in 1861.

In the United States, the Civil War actress Adah Isaacs Menken (1835–68) was inspired by Montez's career and pursued similar strategies of constructing a particularly female celebrity identity. Renée Sentilles (2003: 8) describes Menken as a nineteenth-century Madonna, constantly reinventing herself and flirting with scandal, playing male parts on stage, presenting herself as both respectable and challenging convention, crossing the boundaries of different kinds of celebrity, writing poetry and essays and maintaining friendships with members of the literary elite such as Walt Whitman, Mark Twain and Alexandre Dumas (Sentilles 2003). Sarah Bernhardt (1844–1923) was referred to as 'Sarah Barnum' because of her Barnumesque skill in self-promotion (Eltis 2005: 169; Roberts 2010), and she was only one of a network of actresses which included Lillie Langtry (1853–1929), Mrs Patrick Campbell (1865–1940) and Ellen Terry (1847–1928), who all extended the eighteenth-century theatrical practice of flirting around the boundary between public and private lives, with the effect, regardless of whether it was the intention, of enhancing their capacity to attract and hold public attention (Eltis 2005: 169).

One of the earliest incarnations of the gossip column and its promotion of celebrity was that of Delphine de Girardin, the wife of the journalist and newspaper owner Emile de Girardin. Berlanstein writes that she had noted that tourists were more excited about seeing a star in public than on stage, and she saw the demand there would be for intimate details about celebrities – a new concept at the time – of all types and configurations. For de Girardin, celebrities were 'people who had made a name for themselves in literature, art, politics, or theatre, and who lacked the traditional status accorded to those having inherited noble titles'. Her use of the new concept 'expressed the vision of a changing French society, in which great lords and ladies had to make room for people of talent' (Berlanstein 2004: 69).

After the turn of the century, in what Rein et al. (1997) call the 'industrializing stage' of celebrity production, the growth of the movie industry in Hollywood led in the 1920s to the development of a variety of specialists – 'talent agents, personal managers, publicists, professional coaches, and financial managers' (p. 39), who assess and develop individuals' talents, generate interest from venues, negotiate salaries and fees. The organizational structure was still relatively loose and unintegrated, and this was to change from the 1950s onwards, in the 'factory stage', with a greater concentration and denser networks of specialists – a key example is Berry Gordy's Motown record company in Detroit:

Operating on the same principle that had made Detroit the car capital of the world, Gordy's factory employed specialists to handle songwriting, artist development, repertoires, artist management, production, distribution, even choreography. No aspect of the potential celebrities' images – their songs, sounds, styles, clothes, dance routines, or work schedules – was left to chance.

(pp. 42–3)

Specialists professionalize, setting up barriers to entry and organize to protect and promote their interests. Control shifts more clearly to the managers, backed by larger budgets, with a larger proportion of celebrities' earnings going to the costs of management. Celebrity production characterizes more and more sectors – from movies to music, but then also, say Rein et al., 'sports, politics, art, business, and religion'. These techniques now used to produce a wide variety of 'products' – politicians, sports stars, artists, writers, business leaders. The basic elements are the selection of a potential audience, the positioning and refinement of the aspirant's 'concept and story', and their clothing, appearance and behaviour are reworked to fit the required image. There is more planning and research, and greater integration of research, product development, pricing, advertising, and distribution (p. 44).

Sporting identities such as W.G. Grace (cricket), Gwyn Nicholls (rugby football) and Tod Sloan (jockey) were the earlier examples of sports stars being utilized to focus public attention and sell newspapers (Andrews & Jackson 2001: 6), but it was the spread of film and the developing interest of expanding corporations in the commercial possibilities of sport which provided an important stimulus to the organization of the public sphere around sports heroes in the 1920s. Rader also believes that the increasing complexity of society itself generated a responsive to the sporting star as a 'compensatory hero', providing the dream of a means of vaulting over the normal complex, slow and largely incomprehensible and unpredictable mechanisms of social advancement, 'compensating for the passing of the traditional dream of success, the erosion of Victorian values and feelings of individual powerlessness' (1983: 11). As Rader remarks, George Herman 'Babe' Ruth had a distinctive ability

to project multiple images of brute power, the natural, uninhibited man and the fulfillment of the American success dream. Ruth was living proof that the lone individual could still rise from mean, vulgar beginnings to fame and fortune, to a position of public recognition equalled by few men in American history.

(p. 12)

Ruth became a leading example of the linkage of sporting success with commercial activity, pursuing sponsorship arrangements that enriched his corporate sponsors as well as himself. Corporations and entrepreneurs were quick to understand the commercial possibilities attached to the sports star's capacity to focus the attention of a mass audience, and eagerly promoted other outstanding sportsmen such as the footballer Red Grange and boxer Jack Dempsey (Rader 1983).

It is this factory stage that Richard Rothestein was referring to when he coined the term 'the Josephine machine' to refer to the techniques and strategies used to promote the relatively unknown actress Lynn Whitfield playing in the 1991 film *The Josephine Baker Story* (Gamson 1994: 66–7). The 'pitch' was 'the new discovery' and 'the talented young black actress getting the role of a lifetime', paralleling Josephine Baker herself, and this produced the ideal narrative to attract attention and constitute a celebrity identity. Rein et al. see the period after the 1980s as a 'late-factory stage', characterized by greater decentralization as celebrity production shifts from key centres such as Hollywood, New York and Detroit to a greater number of smaller centres. The various sites of celebrity production have also become more closely interconnected, and as markets expand and become more differentiated, the profits to be made have grown, as have the amounts that celebrities themselves are capable of earning. The take-off of sports celebrity since the 1970s is an important example here, tied to the increasing televising of sport, its impact on fashion, and its relationship to conceptions of fitness and health (Turner 2007: 197).

The field of celebrity

To understand how the production of celebrity works today, it is important to see it as a field of activity which is internally divided into sectors, each with a different balance of representational, public relations skills and other kinds of capacities. Politics, sport, business, the professions and diverse scientific disciplines all demand skills particular to those sectors, and varying degrees of public relations capacity, whereas television hosts need to be primarily good at self-representation. In many sectors, celebrities are only visible internally, and not across sectors (Rein et al. 1997: 84), but some sectors have a dominant position in relation to the others – entertainment, fashion, sport, literature – because their celebrities are visible across the whole field and can generate news more easily and effectively (p. 84). The 2011 Forbes Celebrity 100, for example, consists of 73 celebrities in film, television and radio, including ten personalities (Oprah Winfrey, Donald Trump, etc.), ten in sport, ten in music, four in literature and three in modelling.[2]

One can distinguish between three different *types* of celebrity sectors. First, where there is a relatively high degree of conflict between high visibility and the internal expectations of the group, generally requiring a high level of skill for entry. Becoming a celebrity then creates tension with one's peers and raises the accusation that one is 'merely' seeking publicity, with the presumption that this inherently contradicts the group's values. Amongst academics, for example, the structuring of activity tends to be orientated to an internal conversation amongst one's peers, rather than with a particularly large audience, and celebrity success beyond one's own discipline generally leads to a devaluation of one's status as a scholar.[3] Capturing this orientation nicely, the economist Paul Samuelson declared in his 1961 presidential address 'Not for us is the limelight and the applause . . . In the long run, the economic scholar works for the only coin worth having – our own applause' (Samuelson 1966: 1516). Later Robert K. Merton spoke of distinguishing 'the gold of scientific fame from the brass of popular celebrity' (Merton 1988: 623).

Second, at the other end of the spectrum there are sectors where competition is high (sometimes, but not always, linked to skill levels being low) and where high visibility is central to status within the sector. Rein et al. describe the contrast between these two sectors as follows:

> So many able actresses compete for roles in Hollywood that image-making investments can often make the difference. Conversely, so few people compete to become the leading scholar in the history of Lichtenstein that any competent individual could achieve this reputation without much image-building activity.
>
> (1997: 91)

However, the distance between the two types of sectors has been gradually decreasing with the competitive dynamics of globalization in all fields of activity, as well as the increasing democratization of the relationship between scientists, experts and skilled practitioners on the one hand, and the broader public on the other. In universities, for example, the turn to international rankings as a means of managing global competition for students and for research capacity have generated a concern with performance and impact, in turn creating a focus on a particular kind of celebrity – the citation index. Many of the ranking systems depend on perceived status and quality as much as on objective measures, which means that visibility in the global world of scholarship is an important element of how high or low universities are ranked, and whether the specialist in the history of Lichtenstein will in fact keep their job if there are insufficient student enrolments, or too few citations in leading scholarly journals.

Third, there are sectors lying between these two, where the production of high visibility is more accepted and gives a competitive advantage, but still only a discretionary part of the sector's activity – generally professions such law and architecture – and thus more oriented to a small-scale 'cottage industry' approach than a fully industrialized one. The truly elite sectors are those in the second category which are also able to link all the others together because they can reach audiences in every sector – entertainment, sport and politics. As Rein et al. observe, 'The superstars in these three sectors . . . tower over celebrities in other sectors, no matter how the others stand within their own fields' (1997: 84).

A key example of such an over-arching 'super field' of celebrity is sport, where leading sporting identities have, alongside celebrities in theatre, radio, film, music and literature, come to play an increasingly significant role in the course of the twentieth century. Sports stars are especially effective at becoming global celebrities, since the absence of a language dimension enable them to cross the boundaries of national celebrity frameworks. Chris Rojek argues that soccer stars 'epitomize the disembedded social actors beloved by theorists of later modernity and globalization. They are cosmopolitan flexible accumulators who exchange bonds of city, region and even nation, to participate at the highest levels in their chosen sport and, of course, for the highest salaries' (Rojek 2006: 684). They are also good at linking together the different fields of celebrity: 'with top sports stars moving freely between elite circles in television, pop music, business and fashion' (p. 683).

Rojek observes that sports celebrities can link their prominence in their particular field of endeavour with a variety of other types of concerns, such as health, fitness, and youth, but above all with the social construction of masculinity – sport is a key field for the expression of an ideal masculine identity and ethic. As Rojek puts it, 'sports stars have been adopted as powerful symbolic tokens to negotiate the so-called crisis in masculinity' (p. 682). They also help overcome the hero/celebrity opposition, because it is less arguable that they cannot demonstrate real achievement, as opposed to inauthentic fame. Like music and theatre, sporting events are a vehicle for the expression and manifestation of powerful emotions which have no other outlet in everyday life, adding drama to everyday life and social interaction, and constituting a core narrative of how one leads one's life, overcomes adversity and obstacles, and manages ethical dilemmas.

It is also important to consider that the celebrity production industry is not a single, unified industry, but differentiated into separate sub-industries which operate to 'couple' the celebrity production industry to a wide range of commercial activities. Rein et al. identify nine such industries contributing to the production of celebrity (1997: 42–58):

1   Entertainment: theatre, music halls, dance halls, sports arenas, movie studios, but also museums, fairs and exhibitions.
2   Representation: 'all those who solicit for or negotiate engagement for their clients for a fee, typically a commission' (p. 43 – agents, personal managers and promoters).
3   Publicity: publicists, PR firms, advertising agencies and marketing research firms.
4   Communication: newspapers, magazines, radio, television and film.
5   Coaching: music, dance, speech and modelling teachers.
6   Legal and accounting: legal, accounting and investment counsellors.
7   Appearance: costumers, cosmeticians, hairstylists.
8   Endorsement: souvenir, clothing and games and toys manufacturers: can constitute as much as 90 per cent of a celebrity's income. Andre Agassi 'illustrates an effective visibility model using his major skill, tennis, as a launching pad to obtain endorsements, licenses, and investments' (p. 53). 'The operating principle: the power of visibility' (p. 54).
9   Celebrity service: celebrity tracking services, look-alikes, discrete travelling support services, security.

There is no precise estimation of the contribution of all these commercial activities to the overall economy; Rein et al. simply describe it as 'incalculable' (1997: 57), but given the amounts of money that circulate around celebrities, it is clear that the flow-on value is substantial. Oprah Winfrey herself earned $290m in 2010–11, let alone what her 'brand' has earned for the numerous products with which she becomes associated. One observer, for example, refers to the 'Britney industrial complex' of interconnected economic activity, and in 2008 estimated the 'Britney economy' as being valued around $110 million annually.[4]

The earning power of celebrities often also continues well past their death, continuing to generate significant income for their estates, record companies, publishers and so on. As Rojek remarks, 'death is not an impediment to additional commodification. Once the public face of the celebrity has been elevated and internalized in popular culture, it indeed possesses an immortal quality that permits it to be recycled' (2001: 189). Forbes ranked the top 13 'delebs' (dead celebrities) in 2009 as Yves Saint Laurent ($350m), Rogers and Hammerstein ($235m), Michael Jackson ($90m), Elvis Presley ($55m), J.R.R. Tolkien ($50m), Charles Schultz ($35m), John Lennon ($15m), Dr Seuss (Theodor Geisel) $15m, Albert Einstein ($10m), Michael Crichton ($9m), Aaron Spelling ($8m), Jim Hendrix ($8m) and Andy Warhol ($6m). Continuing good earners remain Marilynn Monroe, James Dean, Steve McQueen, Frank Sinatra and Marvin Gaye.[5] One media licensing consultant, David Reeder, has been quoted as predicting that Michael Jackson would remain the top 'perpetual earner', outstripping Elvis Presley because of his more globalized iconic status (Allen 2010).

The economics of attention

It is clear that there a significant economic dimension to the production of celebrity (Turner 2004) – it is big business, well organized, and large sums of money are involved. This has led many commentators to refer to celebrities as commodities, or more abstractly to the 'celebrity commodity' (Marshall 1997; Turner 2007). Brian Moeran has suggested the concept of the 'name economy', whereby celebrities mediate the relationship between economy and culture. The production of celebrity organizes both attention and consumption in any particular field, turning products into a recognized face, name and body, and also acting as the linchpin between different fields of cultural production: television, radio, film, literature, theatre, music, fashion and politics. Celebrity in any one field can often be converted to another field: actors become politicians, models become actors, fashion designers become film directors, photographers work as actors and journalists, politicians host radio shows. 'It is this ability to function across fields', observes Brian Moeran, 'that enables and sustains a name economy' (2003: 300). This cross-over aspect of celebrity is accentuated by celebrity coupling, so that models, sports stars, actors, politicians, gallery owners and other highly visible individuals link up with each other (pp. 303–4).

Celebrities stand, argues Moeran, at the centre of the intersection between commerce and culture, mediating between the public's desires, needs, wishes and aspirations, and the patterns of economic production and consumption, which both responds to and helps create those desires and needs. The list of examples of the richly rewarded individuals at the top of the celebrity hierarchy, because of their high visibility across all celebrity sectors – models, actors, sports stars, fashion designers – is long and growing; just to pick one, Tiger Woods is reported as having become, in 2006, the first athlete to earn more than US$100 million in one year, of which $90 million was earned in endorsements and appearances, as opposed to US$10 million for playing golf (Lind 2007: 52), and he was instrumental in Nike's construction of a $650 million golf business. As Joshua Gamson observes:

> as sales aids, celebrities are most useful if they can draw attention regardless of the particular context in which they appear. Name recognition in itself is critical for commerce. In fact, the less attached a name is to a context, the more easily it transfers to new markets.
>
> (2007: 150)

For example, in nineteenth-century Paris, writes Lenard Berlanstein, the merchants of the Grands Boulevards 'seized upon the growing power of celebrity cults to sell their wares . . . by placing pictures of theatrical stars in their windows, assuming that the images would attract shoppers to their displays and, ultimately, into their stores' (2004: 72). The economic network surrounding celebrities is extensive, restricted only by the imagination of the celebrity and their management, although there is a tendency not to travel too far from base: models start cosmetic or jewelry lines, swimwear brands or lingerie stores, actors and pop stars establish production and recording companies. The value of the coupling of celebrity identity to particular products is not always certain, but it can be gold-plated: when it became known that Michael Jordan was returning to play basketball for the Chicago Bulls in 1995, the value of the stocks of the companies he was associated with – Nike, McDonalds, Quaker Oats, Sara Lee – increased by around 2 per cent, or roughly US$1 billion (Mathur et al. 1997).

However, there is also an additional sense in which there is an economic dimension to celebrity, in which the commodity being traded is not simply the persons who are celebrities themselves, their image or their persona, but something else related to their position in the broader networks of economic, social and political action. As commodities, celebrities are the real embodiment of a more abstract kind of capital – attention. To understand how this works, we can usefully begin by turning to Robert Merton's studies of the sociology of science and his concept of the 'Matthew effect' (Merton 1968, 1988).

What Merton highlighted was the way in which the Nobel Laureates interviewed by Harriet Zuckerman (1977) consistently observed that researchers who already had a 'name' in the field received disproportionately greater attention for work that was comparable to that done by lesser-known researchers, and that initial advantages of location and resources tend simply to accumulate over time. Those who achieved recognition earlier in their career were more productive later on, the impact of a scientific contribution was greater the more established the reputation of the researcher. In contests over the attribution of new discoveries, the established name generally wins out. Name-recognition plays an important role in the selection of journal articles considered worth reading, and generally reputation – of the researcher themselves and the university where they work – operates as an important cue for selecting the publications worthy of attention from an ever-expanding array of possibilities. This is a dynamic that all academics are familiar with – when one looks at the contents of a journal issue, the names that one recognizes will be the ones that one turns to first. When a conference is being organized, the aim is always to get at least one plenary speaker who is a well-known name in the field, and it is assumed that this will increase the participation levels. Winning a Nobel Prize is a wonderful thing not just for the winner themselves, but also for their university or research institute, since it significantly boosts the institution's global visibility, and makes a significant difference to many of the global ranking models.

Merton described this dynamic in the construction of status and recognition in scientific endeavour as constituting what he called 'the Matthew effect', after the Gospel according to Matthew 25:29: 'For unto every one that hath shall be given, and he shall have abundance: but from him that hath not shall be taken away even that which he hath' (Merton 1968: 56).[6] Merton argued that 'this is the form, it seems, that the distribution of psychic income and cognitive wealth in science also takes' (1988: 609). The Matthew effect was what Boorstin was observing with his 'well-known for their well-knownness' comment, but he got it the wrong way around. It is not so much that celebrities are well known (simply) because of their well knownness, it is that being well known can *generate* greater well knownness, much like scientific reputation can – if properly used – produce still more reputation.

In many respects, Merton's Matthew effect can be explained in terms of the dynamics of post-industrial 'knowledge' or 'information' societies. In a postindustrial world where the supply of knowledge and information threatens to engulf everyone, what is in short supply is the means to discriminate between what is on offer, and the capacity to attract attention – of consumers, voters, students, job applicants, readers, and audiences (Davenport & Beck 2001; Lanham 2006; Franck 1993, 1998). As journalist Leo Benedictus (2011) observes about the impact of celebrities such as Hugh Grant and Stephen Fry on political causes, 'it has never been enough to shed light on a subject. People also have to look.' Herbert Simon explained the basic principle in 1971:

> in an information-rich world, the wealth of information means a dearth of something else: a scarcity of whatever it is that information consumes. What information consumes is rather obvious: it consumes the attention of its recipients. Hence a wealth of information creates a poverty of attention and a need to allocate that attention efficiently among the overabundance of information sources that might consume it.
>
> (1971: 40–1)

The strength and intensity of attention to celebrities is thus a measure of the scarcity of attention, and the oversupply of information and knowledge. The concept of the Matthew effect underlines a central element of the logic of celebrity production, that the capacity to attract attention – demanding expressive and communicative skills that we tend to see as 'superficial' – is itself a self-reproducing form of capital. An Austrian commentator on this question, Georg Franck, suggests in his analysis of what he calls 'the attention economy' that celebrity 'is simply the status of being a major earner of attention' (1993: 748). This can be put more definitively, to say that the secret of the nature of celebrity is primarily a matter of the accumulation and distribution of attention. Attention can be regarded as a form of risk-capital, where risk taking can lead to massive windfalls which can then be converted with new projects into even more celebrity (attention) capital.

Thinking along similar lines, Rein et al. call it 'high visibility', indicating the same 'asset with an independent identity and function, a propellant energizing a wide variety of activities. People in all walks of life no longer find it strange to consider making radical changes in their lives and images in order to gain a high profile and its inherent power' (1997: 9). Franck argues that the logic underpinning celebrity is that of the difference in dynamics between a dyad and a triad: in a dyad, the attention that A and B pay to each other can only be determined by the inherent attention-attracting characteristics of each of their attributes or action; however, in a triad, the fact that C pays attention to B will itself tend to increase the attention A also pays to B, and once C becomes a group, the larger the group, the stronger B's 'pull' on A's attention will be (1998: 98–100).

Paying attention to the individuals to whom everyone else is paying attention also operates, as Clark et al. (2006) argue, as a 'coordination device' in complex societies. Prominent, highly visible people 'help to generate the "common knowledge" necessary for coordination' (p. 370), and provide an indicator for how one can line up one's own appearance, preferences and conduct with those parts of the broader population to which one is most responsive. They draw on Georg Simmel's observations on fashion, that it serves to establish distinctiveness, while at the same time giving 'the individual the satisfaction of not standing alone in his actions' (Simmel 1957 [1904]: 542–3). The appeal to celebrities in the realms of politics, social movements and diplomacy is to a large extent simply about coordinating the ideas, choices and actions of large numbers of people, and there is a sense in which the managers of the celebrity industries can be understood as 'coordination entrepreneurs' (Clark et al. 2006: 385)

The French sociologist Gabriel Tarde made similar observations in relation to political leadership more generally:

> Actually, when a mind acts upon our own thought, it is with the collaboration of many other minds through whom we see it, and whose opinion, without our knowledge, is reflected in our own. We must vaguely on the esteem shown him . . . on the admiration he inspires . . . If he is a famous man, the number of his admirers impresses us, confusedly, *en masse*, and this influence takes on an air of objective solidarity, of impersonal reality, creating the prestige proper for great figures.
>
> (Tarde, *L'Action international*, p. 334, cited in Michels 1911: pp. 78–9)

Earlier in the nineteenth century, John Adams explained how much of the foundation of aristocratic power and authority lies in the attention-focusing effects of a well-known name. Aristocrats, argued Adams, pre-figuring both Boorstin and Merton's Matthew effect, were largely aristocrats because they were (well-known) aristocrats. Why does having a family lineage matter so much, he asked?

> The mighty secret lies in this:—An illustrious descent attracts the notice of mankind. A single drop of royal blood, however illegitimately scattered, will make any man or woman proud or vain. Why? Because, although it excites the indignation of many, and the envy of more, it still attracts the attention of the world. Noble blood ... is held in estimation for the same reason.... When the names of a certain family are read in all the gazettes, chronicles, records, and histories of a country for five hundred years, they become known, respected, and delighted in by everybody. A youth, a child of this extraction, and bearing this name, attracts the eyes and ears of all companies long before it is known or inquired whether he be a wise man or a fool. His name is often a greater distinction than a title, a star, or a garter.... The contempt that is thrown upon obscurity of ancestry, augments the eagerness for the stupid adoration that is paid to its illustration.
>
> (1805: 31–2)

Why do people accord such high regard to 'beauty, elegance, and grace'? Because 'those attractions command the notice and attention of the public; they draw the eyes of spectators. This is the charm that makes them irresistible.' Why do people spend so much more time on 'dancing and drawing, painting and music, riding or fencing', than they do on 'discretion, wit, sense, and many other accomplishments and virtues, of infinitely more importance'? Because, thought Adams, 'they attract more forcibly the attention of the world, and procure a better advancement in life' (1805: 29–30).

Another way of putting it is to say that a central feature of mass psychology is the 'self-accumulating' character of attention and recognition. To a large extent we determine our admiration of a leader not on the basis of careful independent consideration of their virtues and vices, but driven by the cues we get from the social world around us. Robert Michels said of the socialist parties in Germany and Italy early in the twentieth century that, alongside those political leaders who have worked their way up through the party ranks, the rank-and-file remained highly responsive to individuals with pre-existing recognition and admiration in other fields, in 'possession of independent claims to immortality. Such fame won in other fields seems to them of greater value than that which is won under their own eyes' (1911: 80–1).

Celebrity 'attention capital' plays an important role in any 'production', be it a play, a film, a radio programme, an advertising campaign, a university course of study, a conference, a public lecture, a political party or campaign, a social movement, or even a state. We have seen how central 'stars' were to the theatre already in the eighteenth century, and the motion picture industry quickly realized that the principle remained a sound one and that stars had important economic effects. They more clearly differentiated between film industry products, improved the capacity to predict success, and enabled prices to be stabilized and, ideally, increased over time (Klaprat 1985). Celebrity, properly managed, creates profit, driven by 'the attention paid by distant, dispersed, heterogeneous but nonetheless numerous third parties, a corresponding 'network of weak ties" (Wenzel 2000: 462). As Rein et al. put it, a celebrity can be defined as anyone 'whose name has attention-getting, interest-riveting and profit-generating value' (1997: 15), and a great deal of economic activity revolves around the high visibility attaching to parti-cular individuals (p. 27). The capacity of high visibility to generate demand for products is clear – when Kate Middleton or Cheryl Cole wears a particular dress, for example, it will be sold out in the high street within days, and the designer will have their career made. The Australian tourist industry was willing to spend $5m to bring Oprah Winfrey and her show to Australia, precisely because of the sheer size of her audience, even though one could argue the money would have been better spent on a Chinese celebrity.

Richard Lanham (1997, 2006), coming from a different perspective, that of literature and rhetoric, presents a similar account, developing Simon's original point about the scarcity of attention in an information-rich world. For Lanham, our understanding of the transition from an industrial to a post-industrial world requires a sense of how the relationships between different aspects of social and economic life have also shifted. He illustrates his argument (1997: 280) by giving the example of the reasons why one buys a car, let us say there are three: first, Purpose, to get from A to B; second, Game, to show off to your neighbours; third, Play, you get pleasure out of driving that particular car. The first is regarded in an industrial society as 'stuff', 'figure', or 'what is 'real', and the second as 'fluff', or 'ground', secondary and derivative. Stuff is in the foreground, and fluff is in the background. In an attention economy, in contrast, the relationship reverses: Game and Play shift to the foreground, and Purpose to the background. Given Adams's observations in 1805, both Lanham and Simon may be exaggerating the extent to which the importance of attention is a particularly twentieth-century 'information society' phenomenon, so that one needs to see 'modernity' as having emerged much earlier, but it would remain true that these mechanisms have intensified in the course of the twentieth century, along with the expansion of the mass media.

Lanham looks at Marcel Duchamp and Andy Warhol (1997: 276–80) as key examples of how the attention economy operates and how figure and ground can change places. In the normally accepted conception of artistic endeavour, the 'value' lies in the object created – the painting, the sculpture, the novel, the photography, the building. That constitutes the 'figure', and the attention it receives 'follows' it, it comes behind and after it, and in that sense is secondary, the 'ground'. What Duchamp did was reverse this relationship, so that the artistic value lay not in the object itself – the bicycle wheel, the urinal – but in the atten-tion directed at it. That was what constituted 'art'. Andy Warhol's Campbell's soup can and his Marilyn Monroe silkscreen portraits mobilized the same under-standing of the attention economy, applying what he had learned as a commercial artist, that what matters is whether one makes money, not how one makes it. Duchamp and Warhol gave the whole industry of art critics and commentators something to argue about and interpret, and so justify their own existence (Lanham 2006: 50).

Lanham's other illustrations include Christo and Jeanne-Claude Javacheff and their wrappings of Little Bay in Australia, the Pont Neuf in Paris, and the Berlin *Reichstag*, as well as his 40-kilometre-long *Running Fence* in California, and John Cage's 1952 composition 4' 33", in which the pianist walked in the auditorium, sat without playing a note with the keyboard cover closed for 4 minutes 33 seconds, rose, bowed and left. The intention was to reverse the relationship between figure and ground, 'to reverse the usual flow of attention in a concert hall and thus make us aware of the attention itself' (Lanham 1997: 277). Not that this mobilization of attention in music was in fact a twentieth-century invention – listen to Richard Sennett's account of the Italian early nineteenth-century violinist, Nicolò Paganini (1782–1840):

> All his work on stage was focused on drawing attention to himself. The audience at a typical Paganini concert might witness the violinists break one, two, or finally three strings on his violin, so that by the end of a difficult concerto, all the notes were being played off a single string. . . . Paganini liked to appear suddenly in front of his audience from a hiding place within the orchestra . . . once visible, he would wait one, two, or three minutes, staring silently at the audience, bringing the orchestra to an abrupt halt, and all at once begin to play . . . he was universally acclaimed, but the critics could never say that was so extraordinary about him. . . . He made performing an end in itself; his greatness, in fact, was to make his audiences forget about his musical text.
>
> (2002: 200–1)

The jury might still be out on Sennett's verdict that Paganini was 'devoid of musical taste' (p. 200) – one can only assume this was because he was all virtuoso technique, and not much else – but the basic point about his ability to focus the audience's attention remains salient. Franz Liszt was a great admirer of Paganini, and he learned his lessons well, becoming in his own way the celebrity composer of the nineteenth century, a key example of 'the growing taste for individual self-display among artists and audiences alike' (Braudy 2010: 174); when he died in 1886, his face was possibly the best known in Europe (Gooley 2010: 69).

If attention is a valuable resource, then celebrities should also be understood primarily as 'attention-traps', functioning in much the same way as Duchamp's urinal and bicycle wheel, or Warhol's films with no storyline. The effect is that in addition to the attention they attract themselves, celebrities generate potentially enormous and ever-expanding amounts of attention capital in the networks surrounding them – in principle they are merely the tips of celebrity attention icebergs. The strategies adopted by 'the evil genius of this object we have come to know as the Paris Hilton' (Sconce 2007: 330) is a useful illustration of both Lanham's point and the directions currently being taken by the management of large-scale attention-gathering. 'One can only imagine', writes Sconce, 'the levels of irony that would be at play had Warhol lived to meet and interview Hilton' (p. 332). Hilton's strategy is to utilize 'wealth, privilege, ignorance, and lack of talent' in such a way that it leverages ever more attention. Every public event in which she is involved, no matter how ridiculous or silly, 'only further accelerates a vicious circle of fame, wealth, and entitlement that in turn generates its own media gravity, attracting more exposure, opportunity, fame, wealth, and entitlement', what Sconce calls the 'perpetual-motion machine of hype' (p. 331).

For Sconce, Hilton has in fact taken the attention-trap concept to a new level – figures such as Duchamp and Warhol continued to present themselves overtly as artists, and their functioning as attention traps operated beneath the surface of their public image. Paris Hilton, however, makes it clear that this her deliberate objective, and this is a central part of her public image – she is famous for aiming to be famous for being famous, what Sconce calls meta/meta-famous. The artificiality of her celebrity has become part of her celebrity, so that the more she is disliked for her 'fakeness', the greater her stock of attention-capital, 'every detail of her life buttressing a Chinese finger-trap of envy and loathing. The more the public wants her to disappear, the more visible she becomes' (Sconce 2007: 331).

For Franck, the work of science and scholarship is precisely an excellent example of how attention capital operates. Franck takes his analysis back to Merton's original starting point by looking more closely at scientific endeavour, pointing out that the primary 'income' for scientific activity is not money, but the attention 'income' of fellow-scientists in the first place, followed by that of the broader public, possibly including policy- and decision-makers (1999: 53). The value of scientific work is measured to a large extent by the amount of attention it receives – the citation rate of the journal in which an article is published, the number of citations the article itself receives, the status of the book's publisher (which is meant to add an indicator of the quality of the attention received), and how well known the book's reviewers are. Franck argues that citation is essentially a fee in attention capital paid for the licence to use the cited author's information, ideas (p. 54).

This leads to a variety of strategies for maximizing the accumulation of such attention capital, such as the formation of citation cartels, or exploiting one's position as a referee or editor (p. 54). Because academics are always competing in a densely populated market in which no one has time to read everything, there is a strong motivation to capture the attention of one's intended readership with all the ploys of celebrity production – the catchy title and cover, the attention-grabbing event, the radical re-think of all that has been written before, the provocative stance, and of course the association with an established scholarly celebrity, either by making them the topic – by writing still more articles and books on Weber, Foucault, Habermas, Bourdieu, Derrida and so on – or with a foreword or laudatory recommendation on the back cover. In this sense one can speak of a fundamental logic of 'celebrification' in academic life, and this is why there is a degree to which one can describe the pursuit of scholarly 'excellence' as the pursuit of scholarly celebrity.

These kinds of mechanisms illustrate the self-reproducing 'perpetual-motion' character of attention capital, in that both the spender and the receiver 'earn' additional capital – the established celebrity gains even more attention, and the reviewed author gets increased attention because they can bask in the glow of the celebrity. No matter which field of celebrity one looks at – sport, radio, film, television, politics, business, management – the resource being sought, its pursuit underpinning the entire celebrity production process, is attention – eyeballs, as the advertising industry refers to it. From this perspective, it is, to a large extent, a conceptual error to engage only with the concretely 'real' person and their particular biography who is the celebrity – Michael Jackson, Marilyn Monroe, Oprah Winfrey, Paris Hilton and so on. I say 'to a large extent' because the particular skills and talents and charismatic effect unique to particular individuals still remains part of the story. But if one is to understand how the *phenomenon* of celebrity operates in sociological terms, what all celebrities have in common and how they are positioned within broader economic, political and social networks, if one wants to understand what underpins the production of celebrity, one has give equal consideration to the more abstract form of capital that celebrities have gathered in themselves – attention. Layered on top of whatever talents, skills and moral virtues they may have – which is what constitutes their identity as a super-human football player, an incredibly beautiful and moving actress, or an inspiring singer – is their social function as larger or smaller bundles of attention-capital, and this is what constitutes them as a celebrity.

'Sarah Palin's legacy: politics as a path to celebrity and riches'

Until Palin came along, no one realized that a politician could successfully leverage the celebrity gained in a presidential campaign into a multi-million-dollar fortune, and quickly. Less than a year after Palin resigned the governorship of Alaska, ABC News estimated that she'd earned $12 million. . . . Past presidents excepted, did any make as much out of their notoriety? . . . a lot of politicians are going to try to replicate some of what Palin did. . . . Even more failed pols will try to earn money giving speeches. And as job seekers follow financial incentives, perceived or real, it's possible that the prospect of monetizing political celebrity will change not only the way that candidates campaign, but the sorts of candidates who decide it's worthwhile to seek high office.

(Friedersdorf 2011)

3 Celebrity as a social form
Status, charisma and power

At first glance, Mills's account of celebrity, which had appeared four years before Boorstin's (1962) 'well-known for being well-known' portrayal, appears to follow a similar pathway. Mills wrote that the stars of movies, theatre and television 'are celebrated because they are displayed as celebrities', so that '[r]ather than being celebrated because they occupy positions of prestige, they occupy positions of prestige because they are celebrated' (1957: 74). But he also makes a number of other important observations about celebrity that take his account in a very different and much more analytical direction, to reveal far more about the underlying dynamics of celebrity society.

First, Mills argued that that the particular position occupied by celebrities in the distribution of status and prestige took the place of older aristocracies based on power and wealth. 'Printer's ink', he wrote, 'has replaced blue-blood' (p. 73). For Mills, celebrities were 'new types of prestigeful men and women', who 'have come to compete with, to supplement, and even to displace the society lady and the man of pedigreed wealth' (p. 71). But they were also closely intertwined and interdependent with other types of elites, playing a strategic linking role in the various networks in the higher echelons of society. To the extent that the *display* of all forms of status and prestige is central to their nature and dynamics, and celebrities 'as personalities of national glamour' are focal points of 'the means of entertainment and publicity' in an age of mass communication, Mills argued that all the other elites and 'higher circles' are obliged to 'compete with and borrow prestige from these professionals in the world of celebrity' (p. 71).

Celebrities take up a position competing with other types of elites, but also serving particular functions for those other elites in promoting their visibility in the public sphere, in particular to the extent that it could be seen as 'the national scene' as opposed to more localized public spheres. Indeed, that function regarding achieving mass visibility had become such an essential component of the projection of status and prestige on the national, as opposed to merely the local stage, that '[t]hose who would now claim prestige in America', wrote Mills, 'must join the world of the celebrity or fade from the national scene' (p. 77).

Second, he saw the dynamics of contemporary celebrity as closely aligned to that of the historical emergence of 'café society', a term invented by gossip-column journalist for the *Journal-American* Maury Paul (later 'Cholly

Knickerbocker') in 1919 'to indicate a small group of people who mingled in public but would not be likely to visit in one another's homes' (p. 72).[1] For Mills, café society was the American adaptation of the idea of the salons of the seventeenth and eighteenth centuries, which he believed never suited American society, to a large extent because of the dominance of the mass media (p. 79). He defined café society as the world of restaurants, night clubs, coffee shops and parties in the key urban centres such as New York, where individuals in search of a 'name' and public recognition, 'often seem to live for the exhibitionist mention of their doings and relations by social chroniclers and gossip columnists' (p. 72), ensuring that 'the professional celebrities of erotic beauty and transient talent were well-planted at the key tables' (p. 72).

In his book on the seminal gossip columnist Walter Winchell, Neal Gabler elaborates on the social change taking place by observing that café society was not just about the old elite going public, but that it 'seemed to have been born during Prohibition from a combination of Winchell's showy Broadway crowd and a restless group of young socialites', and that this 'Broadway-society axis constituted an unmistakable new social formation' (2003: 184). Winchell did not invent the gossip column, that had been done by Delphine de Girardin in Paris in the 1840s (Berlanstein 2004), but he expanded its audience society-wide. A central feature of this social form was that 'power was really a function not of wealth or breeding or talent or connections, but of publicity . . . where the object was to be seen and known, where the object was to be famous' (Gabler 2003: 184). Gabler quotes Winchell: 'Social position is now more a matter of press than prestige' (p. 185). American production and manufacturing was not being matched by consumption, generating a powerful demand for a variety of brokers in images, information and capital who could construct bridges between manufacturers and consumers (Leach 1991). This was the foundation for the emerging corps of press agents and Winchell's considerable influence and status, making him the best-paid, most widely read and listened-to journalist in the country, confidant to President Roosevelt and J. Edgar Hoover, acting as the central switching point for this new circuit of power, ensuring that he was the linchpin of café society itself:

> A mention in his column meant that one was among the exalted. It meant that one's name was part of the general fund of knowledge. It meant that one's exploits, even if they were only the exploits of dining, rated acknowledgment. It meant that one's life was validated, albeit validated by fame rather than accomplishment.
>
> (Gabler 2003: 185)

The public sphere in America was driven not by considered and thoughtful discussion but by the market in eye-catching stories, pushed by the ever-expanding numbers of press agents, which would underpin mass culture, and the degree of pre-existing visibility – that is, celebrity – of a story's protagonists would be a measure of its effectiveness. Gabler quotes the press agent and publicist Harry Reichenbach – one of the leading creators of the marketing pseudo-events that

Boorstin complained about – indicating how important these mechanisms were for the expansion of mass markets and consumer capitalism:

> Publicity is the nervous system of the world. Through the network of press, radio, film and lights, a thought can be flashed around the world the instant it is conceived. And through this same highly sensitive, swift and efficient mechanism it is possible for fifty people in New York to dictate the customs, trends, thoughts, fads and opinions of an entire nation of a hundred and twenty million people.
>
> (cited in Gabler 2003: 248; as told to David Freedman, *Phantom Fame: The Anatomy of Ballyhoo* (NY: Simon & Schuster, 1931), p. 165)

The very many readers of Winchell's columns and listeners to his radio broadcasts, however, were provided with momentary access to the world of the charmed, golden and beautiful few, as well as making it possible to witness them being pulled down a peg or two by Winchell's razor wit, so that 'the public, far away and trapped in its own travails, would feel that it had, if only briefly, penetrated the very deepest chamber of American society. That was the transaction Winchell brokered' (Gabler 2003: 186).

Similar developments were taking place in Europe – in Germany, for example, Karl Kraus noted in 1927 the increasing role of celebrity (*Prominenz*) in German society. Kraus thought that 'the German soul is possessed by a deep and now homeless "Kaiser-need" ', which demanded after the First World War the restoration of some other kind of elite, and this need was fulfilled in the 1920s by 'comedians, film and cabaret stars, boxers, footballers, parliamentarians, gigolos, women's hairdressers, literary historians, pure personalities', all of whom could and did become celebrities (cited in Wenzel 2000: 452).

Third, Mills had a clear eye for the gendered nature of celebrity, the central role of women, particularly young women, and their public eroticization, as well as the dynamics of prostitution in the commodification of celebrity. He observed that '[a]mong those whom Americans honor none is so ubiquitous as the young girl'; that is, it is 'as if Americans had undertaken to paint a continued national portrait of the girl as Queen':

> Everywhere one looks there is this glossy little animal, sometimes quite young and sometimes a little older, but always imagined, always pictured, as The Girl. She sells beer and she sells books, cigarettes, and clothes; every night she is on the TV screen, and every week on every other page of the magazines, and at the movies too, there she is.
>
> (1957: 82)

For Mills a dominant element of the field of celebrity was the current model of the 'All American Girl', characterized by 'doll face and the swank body starved down for the camera, a rather thin, gaunted girl with the wan smile, the bored gaze, and often the slightly opened mouth, over which the tongue occasionally slides to insure the highlights', always prepared for the camera with the 'professional stance . . . of the woman for whom a haughty kind of unconquerable eroticism has become a way of life', displaying the 'expensive look of an expensive woman who feels herself to be expensive' (1957: 81). Examples date almost immediately, but at the time of writing, one who comes to mind is Miley Cyrus.

Fourth, he identified the underlying logic of *competition* underpinning the production of celebrity, seeing celebrities as 'the crowning result of the star system of a society that makes a fetish of competition'.

> In America, this system is carried to the point where a man who can knock a small white ball into a series of holes in the ground with more efficiency and skill than anyone else thereby gains social access to the President of the United States. It is carried to the point where a chattering radio and television entertainer becomes the hunting chum of leading industrial executives, cabinet members, and the higher military. It does not seem to matter what the man is the very best at: so long as he has won out in competition over all others: he is celebrated.
>
> (p. 74)

Those who stand out in various fields because of their competitive success thus acquire a value and significance for that fact alone.

Finally, although he only touched on this question briefly in referring to John Adams, he noted the role of celebrity in the exercise of power and the governance of a population. In France and England, a line of argument had developed in social and political theory, in the work of Mandeville, Montesquieu and others (Shovlin 2000: 37), about the potential, also understood by legislators in Athens and Rome, for the governance of a population not by encouraging virtue, but by the astute management of vices, including the desire for honour and recognition, a particular problem in a context where the pursuit of economic interest had generated the prospect of the commercialization of all social relations. The controlled distribution of honour and public recognition of merit by the state was thus seen by many as an important device for the purposes of good government and social order. John Adams reiterated these arguments on his return to the United States, in his *Discourse on Davila* (1790), observing of the passion for 'the esteem of others', that government depends on its regulation, since it is 'the only adequate instrument of order and subordination in society, and alone commands effectual obedience to laws, since without it neither human reason, nor standing armies, would ever produce that great effect (1805: 28–9).

In the course of the eighteenth century, this line of thinking had evolved to include the argument that recognition of merit by the public rather than by the monarch was more effective in promoting virtuous behaviour – Jay Smith (1996) calls it the shift from 'the gaze of the sovereign' to 'the sovereign gaze'.

Rather than seeing elites and aristocracies as 'being' more 'powerful', the point is more that their visibility places them in a particular position within a circuitry of power, both constituting them as the *objects* of structures of power, demanding particular kinds of performance, and, as the focus of public attention, operating as *vehicles* for power relations as exemplars for the rest of the population. These arguments focused on particular types of public recognition, the 'engines of fame' (Braudy 1986: 491) organized around formally acknowledged esteem (titles, medals, prizes and so on), but they applied equally to the more informal 'engines of celebrity' (Barry 2008a: 252) – that is, visibility in the media, and star status in theatre, film, radio, television, popular music and sport. Mills's observation on Veblen's critique of the conspicuous consumption among the wealthy was that it failed to take the projection of prestige seriously enough, neglecting to make the connection with their more concrete military, economic and political activities. In Mills's view, Veblen was – and this argument applies to any perception of consumption and celebrity as somehow trivial – 'not quite serious enough about status because he did not see its full and intricate importance to power' (1957: 83).

Celebrity as status and charisma

Alongside Mills's considerations of how celebrities are a constituent part of the power elite, it is also important to link the understanding of celebrity society to two of Max Weber's central concerns: status and charisma. Weber defined *status* as 'a specific, positive or negative, social estimation of honor', with honour characterized by 'a specific style of life' (1978: 932). It attaches to groups, not to individuals, and status groups will devote greater or lesser degrees of effort to blocking entry from lower-status individuals. In its extreme forms, it is regarded as anchored in biology in a way that equates to ethnicity or race. Status groups tend to resist market mechanisms, in defence of their particular economic niche. They display a disregard for economic action – 'Very frequently every rational economic pursuit, and especially entrepreneurial activity, is looked upon as a disqualification of status' (p. 936). '[I]n most instances the notion of honor peculiar to status absolutely abhors that which is essential to the market: hard bargaining. Honor abhors hard bargaining among peers', presumably to reduce competition within the group, 'and occasionally it taboos it for the members of a status group in general' (p. 937). In many respects, Pierre Bourdieu's (1984: 281) highlighting of 'social capital' and 'cultural capital' alongside economic capital constitutes a re-working of Weber's conception of status as a form of social organization which cannot be reduced to class position. As Murray Milner Jr's work shows, wherever you can see a social group developing norms, rituals, aesthetic orientations, distinctive linguistic forms, codes of behaviour, etc. that are used to police its borders, then you are looking at a status system.

There are a number of aspects of celebrity which suggest that it can be understood as a type of status, but also others that make celebrity society a very particular kind of status system. Murray Milner Jr suggests, first, that both celebrity and any form of status are not reducible to economic or political power – one becomes rich or powerful because one is a celebrity, so this argument goes, being rich or powerful does not make one a celebrity. It is worth being a little cautious with this idea, because there is some extent to which it is not true, in the same way that it has in fact always been unstable for any kind of status. Being rich or powerful can in fact attract honour and high regard, or celebrity, one just has to be more careful in how one goes about it. But it is generally true that it cannot be *reduced* to wealth or power.

There is also an associative element to celebrity, like any other type of status – the pursuit of status is enhanced through association with higher-status individuals, and a one's own celebrity can often be enhanced through association with higher-profile celebrities. This is why political leaders are generally keen to be photographed with Bono, as Lincoln was keen to be seen with General Tom Thumb, or Warren Harding with Al Jolson. In any status system, there is a constant concern with ever-changing internal norms, fashion and style as a barrier to entry, as well as with sexual partners, and this is true of celebrity circles to an even greater extent. Gossip is a central mechanism of ordering and interaction, keeping information about constantly shifting relations within the status group circulating and operating as a vehicle for pursuing improvements in one's own position (Milner 2005: 70–1). Status systems are not meritocracies, one's position is not primarily an indicator of one's skill or talent, there is often an unstable relationship to 'genuine' merit as well as a certain inertia about one's status once it has been established and 'hardened'. Like the arguments concerning wealth and power, it is probably worth working with only a weak version of this idea, because merit does have something to do with both status and celebrity, but it does remain true that something needs to be added to merit to constitute any form of status, including celebrity.

Kurzman et al. (2007) also emphasize the way in which celebrities have pursued an aim common to all status groups – the carving out of a particular sphere of legal privilege in the wake of a stabilization of social and economic privileges. The particular legal privilege Kurzman et al. highlight is the 'right to publicity', that is: 'the right of each person to control and profit from the publicity values which he has created or purchased' (Nimmer 1954: 16). Beginning with the recognition of a baseball player's right to ownership of their image on chewing-gum cards in 1953,[2] most states in the USA now recognize a celebrity's property right to their name, image, voice and identity, although the right is less clearly established outside the US. Kurzman et al. also note the informal legal privileges which often flow to celebrities in areas such as criminal law, so that when they are victims, greater attention is given by law-enforcement agencies to the resolution of their cases, and when they engage in illegal acts, it is often possible to say that 'an informal double-standard may have emerged that smirks and winks at celebrity hijinks' (2007: 362).

There are differences, too, making celebrity a very particular kind of status system. The fact that celebrity appears, on the surface at least, to attach to *individuals*, whereas status is generally seen as attaching to *groups*, has undermined a willingness to understand and explain celebrity as a status system at all. Weber also saw status as antithetical to capitalism, gradually being overwhelmed by class, whereas the 'celebrity-industrial complex' (Orth 2004) is precisely tied very closely to the commodification of all human talent and distinctiveness, a vital lubricant of capitalism consumerism rather than a feudal relic. As Kurzman and his colleagues put it, 'Celebrity is status on speed. . . . It is a form of status that serves the interests of capitalism, rather than defending economic niches that capitalism is destined to conquer' (2007: 363). The economic aspects of celebrity are also much more explicit, argues Milner, than they are for other kinds of status systems, which are more likely to define their value and prestige in terms of their distinctiveness from 'mere' economic exchange (Milner 2010: 382–3). Milner further stresses that celebrity is more closely tied than other status systems to the circulation of information and networks of communication, and he believes that the emphasis on visuality means that the moral dimensions of celebrity status are less important than they are for other categories (2005: 74). The boundaries around celebrity groups are more porous, with more constant turnover and recruitment of new members, so that celebrity is less of a zero-sum game compared to other types of status.

Unlike other status systems, there are strong parallels with religion – the worshipping of celebrities/saints and everything associated with them, the attachment to holy locations – birth, key turning points, death – and to relics (autographs, former possessions, clothing, etc.). As Milner points out in relation to Emile Durkheim's analysis of religion, it identified two mechanisms operating in religion to promote social solidarity: first, the establishment of a relationship of all human beings to a sacred being that is both completely external and superior to the human world, thereby reducing the significance of differences among human beings; second, the creation of meaningful shared experience through ritualizing worship, generated a common bond between the members of the worshiping group (2005: 71). The role of sacredness in the production of celebrity suggests that its socially integrative effects may be similar to those of religion. Both of these mechanisms also characterize the celebrity–fan relationship, and this one of the reasons why writers such as Braudy (1986) and Rojek (2001) emphasize the parallels between the practices associated with religion and people's relationships with celebrities.

The construction of the celebrity/saint as charismatic (Rojek 2001; Alexander 2010a) is especially important, and raises the question of how the analysis of celebrity relates to another of Weber's central concepts – charisma. His analysis of charisma was bound up with the problem of explaining the differing foundations for societal authority, and he distinguished between three types of authority – traditional (dynastic or genealogical), rational-legal (bureaucratic), and that which fits into neither of these two categories and needs to be explained in terms of some personal quality, charisma. He defined charisma as follows:

> The term charisma refers to a certain quality of an individual personality by virtue of which he is considered extraordinary and treated as endowed with supernatural, superhuman, or at least specifically exceptional powers or qualities. These are . . . not accessible to the ordinary person, but are regarded as of divine origin or as exemplary, and on the basis of them the individual concerned is treated as a leader.
>
> (1978: 241)

Charisma is a somehow 'magical' quality, a kind of indefinable 'grace' and capacity to fascinate, driven by an underlying passion and often uncompromising commitment to a particular ideal or cause. For Weber, the relevant figures in traditional societies are magicians, prophets and warrior heroes, but more generally he is concerned with demagogues and political leaders, and their role in significant social and political change. Apart from Jesus, his political examples include the Athenian statesmen Cleon and Pericles through to Napoleon.

It does depend to some extent on performance and its acknowledgement by the audience; as Weber puts it, 'Recognition on the part of those subject to authority is decisive for the validity of charisma. . . . If proof and success elude the leader for long . . . it is likely that his charismatic authority will disappear' (1978: 1:241). But he did still tend to emphasize an account which stressed its psychological dimensions, and it is not always clear how the immanent qualities of an individual can be related to the clear sociological requirement that they be acknowledged and recognized as such by a particular audience (Friedland 1964: 20). As Friedland notes, there are charismatic individuals aplenty, but if they are not to be regarded as merely peculiar or perhaps insane, their charisma has to be rendered legitimate, and this is only understandable in sociological terms.

In the process of routinization and rationalization, Weber felt that over time charisma is destined to give way to either traditional or rational–legal authority. He saw it as having a limited lifespan, destined to play a reduced role in complex modern societies. As Weber observed, 'It is the fate of charisma to recede before the powers of tradition or of rational association after it has entered the permanent structure of social action' (1978: 2:1148). 'Only extraordinary conditions', he wrote, 'can bring about the triumph of charisma over the organization' (2:1132). Even if a charismatic individual can outmanoeuvre organizational imperatives, by definition it is restricted to their lifespan at most, and dies with that individual person, rather than continuing, as both traditional and rational–legal authority do, in an institutionalized form.

The difficulty in drawing on Weber's account of charisma to understand celebrity has always been his concentration on its linkage with political power and authority. Weber's ideal types were revolutionaries and politicians – Braudy lists Oliver Cromwell, the Duke of Malborough, Frederick the Great, Catherine the Great and George Washington – not musicians, actors and actresses, or writers, not Rousseau, Liszt, Byron or any of the other many household names of the nineteenth and early twentieth centuries. In addition to arguing for the inclusion of cultural alongside political authority figures, then, Braudy (2010: 170) also suggests making a distinction between '*instrumental charisma*, which is linked to the realm of action, especially political and military, and *intrinsic charisma*, the outcome of skilled performance and representation, what we would normally associate with celebrity'.

The way in which the relationship between the different forms of authority is understood by Weber is also destabilized once one includes an analysis of celebrity. Instead of seeing them as alternative bases of authority, it may be that they are in fact interlocking and mutually reinforcing. Braudy sees rational–legal and charismatic authority – or at least celebrity – as developing hand in hand with the explosion of a wide variety of different types of celebrity identity associated with the massive expansion of the mass media in the nineteenth century, indicating precisely that processes of rationalization and bureaucratization in the context of increasing density and complexity generated a greater variety of ways of making one's mark, and a greater interest in how that was achieved – hence the interest in figures such as Paganini and Liszt (2010: 180). Looking at charisma through the lens of celebrity shows that the *intersection* of charismatic, traditional and rational–legal authority is precisely what is interesting about politics, culture and society in the nineteenth and twentieth centuries.

Paying attention to celebrity additionally highlights the importance of what Berenson and Giloi (2010) call 'celebrity from below', the proliferation of various forms of charisma in addition to the political, with the demands and expectations of the audience as a driving force for the social 'construction' of charisma. Including a discussion of celebrity brings the gender dimensions of charisma much more clearly into view, requiring us to take account of Lola Montez and Sarah Bernhardt as much as Napoleon, and to consider the dynamics of the relations between masculine and feminine spheres of celebrity. Thinking about celebrity is useful, too, in understanding how charisma evolves; celebrity can outlive, for instance, the charisma that was originally its foundation – Berenson and Giloi (2010) give the example of Henry Morton Stanley, whose reputation for violence undermined his charismatic authority, while remaining a celebrity for 'Dr Livingstone, I presume?' and numerous biographies and commentaries (p. 4).

To understand charisma, then, it is useful to go beyond Weber's own account and include an analysis of the mechanisms and logic of celebrity – in some contexts, it is possibly more useful to think in terms of celebrity than charisma. There certainly appears to be a mutually interactive relationship between charisma and celebrity – charisma will often get turned into celebrity, because of the charismatic individual's capacity to draw attention to themselves. But what we experience as 'charisma' can often in fact be celebrity, because the self-reproducing nature of celebrity's attention-capital (the Matthew effect) means that celebrity itself can be experienced as the individual's superhuman and exceptional characteristic. One can generate allure because of immanent attributes – think of Giuseppe Garibaldi, Che Guevara, Muhammad Ali, or Bill Clinton – but also additionally, or even simply, because one is already attracting the attention of a multitude.

Power in the viewer society

Michel Foucault argued that the operation of mechanisms of power became specifically modern at the point where it moved from spectacular but disparate and unsystematic displays of sovereign power (such as public executions) to more regularized, extensive and invisible techniques based on the accumulation of knowledge about the relevant aspects of a population and the behaviour of its members. He referred to Jeremy Bentham's prison model, the 'Panopticon', to capture this idea of the many (the people) being visible to the few (state officials), as opposed to the

Absolutist model of the few (the king and the aristocracy) being visible to the many (the people). 'Our society', wrote Foucault, 'is not one of spectacle, but of surveillance', in which the 'necessarily spectacular manifestations of power; have been 'extinguished one by one in the daily exercise of surveillance, in a panopticism in which the vigilance of intersecting gazes was soon to render useless both the eagle and the sun' (1977: 217). The point was not so much that the population was in fact being kept under surveillance by a smaller number of observers, but that because one never knew if one was being observed, this had an 'as if' effect, one behaved as if one were under observation, thus internalizing the surveillance.

The Norwegian criminologist Thomas Mathieson has suggested that this argument needs to be modified to take account of the role of the mass media in contemporary society, which underpins a crucial counterpart to panopticism, namely 'synopticism', where the viewing relationship is reversed so that the many watch the few, that is, celebrities – 'the VIPs, the reporters, the stars, almost a new class in the public sphere' (1997: 219). Mathieson does not see any historical transition from one model to the other, but more that they both have long historically roots going back to the ancient world, and that organization and technological transformations in the nineteenth and twentieth centuries 'advanced the use of *both models* by leaps and bounds, thus making them into two basic characteristics of modernity' (pp. 222–3). Indeed, panopticism and synopticism have developed more or less hand in hand, and he points out that all the institutions which have been presumed to constitute examples of panopticism – the Roman Catholic Church and the Inquisition, the state, the military, prisons – actually simultaneously have important elements of synopticism, in the sense that they also project themselves powerfully into the symbolic realm, with churches and cathedrals, saints' processions, spectacular Inquisitors, Royal pageantry, the celebration of military heroes, and the overwhelming physical presence of prisons (p. 223). 'In a two-way and significant double sense of the word,' writes Mathieson, 'we thus live in a *viewer society*' (p. 219)

The concerns are different, but a similar argument about a need to take greater account of spectacle and display in analysing the operation of power in modern social life was developed by Tony Bennett in his account of what he calls the 'exhibitionary complex', referring to the variety of institutions developed to display artistic, cultural, natural and scientific artefacts in museums and exhibitions. By providing 'object lessons in power – the power to command and arrange things and bodies for public display', wrote Bennett,

> they sought to allow the people, and en masse rather than individually, to know rather than be known, to become the subjects rather than the objects of knowledge. Yet, ideally, they sought also to allow the people to know and thence to regulate themselves; to become, in seeing themselves from the side of power, both the subjects and the objects of knowledge, knowing power and what power knows, and knowing themselves as (ideally) known interiorizing its gaze as a principle of self-surveillance and, hence, self-regulation.
>
> (1988: 76)

Like synopticism more generally, one can see the same mechanism of power organized around the focusing of the attention of large numbers of people on central objects, ideas and representations, what Richard Lanham (1997) calls the 'centripetal gaze'.

The advent and spread of television has simply reinforced the interdependence of panopticism and synopticism, so that the televisual observation of human behaviour is actually a two-way process to the extent that the form taken by the observed situation, its structure and grammar, has a 'return effect' on the viewer in structuring their consciousness, beliefs, values and normative orientations, to a large extent because of the human tendency towards identification with the other. Freud refused to allow himself to be simultaneously recorded and filmed, for fear of losing his soul, and Braudy remarks that Freud had clearly 'learned the performer's lesson that to be caught in the attention of others is in great part to mean what they want you to mean' (1986: 583). However, this dynamic works in both directions, so that having one's attention caught by others is also in great part to mean what they want you to mean. In relation to celebrity gossip magazines, Julie A. Wilson argues along related lines that the constant attention paid to the minute details of celebrities' personal life-style choices constitutes 'a mainstream cultural testing center for the development of appropriate gendered selves' (2010: 30), so that the ongoing evaluation of celebrities' conduct operates as continuous self-evaluation, star-testing needs to be understood as simultaneously surveillance and normative adjudication of one's own conduct and identity.

The proliferation of reality TV since the 1990s is a central example of the role that the media construction of both short- and long-term celebrity identities plays in shaping the process of self-formation. Nick Couldry (2008, 2010) has argued, for example, that the logic and structure of reality TV shows such as *Big Brother* are closely linked to the modes of governance characterizing the neoliberal market and workplace. He highlights the core features of the *Big Brother* format: absolute external authority, the validity and rationality of which are beyond question, which includes acceptance of arbitrary decisions; team conformity, requiring almost complete conformity to group norms; enforced authenticity, demanding performance that is both constant and always genuine, blurring if not completely eliminating the boundary between public and private life; the demand for positive passion, with no space left for criticism, doubt or anxiety; and complete individualization, crowding out any sense of the collective or social dimensions of experience, expressed above all in the mechanism of voting-out individual household members one at a time. A similar analysis can be applied to other reality TV shows (Hearn 2006, 2008) – *Survivor, The Apprentice, Pop Idol, Britain's Got Talent, Masterchef, The Biggest Loser*, in China, *Super Girls Voice*, in that they all are premised on a particular kind of subjectivity, scripting a particular *habitus*. To the extent that this remains implicit and unconscious, built into the structure of the affective experience of the television programme, they have the capacity to plays a powerful role structuring viewer's cognition and identity in very specific ways.

The dynamics of ever-intensifying competition and constant organizational change in the post-Fordist economy of flexible accumulation and the networked organization (Harvey 1990; Boltanski & Chiapello 2006) also underpin the increasingly central role of celebrity in the construction of one's identity in the workplace. Ernest Sternberg points out that the mere possession of skills, expertise, training and experience is decreasingly effective in a dense, overcrowded competitive field, requiring greater attention to 'calculated self-presentation, using techniques originally meant for the making of celebrities' (1998: 4). The core problem becomes one of turning one's self into a brand (Hearn 2008) and adapting one's persona to the every-changing demands of the labour market, especially that of permanent flexibility and adaptability (du Gay 1996a, 1996b). The ever-expanding and shifting field of celebrity conduct is an invaluable resource, guide and model for the ways in which emotional labour can – and indeed is expected – to be performed. 'In every industry and line of business', writes Sternberg, 'each of us must learn from celebrities, those human icons whose successes in presenting the persona are verified through their renown' (1998: 11). As Alison Hearn argues, 'celebrity functions not only as cultural resource in and through which individuals construct their identities, but becomes a generalizable model of profitable self-production for all individuals' (2008: 208). Ordinary appearance, wallflower personalities, unmemorable faces and inflexible characters just do not cut it anymore; to stand out from the crowd in a celebrity society as an 'entrepreneur of the self' (du Gay 1996a: 70), one needs the 'X-factor', so it is little wonder that so many people are so consistently fascinated by the do's and don't of that aspiration.

The power relations between celebrities and their audiences are thus complex and multi-layered, moving in a number of directions at the same time. On the one hand, celebrities are indeed 'powerless', dependent on the allocation of attention from their audience, which can at any time be withdrawn if a celebrity fails to perform adequately, the criteria for their recognition entirely under the control of an anonymous 'public' which can be ruthless if one does not measure up (Kirby 2006). David Kirby gives an example of this dynamic, with fans of US stock-car champion Jeff Gordon, who, when he failed to respond to their approaches, 'turned on him viciously, screaming their hatred and making lurid gestures toward the man who, a few minutes before, had been as a god to them'. Celebrities may be well paid, but part of the exchange is a demand for almost infinite responsiveness to the expectations of their audience. On the other hand, the celebrity power relation works in the other direction as well, in the sense that our consciousness is structured and organized in a particular way, around ideals of gendered identity, appearance and behaviour. Our sense of self is always strongly influenced by those we are attached to and with whom we have an intimate relationship, and celebrities are a focal point for what Steven Lukes (2005) calls the 'third face' of power: the myriad ways in which cognition, perceived needs, preferences, desires and aspirations can be shaped in particular ways.

Mathieson thus suggests that the 'pincer movement' performed by the combination of panoticism and synopticism confines life to the generally accepted and taken for granted, and steers us away from any 'difficult' questions subduing or even making silent discussion of

> the basic critical questions concerning the very foundation of our life and existence. We are left [instead with a situation] . . . where the answers to the basic questions are taken for granted, and the debate concerns details and remains on the surface. In bold relief: surveillance, panopticon, makes us silent about that which breaks fundamentally with the taken-for-granted because we are made afraid to break with it. Modern television, synopticon, makes us silent because we do not have anything to talk about that might initiate the break.
>
> (1997: 230–1)

While this formulation may overemphasize the extent to which silence is in fact imposed, it is probably fair to see celebrity as having a significant 'bread and circuses' effect, so that the attention devoted to celebrities can only subtract from the attention being paid to issues connected with politics, economics and the distribution of other forms of power.

It may be difficult to describe any particular celebrities *as individuals,* or even as a group, as being 'powerful', but there is a great deal of salience to the idea that there is a power relationship between individuals and the *field of celebrity* as a whole. This is because of the standardizing effect associated with synopticism: the attention of large numbers of people converges on a relatively small number of celebrities. In Theodor Adorno and Max Horkheimer's 1944 critique of the 'culture industry' and the twentieth-century commodification of culture, they made the point that the production of pseudo-individuality has the effect of standardizing individuals' conceptions of what it means to be individual, turning even distinctiveness into a standard 'product' which can be bought and sold. 'The defiant reserve or elegant appearance of the individual on show is mass-produced like Yale locks', they wrote, 'whose only difference can be measured in fractions of millimeters' (1979: 154). To the extent that celebrity turns into permanent advertisement, of itself if not for products being endorsed, the celebrity society is a powerful force towards the standardization and commodification of everything.

The point at which synopticism can be linked back to other aspects of Foucault's work is his account of the various ways in which individuals reflect and act upon themselves in constantly monitoring, revising and reworking their answers to fundamental questions of identity, virtue and morality. Such questions can never be answered definitively, and need ongoing engagement, because every different situation will generate more or less significantly different answers, and this underpins the fundamental instability of any self-assessment and the nature of self-formation as a never-ending project. In addition to the technologies of production, signification and power, Foucault argued that it is useful to examine the 'technologies of the self', by which he meant techniques and practices enabling individuals, either on their own or in interaction with others, to perform 'a certain number of operations on their own bodies and souls, thoughts, conduct, and way of being, so as to transform themselves in order to attain a certain state of happiness, purity, wisdom, perfection, or immortality' (1977: 225).

Foucault thought that one of the central technologies of the self, alongside self-examination, self-reflection and confession, is 'a review of what was done, of what should have been done, and comparison of the two' (p. 238). One important way in which one can enter into a dialogue both with oneself and with others about such an examination is to expand the range of 'things which have been done' beyond oneself, to include those of figures and characters with whom one's interlocutor (even if just oneself) is familiar, and whom one knows to be reference points for other members of one's larger or smaller social group. Nikolas Rose argues that the 'enterprising self' in advanced liberalism is oriented towards autonomy, 'it is to strive for personal fulfilment in its earthly life, it is to interpret its reality and destiny as a matter of individual responsibility, it is to find meaning in existence by shaping its life through acts of choice' (1996: 151). Rose himself emphasizes the central role of experts of subjectivity in forming the ways in which individuals navigate the waters of heterogeneous choice, but one can add to that analysis a sense of how the repeated exposure to continuous reflection on the conduct of highly visible prominent individuals is also an important arena for the alignment of individual aspirations and personal preferences with the broader 'conduct of conduct'. A central element of reviewing and reflecting on oneself is comparison with 'significant others', and celebrities are particularly important here, being already widely recognized and the object of ongoing critical scrutiny by other members of society. This is the social and intersubjective 'space' into which celebrities of all types step, and this is what elicits the celebrity role and identity in ever-changing ways.

The legal construction of celebrity

Kurzman et al. (2007) refer to the legal dimensions of celebrity status, and it is useful to go into the legal regulation of celebrity identity in some more detail, as well as reflecting on the varying forms it takes in different national settings and jurisdictions. Law can play a role in relation to celebrity in a variety of ways, including defamation, trespass and nuisance, and the ways in which common law principles and differing legislative provisions interact can be complex (Loughlan et al. 2010), but here I will focus on two particularly important arenas: the regulation of celebrity identity as a form of property with commercial value, and the regulation of privacy. In practice, the two will sometimes overlap, with particular jurisdictions making it possible to pursue more or less the aims of one concern in terms of the other. For example, if a magazine publishes information about a celebrity's private life, that can either be regarded in commercial terms as gaining an economic benefit from that celebrity's identity and 'attention-capital' in the absence of appropriate monetary compensation, requiring financial restitution (more likely in the USA), or it can be regarded as an illegitimate intrusion into their private lives, also demanding compensation (more likely in the UK and France), probably at a similar level. Still, to begin with it is useful to keep them analytically separate, and the legal regimes are generally distinct.

In relation to the legal regulation of celebrity identity understood as commercial property, there are two models that structure its operation – misappropriation, or the tort of 'right of publicity', and misrepresentation, or the tort of 'passing off'. The first is characteristic of North American law, and the second of Anglo-Australian law. In the misappropriation model, one's identity as a celebrity is treated as property which has commercial value and can be traded. An early example is Johnny Carson and his trademark phrase, 'Here's Johnny', which was used in promotional material by a trader in portable toilets. Carson sued saying that his identity had been commercially appropriated, and won (2010: 35). 'The concept of 'use of a celebrity identity does appear', argue Loughlan et al. (p. 380), 'in the exercise of the right of publicity, to stretch to cover a trader's use of anything which evokes the celebrity in the mind of the target consumer.' Its operation is not, however, uniform across all the American states – in relation to dead celebrities, for example, Elvis Presley's rights of publicity are protected in Tennessee, but not Marilyn Monroe's in New York and California (p. 39).

For misappropriation, the concern is 'prohibiting marketplace misrepresentations to the public and preventing consumer confusion' (p. 35). Use of a celebrity identity in an advertisement without their consent misrepresents the goods as being endorsed by the celebrity. But this is not the same as 'owning' one's identity. A useful illustration of the difference is that Elvis impersonators would not be regarded in Australian and UK law as attempting to 'misrepresent' themselves as Elvis, whereas the concept of misappropriation would lead to the treatment of Elvis's identity as property owned by Elvis's estate (p. 48). Underlying both models is a tension between the commercial control of celebrity identity and the fan–celebrity relationship, but where money is being made, there is general consensus that some legal regulation is required – it is a matter of determining exactly where the boundaries lie.

Celebrity is by definition about high visibility, but there can also be disputes and differences of opinion about exactly where the boundaries of that visibility should lie, and these often manifest themselves as legal disputes about privacy. There is a particular kind of relationship between some celebrity figures and their audience, where the audience has the usual strong interest in blurring the boundaries between public and private life, but not the celebrity themselves. The situation is usually framed as concerning the tension between the individual's right to privacy and freedom of expression, but often it can be better understood as revolving around the limits to the freedom to make use of a public personality's attention-capital, when they themselves have no interest in increasing their own visibility. The question of privacy raises the question of exactly where the boundaries between the public and private spheres lie, and whether that boundary can lie in different places for individuals engaged in different kinds of activities. This is an especially important question in relation to celebrity society, since celebrity is often – but not always – precisely about the blurring of the boundary between the two realms.

There are two key aspects to the place of privacy in the legal regulation of celebrity: intrusion, 'the protection of a person from unwanted or unreasonable physical intrusions and surveillance'; and disclosure, 'the protection against the disclosure of private information' (Loughlan et al. 2010: 102). The first concerns an individual's physical surroundings, the second concerns the flow of various types of information – oral, written and visual (p. 103). In the United Kingdom, the question of privacy is read through the lens of the concept 'breach of confidence', so that settlement of the issue depends on whether the information concerned can be regarded as confidential. For example, John Lennon brought action against his former wife Cynthia to stop the *News of the World* from publishing an article on John and Yoko, which failed on the basis that Lennon had already made much of his private life a public matter. The distinction was subtle – the court went the other way in relation to the Duke of Argyll and his former wife, handing down an injunction against him revealing details of the Duchess of Argyle's personal affairs despite her own previous disclosures (p. 121). The settled position in UK law became that it was not necessary for the confidential nature of the information to have been made explicit, it was a matter of determining whether a person would have had notice of its confidentiality, and whether 'it would be just in all the circumstances that he should be precluded from disclosing the information to others'.[3]

The passage of the Human Rights Act in 1998, giving effect to the provisions of the *European Convention on Human Rights*, transformed the regulation of privacy in the UK, framing it in terms of striking a balance between respect for private life and countervailing concerns such as right to freedom of expression, freedom of the press, and the public interest. The duty of confidence remains central, as in Naomi Campbell's action against *The Mirror* in 2001 concerning photographs of her leaving Narcotics Anonymous. The House of Lords ended up ruling in Campbell's favour, arguing that the duty of confidence arises whenever the party subject to the duty is in a situation where he knows or ought to know that the other person can reasonably expect his privacy to be protected. Significantly, the 'confidence' was held to be the location of Narcotics Anonymous, not the fact that Campbell was undergoing rehabilitation treatment for drug use.

But the overall shift that has taken place in UK law has been away from requiring a preceding confidential relationship, towards focusing on the nature of the information itself and its impact on human dignity. As Lord Hoffman put it,

> Instead of the cause of action being based upon the duty of good faith applicable to confidential personal information and trade secrets alike, it focuses upon the protection of human autonomy and dignity – the right to control the dissemination of information about one's private life and the right to the esteem and respect of other people.[4]

French law provides vigorous protection of the private lives of public figures. Legal construction of celebrity privacy based on a 1858 'celebrity deathbed' case, the *Rachel* case (Hauch 1994). The actress Rachel Felix (1821–58) was a leading nineteenth-century French celebrity, the mistress of Louis I's son, with whom she bore a son, after which her lovers included Louis Napoleon Bonparte, later Napoleon III. When she lay dying, Rachel's sister had a photograph taken, on the understanding that it would not be publically revealed. When a sketch clearly derived from the photograph came on sale, Rachel's sister successfully sued both photographer and artist and secured destruction of all the copies. The French court's position was that it did not matter how much of a celebrity one was, consent was always an absolute requirement. In a sense, the French requirement for consent approached that of the American concept of celebrity identity as 'property' (Hauch 1994: 1233), since 'the absolute nature of the restriction on publication without consent meant that, in France, a person could prevent publication of facts even if they had previously been made public' (Loughlan et al. 2010: 127). This principle underpins the French approach to celebrity privacy more or less to the present day.

The idea that, as Hauch sums it up, 'the extent of the right to privacy is defined by its central goals: to protect individuals from the interference of others and in their relations with others' (1994: 1245), runs through cases such as Marlene Dietrich's action in 1955 against *France Dimanche* for revealing aspects of her private life, Gérard Philipe's action in 1965, also against *France Dimanche*, for an article on his young son's illness, as well as a range of subsequent cases concerning images of naked or partially clothed bodies, illness or death, physical deformity, surgical operations, familial relations, pregnancy, contraception and childbirth, illegitimacy, marital quarrels and prostitution, and the fictional representation of real people and events (pp. 1246–9). Activities that are themselves clearly public are not protected, but being a public figure does not by itself grant access to those parts of one's life that are not, such as being on holiday or at home. Other exceptions include the public interest in public figures after their death, especially if the information is already in circulation, which is why President Mitterand's family failed to prevent disclosure of the fact that Mitterand had kept his cancer secret from his family. It also seems that French courts may be less responsive to celebrities' claims of breach of privacy if they have already been quite active in exposing their private life – Princess Stephanie Monaco, for example, was not successful in an action over photographs of her and her ex-husband in public for this reason (Loughlan et al. 2010: 130).

In Germany the balance struck between the various concerns is different – for example, Princess Caroline of Monaco (then von Hannover) failed during the 1990s in preventing the circulation of photographs of her and her family in everyday activities – in restaurants and cafes, shopping, on holidays, swimming. The German court's position was that she was a 'figure of contemporary society *par excellence*', that her family had always sought media attention, that her reputation had not been damaged, and that the locations could not be considered 'private'. However, the European Court of Human Rights took a different view, finding that the German courts' criteria for a 'figure of contemporary society' and what constituted a private location were too vague, and implied that Princess Caroline would be photographable at any and every opportunity. It argued, in contrast, that the decisive factor in balancing the protection of private life against freedom of expression should lie in the contribution that the published photos and articles make to a debate of general interest. It is clear in the instant case that they make no such contribution since [Princess Caroline] exercises no official function and the photos and articles relate exclusively to details of her private life.[5]

It held that Article 8(1) of the *European Convention for the Protection of Human Rights and Fundamental Freedoms* of 1950 (Everyone has the right to respect for his or her private and family life, his home and his correspondence) was of equal weight to Article 10(1) providing for freedom of expression, that the activities portrayed were of a private rather than public nature, and that she was not in fact a 'figure of contemporary society *par excellence*', because she fulfilled no public function.

Unjust enrichment?

One of the key recent UK cases has been that of Max Mosley and *News of the World*, which, in March 2008, published an article, photographs and video footage of Max Mosley – the son of Oswald and Diana Mosley, well-known British National Socialist sympathizers – engaged in various sexual activities involving bondage and sado-masochism. Justice Eady ruled in Mosley's favour, remaining unpersuaded by the public interest arguments, which revolved around the argument that Mosley's actions were criminal and Nazi-like, and around Mosley's position as president of the International Automobile Federation, all of which Eady J rejected. The press complained about censorship and restriction of the freedom of the press, but of course the full extent of the *News of the World*'s willingness to breach celebrities' privacy in the name of 'press freedom' was revealed in the course of the 2011 phone-hacking scandal, with many of the cases reportedly enjoying Mosely's financial backing, finally leading to the *News of the World*'s closure.

However, the underlying concerns are also made clearer by another case, run by *OK!* magazine and Michael Douglas and Catherine Zeta-Jones against *Hello!* magazine in relation to photographs of the wedding of Douglas and Zeta-Jones. This was a relatively unusual case because it involved protection of commercial interests relying on breach of confidence – *OK!* magazine had purchased exclusive rights to the wedding photographs, and understandably they wished to protect their £1million investment. The House of Lords ruled in *OK!* Ltd's favour, on the basis that *Hello!* and their photographer were fully aware of the confidential nature of the images, in the sense that exclusive rights had been granted to *OK!*

Although in this case Douglas and Zeta-Jones had in fact exchanged their privacy for money, in a way that is not true of these other cases, the underlying dynamics are very similar, and highlight in a very useful way the arguments concerning celebrity as a form of 'attention capital' developed in the previous chapter. For example, it was not expressed this way, and it was not how Princess Caroline herself framed her concerns, but it is clear that essentially the magazines

– *Sieben Tage, Frau im Speigel* – were free-riding on Princess Caroline's attention capital, without her permission and without paying for it. Royalty sells as many magazines in Germany as it does anywhere else, and it is this commercial interest which had been restricted by the European courts, and then, stepping into line, the German courts, not freedom of expression.

> While it's hard to put a concrete figure on the popularity of all things aristocratic in Germany . . . interest is growing. . . . The media are all too happy to help sate the public's appetite for the royals. All the major German stations have programs devoted to the more sensational side of the things, including royals, or, better yet, royal scandals. . . . Or walk into any shop selling newspapers and magazines, and one row will be devoted to what the Germans call the 'rainbow' press – weekly gossip magazines aimed largely at women that feature stories about the royals.
>
> According to a 2003 survey, 9 million copies of these kinds of magazines are sold a week. Although when many people are asked, they won't admit to reading them, or even being the slightest bit interested in what colors Princess Mary of Denmark chose for her new bathroom. . . . 'When you ask someone, no one says they're interested in them. It's like with porn magazines; they sell like crazy, but no one admits to buying them,' said Peter Schaumberg, who owns a flower shop in Berlin.[6]

In all the other cases, too, the fundamental interest of the mass media is in the attention-capital of the celebrity concerned, and in how that can be leveraged into sales and viewers. The legal disputes thus concern situations where that attention capital has not been paid for and usually where its possessor has not wanted to exchange it at all. What the legal regulation of celebrity identity is very often about, then, is the management of disputes and breakdowns in the circulation of attention-capital, and this suggests that 'unjust enrichment' might be the cause of action that more accurately reflects the underlying conflict.

4 Imagined community and long-distance intimacy

I think we can say that men and women do wish to talk about personal matters, for reasons on which I am not clear, and in the great conurbations the discussion of, for example, stars of film and sport, produces a basis on which people transitorily associated can find something personal to talk about.

(Gluckman 1963: 315)

A central aspect of living in a social world organized around various forms of mass communication, beginning with the printed word but then including the telegraph, film, radio, television, and today the Internet, what Marshall McLuhan (1962) called the 'Gutenberg Galaxy', is that a large proportion of the social network exists in the realm of imagination rather than direct face-to-face contact. As the German sociologist Niklas Luhmann once remarked, 'Whatever we know about our society, or indeed about the world in which we live, we know through the mass media' (2000: 1). Life in large-scale, industrialized and urbanized nation-states is such that any sense of having a shared identity beyond the realm of direct contact – as an Australian, French, or American person – is inherently 'virtual'. People can only know about their fellow citizens in the world of the imagination, the written word, images and sounds conveyed over the mass media, such that a 'nation-state' is inherently an 'imagined community' (Anderson 1983).

Another way of characterizing the issue is to draw a contrast between *gemeinschaft* (community) and *gesellschaft* (society), first formulated in 1887 by the German sociologist Ferdinand Tönnies (2001). The concept *gemeinschaft* refers to a world of communal bonds, where direct face-to-face ties are strong and individual identity is strongly structured by the collectivities people are part of, particularly their family and village or small town. The term *gesellschaft*, in contrast, refers to a mode of structuring social life where communal norms are weaker, individual identity is stronger, and social networks are held together in more volatile ways, sometimes indirectly through the construction of discourses of supra-local identity such as the nation or the Christian Church, and sometimes more directly through institutional forms such as education systems, police and security forces, and the legal system.

Life in modern urbanized societies is characterized by a complex division of labour consisting of numerous contacts with people one only knows partially and to a limited extent, and of segmented social contexts that may never come into contact with each other. The most obvious example would be the possibility of being one person in one's family life, another in the workplace, and still another in one's social life outside the family. Modern 'society' in this sense is thus characterized by what Mark Granovetter (1973) termed 'weak ties'. This concept refers to the ways in which clusters of individuals more directly bonded to each other by high-density 'strong ties' are in turn linked to each other by low-density 'weak ties': either those of acquaintance, or of mutually shared strong ties. Granovetter pointed out that it is these weak ties that constitute the communicative links between clumps of strong ties, and this is their 'strength' in a large-scale social world. As he put it, 'social systems lacking in weak ties will be fragmented and incoherent. New ideas will spread slowly, scientific endeavors will be handicapped, and subgroups separated by race, ethnicity, geography, or other characteristics will have difficulty reaching a *modus vivendi*' (1983: 202)

As an example of weak ties, the bonds that people form with celebrities as 'intimate strangers' (Schickel 1985) can be very significant in themselves, constituting an important dimension of their sense of self and their everyday experience. They underpin individual and collective identity as a fan, enthusiast, devotee or connoisseur of varying degrees of commitment and obsession (Pearson 2007), sometimes spilling over into stalking (Nicol 2006) and occasionally as far as killing the celebrity object of their attentions (Elliott 1998). However, of broader significance is the role that celebrities play – as highly visible to a large number of otherwise disconnected individuals – as 'weak ties' binding disparate, segmented individuals together. One can put it quite firmly – one needs to have some knowledge of a reasonable range of core celebrities to be regarded even minimally as a socially competent member of society (Alperstein 1991; Caughey 1984), and membership of particular sub-groups will require a familiarity and discursive competence about the celebrities linked to that group. As John Caughey put it, every person in America 'is expected to be familiar with an extensive series of artificial beings, and these mutual acquaintances often give strangers (e.g., in bars, taxicabs, airplanes) a basis for socializing' (1978: 84). Celebrities have an important socially integrative effect, constituting significant 'nodes' which hold together a communicative social network, analogous to the 'buttons' in a mattress. They provide an important type of *lingua franca* and shared experience for otherwise disconnected social networks, and act as focal, reference points for imagined, virtual communities stretched around the globe.

Richard Schickel (1985: 275) has suggested that a useful analogy is the definition of 'The Force' given in the film *Star Wars* by Sir Alec Guinness as Obi-Wan Kenobi – 'It's an energy field created by all living things. It surrounds us, and penetrates us. It binds the galaxy together.' Since celebrities also bind our social world together, providing much of the sense of social connectedness has become more and more difficult to sustain in terms of direct face-to-face interaction. In a study of the political dimensions of celebrity, Marks and Fisher come to a similar conclusion, arguing that the universal recognition achieved by celebrities today has analogous effects to that of absolutist monarchs, and that 'when the people identify as a collective with media created celebrity figures, this is the first step towards the creation of a simulated political community' (2002: 394). Jason Goldsmith similarly comments on the centrality of celebrity to the development of nationalism in the nineteenth century, operating as 'one of the mechanisms through which national sentiments were fostered among a diverse and heterogenous populace' (2009: 22). As vehicles of emotional formation in art and literature, 'celebrities elaborate nations and national identities' (p. 22). Today sports stars play an important role in the elaboration of increasingly complex national, gender and cultural identities in the context of the forces of globalization – the examples examined in Andrews and Jackson (2001) include Michael Jordan, Venus Williams, Ian Wright, Tiger Woods, Diego Maradona, Martina Hingis, Imran Khan and Cathy Freeman. Celebrity can be understood, writes Goldsmith, 'as an extensive, industrialized and intertextual mode of gossip, disseminating information, facilitating identifications, channelling desires, defining relations within a community, proscribing behaviours and legitimating values' (2009: 22).

Para-social interaction, long-distance intimacy

When one goes further, to look at the actual substance of the role that celebrities play in everyday life, more can be said about the role that the theatrical acting-out of imagined situations – in literature, certainly, but more powerfully in films, on radio and on television – plays in the construction and development of the self in contemporary social life. The mass media expose people to an endless flow of imagined, hypothetical scenarios in everyday life, ranging from the extreme to the mundane, which play the same role as story-telling does in any cultural context – providing models, examples, parables, cautionary tales that embrace viewers and listeners in what Donald Horton and Richard Wohl (1956) called 'para-social interaction' and 'intimacy at a distance', or, as I prefer to call it, 'long-distance intimacy'.

'One of the most striking characteristics of the new media – radio, television, and the movies', wrote Horton and Wohl in 1956, 'is that they give the illusion of face-to-face relationships with the performer' (p. 215). They decided to refer to this type of virtual encounter as a 'para-social' relationship, and used 'para-social interaction' to capture the 'simulacrum of conversational give and take' (p. 215) in people's relationships with radio and television personalities. Their focus was particularly on 'personalities' or 'personae' – that category of performer that only the mass media can produce, the announcers, quiz masters, interviewers, masters of ceremonies and so on, who mediate the relationship between the particular radio or television programme and the audience, but then also take on a central defining role themselves. The work of media personalities is to create a 'bond of intimacy' with the audience, constructing the programme as a spontaneous experience in which those in the audience feel they are active participants, reinforced with deliberate informality (first names or nicknames, casual conversational speech, treating all the cast as close friends), stepping outside of frame, use of camera angles, use of live (coached) studio audiences.

Such long-distance intimacy, suggest Horton and Wohl, constitutes a particular kind of social pedagogy regarding everyday conduct and the management of the enormous variety of issues, problems, dilemmas, and choices that make up daily life. It is characterized by

> the exemplification of the patterns of conduct one needs to understand and cope with in others as well as of those patterns which one must apply to one's self. Thus the spectator is instructed variously in the behaviors of the opposite sex, of people of higher and lower status, of people in particular occupations and professions. In a quantitative sense, by reason of the sheer volume of such instruction, this may be the most important aspect of the para-social experience, if only because each person's roles are relatively few, while those of the others in his social worlds are very numerous.
>
> (1956: 222)

Viewers come to 'know' media characters, observed Horton and Wohl, 'in somewhat the same way they know their chosen friends; through direct observation and interpretation of his appearance, his gestures and voice, his conversation and conduct in a variety of situations' (p. 216). This type of mediated intimacy had already been experienced with radio, but the addition of live images with television significantly heightened its psychological impact.

Building on Horton and Wohl's piece, there is now a considerable literature on para-social interaction (Caughey 1978; Leets et al. 1995; Houlberg 1984; Levy 1979; Rubin, Perse, & Powell 1985; Rubin & McHugh 1987; Perse & Rubin 1989), extending their original arguments to respond to the challenge they posed at the end of that paper, to understand in more detail how para-social interactions 'are integrated into the matrix of usual social activity' (Horton & Wohl 1956: 228). John Caughey argued that it is important to place alongside the 'real social world' of average Americans the 'artificial social world' known to them 'via television, radio, movies, books, magazines, and newspapers, populated by a far larger number of characters – actors, musicians, authors, politicians, columnists, announcers, disc jockeys, talk-show hosts, and other "celebrities" as well as all the characters in all the novels, biographies, plays, movies, TV shows, and comic strips' (1978: 71). Caughey noted that many viewers of soap operas see these as providing them with knowledge that is useful in everyday life, and that they use the televisual material 'as a script for conduct in the real world' (p. 80).

Helen Wood and Beverley Skeggs (2004) similarly focus on the pedagogic elements of the ever-expanding variety of more recent reality and lifestyle television programmes, providing viewers with a 'grammar of conduct' and a set of repertoires for everyday existence and identity structuring their self-fashioning (Stacey 1994), involving an endless array of how-to's and what-not-to-do's – how to be feminine or masculine, acquire and perform social capital, understand the workings of class, engage in appropriate sexual behaviour, lead a more efficient clutter-free life, display appropriate taste, manage emotions and make moral choices. Once one begins to look at the various forms which can be taken by people's relationship to media characters, there are a number of dimensions of such para-social relationships – fandom, gossip, integration into 'real' relationships, involvement in studio audiences or as participants in the ever-expanding forms of reality TV, and of course stalking.

M.S. Picirillo has drawn out the extent to which para-social interaction shares many features of everyday real-life interaction in her study of the closing episodes of long-running television series such as *M*A*S*H*, *The Mary Tyler Moore Show*, *Barney Miller* and *Alice*, in the sense that they all display a particular 'rhetorical aesthetics' in introducing, forming, developing and re-working the personalities and conduct of all the characters in the programme so that '[c]ollected instances of intimacy allow viewers to share a common history with a television series, one which parallels the history imbedded in the practice of everyday lived experience' (1986: 345). Picirillo identifies three arguments against simply seeing televisual para-social interaction as somehow neurotic and dysfunctional (p. 352). First, there is considerable originality and creativity in the structuring and development of character, social relations and social interaction in the narratives of television programmes, constituting a more significant contribution to the social imagination than mere third-rate theatre or film. Second, there is a distinctive authenticity to televisual experience in its own right, both in the programmes themselves and in the viewers' response to them. Third, televisual experience is 'rhetorically aesthetic', in that television programmes develop a distinctive rhetoric of everyday life that have their own particular aesthetic value, and this is what underpins much of the para-social relationship that viewers are invited to develop with the main characters. Para-social interaction should not be seen as a false substitute for 'real' interaction, but as co-extensive with it, sharing many of its features, and in fact expanding and developing in ever-changing ways every individual's social world.

Leets et al. (1995) have highlighted three ways in which para-social interaction operates alongside real relationships. First, like face-to-face relationships, personal engagement is closely linked to uncertainty reduction. The fact that viewers gradually 'get to know' the characters in a television programme in itself will establish a relationship; 'as viewers reduce their uncertainty of media personalities', write Leets et al., 'they will perceive deeper intimacy with, and liking for, mediated characters' (p. 104). Second – and this is similar to Horton and Wohl's point – viewers used para-social interaction as a testing ground for the mobilization of their criteria for evaluating any interpersonal relationship, it is a significant resource for making sense of their social world. Third, para-social relationships offer relatively high possible rewards in the sense of enjoyment and pleasure, and a basis for communication and interaction within one's real-life relationships, but at very low cost, where costs refer to the possibility of embarrassment, anxiety, the requirement of physical or mental effort. They are a relatively cheap and easy way, in other words, of acquiring cultural knowledge and capital that can then be converted into other forms of capital within one's real-world relationships.

It is important here to stress the group nature of much para-social interaction, and the ways in which it functions as social cement and a basis for community formation. The value of the para-social interaction is most fully developed in its linkage with real-life relationships, in talk about what happened in whichever programmes are currently capturing broad attention (it was tempting to mention particular programmes here, but there is such rapid turnover that they would be dated very quickly) with one's family, work colleagues, friends and so on, testing out the understanding of the television 'grammar of conduct' in interaction with one's real social network. The continuation of the relationship with the imaginary character(s) takes place precisely in interaction with the real human beings around us, they mediate those relationships – lubricate, facilitate, give shape and form to, trigger, provide cues and so on. This has a lot to do with why the boundary between the real and the imaginary is so porous, why flowers and letters are sent when characters in a television soap series experience some trauma or misfortune – not in their real life as actors, but in their imaginary life as characters (Giles 2000: 64).

The para-social relationship with the celebrity is in turn 'experienced as of the same order as, and related to, the network of actual social relations', and this long-distance intimacy with any celebrity persona is of increased relevance 'when the persona becomes a common object to the members of the primary groups in which the spectator carries on his everyday life' (Horton & Wohl 1956: 226). This is another sense in which celebrity society operates as 'court society in an age of mass communication': instead of reading etiquette manuals, people today attend to the behaviour of a variety of celebrities providing negative as well as positive models to pick and choose from. They also provide an important conduit and framework for our relationships with each other.

Sheryl Garratt emphasizes these aspects of her time as fan of the 1970s Scottish pop band the Bay City Rollers, observing that 'comradeship' was a key concern, and that Roller fans were not that interested in the music, they simply wanted to be part of the action that happened to be current. Group identification was central – they were 'a gang of girls having fun together, able to identify each other by tartan scarves and badges' (1984: 144). As Garratt explains:

> Looking back now, I hardly remember the gigs themselves, the songs, or even what the Rollers looked like. What I *do* remember are the bus rides, running home from school together to get to someone's house in time to watch Shang-a-Lang on TV, dancing in lines at the school disco, and sitting in each others' bedrooms discussing our fantasies and compiling our scrapbooks. Our real obsession was with ourselves: in the end, the actual men behind the posters had very little to do with it at all.

> (p. 144)

Sigmund Freud explained the psychodynamics of this kind of fan–celebrity relationship with his observation on what he called the 'formula for the libidinal constitution of the mass', referring to a grouping of people without any leader, and not sufficiently structured and organized to start behaving 'as if' it was a unified individual – exactly the structure of any celebrity's audience. He wrote that in the process of making the same individual the object of their attention and affection,

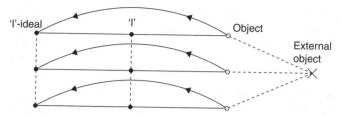

Figure 4.1 'I'-ideal diagram by Sigmund Freud.

Source: 'Mass psychology and the analysis of the "I"', in *Mass Psychology and Other Writings*. Harmondsworth: Penguin (2004 [1921]). By permission of The Marsh Agency Ltd on behalf of Sigmund Freud Copyrights.

placing them in the position of their 'I-ideal', the members of such a human group have '*consequently identified with one another in terms of their "I"*' (Freud 2004: 69). In paying attention to celebrities, it can be useful to think, then, of the relationship with the celebrity as often – not always – constituting a *secondary* aim, the primary one being one's relationship with one's surrounding social network – friends, colleagues, occasionally family members.

In order to understand the various ways in which celebrity conduct is attended to and communicated about, the actual operation of the linkage between long-distance intimacy and everyday individual experience, and the ways in which the attention paid to celebrity underpins people's social and emotional relations with each other and their self-formation, we need to take a closer look at one of its more important central characteristics – its nature as gossip.

Celebrity gossip

A number of observers of gossip have outlined the role that it plays more generally in 'lubricating' and sustaining social relationships, conveying and teasing out values, norms and viewpoints, and acting as a sounding-board for strategies of survival and advancement (Stirling 1956; Spacks 1985; Jones 1980; Eggins & Slade 1997: 273–311; Bird 1992; Hermes 1995; Doyle 2000; Goodman & Ben-Ze'ev 1994; Baumeister et al. 2004; Wert & Salovey 2004; Merry 1984; Paine 1967; de Backer et al. 2007). Rebecca Stirling (1956) was one of the earlier commentators, and her analysis drew out many of the themes that have continued through the accounts of the functions of gossip since, and which play an equally important role in celebrity gossip. Gossip operated to communicate useful information, but also simply to pass the time. Ronald Frankenberg, for example, is reported as recounting how, when he began his study of a Welsh village, he went to buy a loaf of bread and was back in five minutes. His landlady was dismissive: 'Back already? It takes me an hour to buy a loaf of bread' (Gluckman 1963: 315). As a socially binding activity, wrote Stirling, it 'tends to solidify group-member identification', contributing to group cohesion by providing 'a common target and a common cause [and] as a generalized catharsis of hostile aggressions' (1956: 262).

Gossip is a vehicle for demonstrating one's moral credentials: 'An impassioned tirade against so-and-so for doing such-and-such shows what a very upright upholder of standards the speaker is' (p. 266). It enable the redirection of aggression: 'Often the individual is not aware of the cause of his vague dissatisfaction. . . . Gossip allows a striking out, even though the target may not be the immediate cause of the frustration or irritability' (p. 264). Such aggression can at times constitute a projection of one's own misdemeanours – a useful way to obscure one's own marital infidelity is to take up the high moral ground in relation to someone else's, as an apparently endless parade of American fundamentalist preachers shows. There is often an element of 'protesting too much', in the sense that people pour scorn on those individuals doing exactly what they would like, but feel too constrained, to do themselves. Gossip, perhaps above all, is driven by the social value of being the first 'in the know', being 'an attempt to enhance one's self-image and also one's social self in the eyes of others', providing 'a sense of spurious importance' (p. 266).

Max Gluckman (1963) reiterated these themes and expanded on them by saying that gossip has three collective functions: (a) to create group morale, establishing and vindicating group norms and values; (b) to exert social control over newcomers and dissidents; and (c) to regulate conflicts with rival groups. He noted the importance for group membership of being able to gossip not just about the group's current membership, but also their ancestors, and the inability to do so weaken one's position. The absence of ancestors reduced the amount of gossip one is exposed to, but still, every time someone mentions a scandal involving someone's ancestor, 'he is gently rubbing in the fact that you have no ancestors and do not belong properly to the group' (p. 309). Not only does gossip strengthen group identity, to a large extent it constitutes that identity. As Gluckman puts it, 'the right to gossip about certain people is a privilege which is only extended to a person when he or she is accepted as a member of a group or set. It is a hallmark of membership'. Gossip rights, says Gluckman, 'serve to mark off a particular group from other groups' (p. 313). He did not explore it in any detail, but he also had a vague sense of the distinctive role that celebrity gossip could play, observing that 'the discussion of, for example, stars of film and sport, produces a basis on which people transitorily associated can find something personal to talk about' (p. 315).

The dynamics of the socially integrative effect of celebrity gossip is clearly visible in Joshua Gamson's (1994) discussion of the playful pleasure that celebrity watchers get from gossip about celebrities. Gamson observes that celebrity gossip has the enormous advantage of having no consequences for anyone with whom one has any 'strong ties'. He quotes one participant in his study describing the freedom of celebrity gossip:

> The whole field of gossip and that kind of stuff is relaxing. If you were to say to her right now, and you heard me, "That guy is funny looking," God, I can

be in big trouble. But I can say Debbie Reynolds is a lesbian, which I understand she is, and no one's going to yell at me for it. This is the whole thing of gossip as far as I'm concerned, because it's totally irresponsible. . . . I can enjoy myself with no culpability whatsoever. You can't do that in everyday life. I mean, you can, but there could be repercussions. And even if I knew something terrible about somebody I mightn't say it because I wouldn't want to circulate it, or I wouldn't want it ascribed to me, or maybe I'm not right about it. But I can say it about Debbie Reynolds because who gives a damn? Now, I'd rather not see Oprah marry this guy. I don't like him. That's her business, but I have an opinion, and I'm free to have an opinion, what the hell. It's total freedom. Which you don't have in a lot of other things you do in this world. That to me is what gossip is.

(1994: 176–7)

Like P.T. Barnum's revelation of the mechanics of his stunts, knowledge about the artificiality of celebrity identities and stories is actually not relevant; indeed, it is part of the game being played, and the field of celebrity is essentially playful, entirely agnostic about authenticity (Gamson 1994: 178). Celebrity-watching thus operates as playful, in many senses 'deconstructive', engagement with the variety of ways in which public selves are produced, with the nature of that production process, and the complex relationship between prudence and sincerity, artifice and authenticity, actor and role, front stage and back stage. Celebrity watching 'makes these central experiences visible and comprehensible, takes them out to look at, play with, consider, practice, and master' (Gamson 1994: 185).

In Rebecca Feasey's (2008) study of readers of *heat*, she found that young women made dual use of celebrity gossip: to gain respect and recognition among their friends, colleagues, family, but in the context of connecting with them in an egalitarian way. Bourdieu (1984) spoke of the status attached to knowledge of food, art, music etc., but it is also true that knowledge about the most recent scandals surrounding current celebrities confer recognition and respect. Feasey observes then, that 'the real reason why the readers were so desperate to be "the first in the know" was because they wanted to find a way to instigate female dialogue and encourage women's talk' (2008: 691). Feasey quotes one of her respondents, 'what I really like is that after you've read it, it gives you something to talk about. So it's a way of socialising, having a topic of conversation' (p. 691). It was important to be first 'in-the-know', as Stirling suggested. One of Feasey's participants described the aim of getting hold of the magazine as soon as possible as being able to say that

I've got gossip that you're not going to know because you've not bought *heat* yet. And I'm going to read it and then when I come downstairs and we're watching EastEnders tonight, I can tell you that so and so has actually had a big fight with so and so and now they're going out with them, but you don't know that because you didn't read the magazine first.

The rule in the house was that if someone had brought the magazine home, they had rights to 'first reading', even if they left it on the table while they went to the toilet or made a cup of tea (p. 691).

Celebrity gossip is also a safe and effective way of breaking the conversational ice, whether it be with old friends, casual acquaintances or strangers (p. 692), and more generally a central aspect of the public sphere – pubs, workplaces, cafes – alongside private social interaction (Johansson 2006: 349; de Backer at al. 2007: 347). In her study of how people read tabloid newspapers, Sofia Johansson similarly observes that the coverage of celebrities operates as 'gossip-fodder' which in turn nourishes informal conversation. She emphasizes how social tabloid reading is, 'exemplified in how some of the participants would read the paper together, for instance "for a banter at work", and celebrity stories were described as especially good 'talking points' (2006: 348). She quotes Nicole, a 21-year-old unemployed *Sun* reader:

> Like, my boyfriend works and I'll . . . If I've read the newspaper today . . . If he phones me, I go, 'have you read the newspaper today?' We generally read the same thing or we watch the same news, if we haven't seen each other. And, he'll say 'yeah, I heard about so-and-so,' And we might discuss it for a couple of minutes. But it's something . . . I don't know. It's like something to talk about. It generates conversation between people.
>
> (p. 348)

Johansson found, too, that celebrity stories operated as an arena for testing and working though various social norms: how should infidelity be dealt with, or domestic violence, when is the right time to marry, how does one deal with serious illness, in oneself and close friends or relatives, and so on, operating as a key social space where community and social identity is created and re-created on a everyday basis. Celebrity gossip can help smooth cultural differences because discussions of celebrity and morality 'can serve a normative function, in that a sense of togetherness is established through common evaluation of easily identifiable subjects' (p. 349). For Jeffrey Alexander (2010a) and Elizabeth Breese (2010a), it is useful to draw on Durkheim's account of the role of totems in moral community-formation, to see celebrities as 'icons', so that 'celebrity icons . . . represent the boundaries, ideals, solidarities and morality of the collective' (Breese 2010a: 344). Breese gives the particular example of the public scrutiny of the Jamie Lynn Spears, which operated as an arena for working through divergent moral evaluations of that particular issue – underage pregnancy, how it should be responded to, how it can be prevented, and how the conduct of the people surrounding Spears should be assessed – but it is generally true that celebrities constitute reference points and testing-grounds for the continuous negotiation and development of cognitive and moral orientations.

The pedagogic role of celebrity gossip is central, acting, as de Backer et al. suggest, as 'a fast and cost-effective way to fill in our knowledge gaps about strategies important to succeed in daily life' (2007: 338). Engaging in an ongoing testing-out dialogue about highly successful individuals is 'a cheap way to get information about successful and unsuccessful behavior strategies' (p. 339). It provides useful information about success and failure relatively cheaply, substituting in a low-cost way for experience, which is why de Backer and her colleagues also argue that interest in celebrity gossip is strongest among younger people and likely to decline with age, a hypothesis which was supported by both the questionnaire study of 1000 Belgian respondents' responses to a variety of stories about celebrities and their focus group discussions. The conclusion was that adolescents spent most time talking about 'the behaviors of celebrities from which they can learn something. Celebrities are "teachers" from whom they learn how to dress, how to impress, from whom they learn what is right and what is wrong to do in a society' (p. 346).

These accounts of celebrity gossip also connect with George Herbert Mead's arguments concerning the role of what he called 'the generalized other' in the constitution of the self. Mead argued that a crucial means by which social influence was exercised on individuals was through our understanding of what the broadly accepted norms of conduct are likely to be, captured by the concept of the 'generalized other'. He wrote that 'It is in the form of the generalized other that the social process influences the behaviour of the individuals involved in it . . . that the community exercises control over the conduct of its individual members' (1934: 155). Celebrities rarely represent or stand for the generalized other – people's relationships with them are too contradictory, variable and heterogeneous – but the very fact that they lie at the intersection point of the cognitive maps of large numbers of people means that they are a useful guide, either positively or negatively. In the latter case, constituting a counter-self instead of an ideal self, they provide a dynamic opportunity to rehearse one's sense of the generalized other, fine-tuning it by setting it alongside the broader public evaluation of celebrity conduct.

There is a thread of a particular kind of *democratic ethos* running through the accounts of reading and talking about celebrity gossip. People focus on the ordinariness of some celebrities, the ordinariness of their everyday lives, as well as engaging in celebrity-bashing (Johannson 2006: 352–5), and gaining enjoyment from celebrity misfortunes or mishaps (p. 354). As Joseph Epstein observes, all the celebrity magazines could 'just as easily travel under the generic title of *The National Schadenfreude*', so many of their stories 'come under the category of "See how the mighty have fallen" ' (2005: 12). Reflecting Stirling's (1956) observations, indulgence in celebrity-bashing is experienced, then, as a way of coping with one's less fortunate situation, a means of empowerment, or as Johannson puts it, 'reversing' a general sense of disempowerment (2006: 354; see also Connell 1992). This is also consistent with studies of the role of gossip in the lives of secretaries (Kanter 1977; van Iterson et al. 2010: 383).

The critical dimensions of celebrity gossip seems to have become accentuated over recent decades, and for Julie A. Wilson (2010) there is clearly a shift of emphasis taking place, away from adoration and identification, towards moral critique and evaluation – from star-gazing to star-testing, as she puts it. The discursive construction of celebrity gossips has become increasingly orientated towards questions and issues of choices concerning a range of personal concerns – marriage, parenthood, self-image, work–family balance, friendship, body-image – that operate as an arena for readers' permanent self-evaluation against a constantly shifting range of evaluative criteria, constantly being trialled and tested in conversations with both one's real-life conversation partners and the imagined community of magazine readers. The variety of do's and don't offered by celebrity magazines are not rigid prescriptions – indeed, central to current forms of celebrity gossips is the emphasis on how one's life is entirely one's own choice and responsibility – but they do operate to set the cognitive framework for how one thinks about personal responsibility. Wilson's analysis sometimes presents the concern with personal responsibility as an instrument of neoliberal rationalities of government (p. 32), at other times providing sociocultural resources for navigation through the neoliberal orientation towards personal autonomy and responsibility (du Gay 1996a; Rose 1999), and elsewhere as more simply as providing women with 'ongoing standardized testing centers for negotiating their other social roles as homemakers, mothers, wives, girlfriends, and daughters' (Wilson 2010: 36). Whichever of these emphases one chooses, the observation they share is that if celebrity gossip is a vehicle for the formation of moral community, then shifts in the nature, structure, and dynamics of that community are likely to be related to shifts in the way in which celebrities' private lives are publically scrutinized.

Fandom and self-formation

In addition to gossip, central to the structure of the relationship between celebrities and their audience is the construction of oneself as a 'fan', whereby the relationship with a smaller range of celebrities, often only one, becomes a key aspect of identity and self-formation. In many respects, being a fan can be a kind of celebrity-at-one-remove; as Braudy observes, one can set about 'gathering reflected glory by carefully monitoring the rise and fall of those more avid for the absolute prizes, but allaying the ambition to be personally great by assuming a pose of involved detachment from their triumphs and tragedies' (Braudy 1986: 589–90). The extent of incorporation of one's 'enthusiasm' for a musical band, actor or actress, sportsman or woman, composer, writer and so on, can be regarded as an indicator of whether one should be seen as a 'fan' or a 'connoisseur', although often the distinction is tied to that between low and high culture. Rebecca Pearson (2007), for example, explores how one would distinguish between 'Bachies' and 'Trekkies'. The weight and significance of the role played by celebrity in the constitution of identity over one's lifetime (Harrington & Bielby 2010) increases with the degree of self-perception as a fan and the extent to which the relationship with the celebrity can be understood as a social relationship operating alongside real-life relationships.

Imitation of stage personalities is not especially new – Cheryl Wanko points out how in eighteenth-century London, leading actors and actresses would have distinctive aspects of their appearance imitated by fans – well before Jennifer Aniston, women's hair was 'Catlified', copying singer and dancer Anne Catley's (1745–89) hairstyle, and Frances Abington's (1737–1815) headdress became known as the 'Abington cap' (Wanko 2009: 217). Highly visible figures such as actors and actresses operated as guides to fashion, and aristocratic patrons sought out the company of stage celebrities because, as Wanko points out, such company constituted public confirmation of their taste and style (Wanko 2009: 219–20). In the age of motion pictures, Jackie Stacey's (1994) study of women's experience as viewers of Hollywood films in Britain in the 1940s and 1950s indicates a similar, albeit more emotionally laden relationship between celebrities and their fans, and celebrities' central pedagogical role in the acquisition of cultural competence, character, style and overall image. Films were relatively infrequent, and had no competition from DVDs, television films, or the Internet, so women's emotional experience of film stars was particularly intense, and Stacey's respondents can vividly remember the core elements of how Doris Day or Lauran Bacall dressed, their shoes, accessories and haircuts, how they carried themselves and behaved, all of which was incorporated into their own identity and self-presentation to a greater or lesser extent. 'I think we all liked to identify with our favourite entertainers', observes one respondent. 'Why else did we copy their styles and clothes. During the forties there were thousands of Veronica Lakes walking about' (p. 203).

It was not just a matter of appearance, but character as well, with actresses providing exemplary models of self-confidence, sophistication, and independence – Bette Davis, Joan Crawford and Katherine Hepburn are just some examples (p. 154). The importation of Hollywood styles of femininity to Britain was especially important in bringing about transformations in acceptable forms of feminine appearance and behaviour. As Stacey puts it, 'the reproduction of self-image through consumption was perceived as a way of producing new forms of "American" feminine identity which were exciting, sexual, pleasurable and in some ways transgressive' (p. 204). The range and variety of models for female – and male – self-representation may have multiplied in the meantime, and there may be more irony and nuance in how one relates to fashions in appearance and behaviour, but the logic of people's relationship to celebrity image-modelling remains more or less the same.

At the point where attention concentrates more fully on one particular celebrity, the concept 'fan' becomes more salient than simply 'consumer' or 'viewer'. There has been a good deal of research undertaken on the pathological elements of fans' relationships with celebrities (Jenson 1992), the extent of mental health problems characterizing fan behaviour, especially when real-life encounters are sought, and when they can become characterized as stalking (Nicol 2006). Certainly many fans devote an enormous proportion of their time, emotional energy and finances to accumulating their celebrity's artefacts, going to their concerts, meeting with other fans, maintaining fan clubs, organizations, activities, websites and blogs, and more recently following them on Twitter. Many fans themselves think that all other fans are too obsessive, too hardcore (Jinda 1994: 47–8). But fandom is also a more routine part of emotional and social life, a building block for the formation of identity, the establishment of social relations, and the navigation of rocky emotional and psychological stages in one's life. As a part of adolescent identity-formation, some studies refer to 'secondary attachment', in the sense that fans are emotionally engaged with an idealized internal representation of the celebrity, rather than the real person themselves (Adams-Price & Greene 1990; Caughey 1988).

Sue Wise (1984), for example, having moved from being an Elvis fan to rejecting his machismo image with her discovery of feminism, found it hard to explain her emotional reaction to his death in 1977. Although she had come to think of him as a 'relic of past "false consciousness" ', she says that 'his death was terribly significant to me and it made me very sad'. In attempting to understand this emotional response, Wise found that 'the overwhelming feelings and memories were of warmth and affection for a very dear friend' (pp. 16–17). Above all, Elvis was 'another human being to whom I could relate and be identified with'.

> When I felt lonely and totally alone in the world, there was always Elvis. He was a private, special friend who was always there, no matter what, and I didn't have to share him with anybody. He was someone to care about, to be interested in and to defend against criticism. In my own private Elvis world I could forget that I was miserable and lonely by listening to his records and going to see his films. Some people who feel so alone in an alien world turn to religion or to drink or to football teams to give their lives purpose. I turned to Elvis; and he was always there and he never let me down.
>
> (p. 17; see also Fogo's (1994) discussion of the response to John Lennon's death)

In this sense, the relationship with a celebrity is primarily a private and individual one, which in Wise's case did not extend to real-life interaction with like-minded fans, but which can often constitute an important basis for real-life social interaction and the construction of shared meaning and emotional response, so that fans will often describe their network of fans as their family, friends and community. Michael Jinda, for example, refers to the network of Star Trek fans as forming 'a type of "symbolic community"', where people seek to form identities distinct from the outside world', and that 'it is frequently reported among fans that a group of strangers found common ground in their love of ST' (1994: 38). Roberta Pearson makes similar observations about Sherlock Holmes fans, or Sherlockians:

> Members of scion societies meet on a regular basis to eat, drink, take quizzes, listen to talks, engage in theatrical presentations, sing, play games, and, most importantly, escape into a world where all the inhabitants share a similar passion. Individual Sherlockians produce sherlockian 'art' – ranging from paintings to hand-painted sweat-shirts – for their own pleasure or for sale. Sherlockians write what others would call fan fiction, pastiches of the original stories and novels, and what they themselves call Sherlockian

scholarship, nonfiction that employs the techniques of textual hermeneutics and historical contextualization to clarify the contradictions and lacunae that stemmed from Conan Doyle's writing in the serial format.

(2007: 105)

Not that Sherlockians themselves would use the word 'fan' to describe themselves, they prefer 'admirer', 'enthusiast', 'devotee' or 'aficionado'. Pearson reports one Sherlockian as saying 'I would prefer to separate myself from teenagers and testosterone-charged boys of all ages' (p. 105).

There are numerous studies of different types of fans, including eighteenth-century English actresses (Wanko 2009), Elvis (Wise 1984; Hinerman 1992; Fraser & Brown 2002), the Beatles (Ehrenreich et al. 1992), Star Trek (Pearson 2007; Jenkins 1992; Jindra 1994), Sherlock Holmes (Pearson 1997, 2007), Shakespeare (Pearson 2002), Chekhov (Tulloch 2007), David Bowie (Stevenson 2009), Avril Lavigne (Vannini 2004), among many others, and of celebrity–fan encounters (Ferris 2001). Just picking one example, Susie Boyt's (2008) discussion of her almost lifelong attachment to Judy Garland is an interesting case-study in how self-formation is constituted by identification with others – in the case of celebrities, physically absent but no less real. Celebrity personalities can be an important vehicle for the constitution of the self and the management of one's life history. The concept of a 'role model' is probably too broad and vague, it is more useful to see the relationship as pedagogical – 'I always say I learned my manners from the musicals of MGM' (p. 196) – encompassing inspiration, philosophy, examples of how to overcome overcoming obstacles, emotional sustenance, suggestions for how to dress and how to behave in various situations.

As Boyt writes, 'Judy teaches us to be unpretentious and to laugh at ourselves, to be like the lady in "The Lady is a Tramp" who has no truck with airs and graces'. Judy showed young women how to combine 'glamour' with ordinariness – 'Judy . . . is both the epitome of a very theatrical brand of glamour and an approachable, natural, hard-working champ' (p. 189) – as well as talent and modesty. Judy suggested the possibility of by-passing the requirements of 'selling' oneself, where one's self-worth is intrinsic and capable of generating recognition on the basis of its own virtuousness, the triumph of profound authenticity over shallow instrumentalism. For Boyt she provided an inspirational 'soundtrack to life', both her voice and her lyrics constituting an emotional guide to overcoming hardship and obstacles.

Boyt gives an illustration of how para-social interaction with celebrities links up with, supports, sustains and gives shape to real-life interaction: another fan, Marc Chabonnet, wrote to Boyt about his relationship to Judy, recollecting how he had bought an album of hers, *Forever Garland*, as a gift, and showed it to his father, who had more of a habit of making snide remarks about his choices and preferences. But not this time: he'd grown fond of 'Over the Rainbow' during the Second World War, and told of a friend who was 'crazy about Judy Garland', and hoped one day to meet her. 'My father told me more', wrote Chabonnet, 'and I listened. It was an unusual connection between my father and me' (pp. 216–17). He goes on to recall watching *The Judy Garland Show* on Sunday nights:

I remember, on the show, her crying at the end of her runway with the light bulbs and the wobbling vibrato and all of the emotion – it was like a kind of supreme voltage reaching out of the television set and grabbing me by the eyes and ears. While I would sit there, pretending not to be transfixed, my father would begin talking about Judy again. He told me how it was so sad that such talent had withered, and we discussed it. These were the first conversations that I had with my father about something outside our lives . . . Judy talk ended up being the familial glue between my father and me, in place of the sports talk that is for other dads and sons.

(p. 217)

In this kind of example (for others, see Harrington & Bielby 2010; Harrington et al. 2011) the emotional incorporation of the performer into the process of self-formation is organized around a single individual, and this is what makes it recognizable as 'fandom', but the same mechanisms are at play, in a lower-key way, in any film, TV programme, novel or play which succeeds in touching the souls of its viewers. Celebrity performers are simply those who manage to assemble more of that kind of interaction with their audience more frequently and to a greater extent.

Celebrity-watching as 'equipment for living'

The social role of celebrity-watching is very similar to that of reading literature, as 'equipment for living' (Burke 1938), providing conceptual and symbolic 'raw material' for the assembly of the self in a world where its contents and contours are not pre-determined by family, community or religious prescriptions. It can be the lives of celebrities themselves that are reflected on in this way or, if they are actors, the characters they play, sometimes to the point where the imagined character is more powerful than the actor themselves – George Castanza, the character in *Seinfeld*, for example, in many respects has greater resonance for his audience than Jason Alexander the actor, and it is often an issue for actors to break free from especially strong roles. An extreme of identification with a celebrity is the case of Mark David Chapman, who had gone further than the millions of people who mourned John Lennon's death to believe he was the real John Lennon, and that Lennon was an impostor denying him the recognition he deserved (Schickel 1985: 21). As the intensifying competition accompanying democratization makes appearance and performance become increasingly important, celebrities likewise gain in significance for the *bricolage* that is the modern self, as guides, reference points, models and 'raw material' (Milner 2005: 73).

Chris Rojek (2001) goes on to argue that the social and psychological space vacated by organized religion is in many respects occupied by celebrity, which produces 'one of the replacement strategies that promote new orders of meaning and solidarity' (p. 99), the long-distance intimacy with celebrities taking the place of that with God and the saints, displaying many of the same dynamics – reverence for relics and icons, visits to celebrity homes, locales and graves, even a belief in reincarnation, in the case of Elvis Presley. He also argues that celebrities should be understood as offering parables for how to live one's life in modern society, taking the place of organized religion and family life, with sports stars only one of the central examples (2006: 687).

As Neal Gabler emphasizes, a defining element of celebrity is narrative, having an engaging story to tell, made more interesting than purely fictional characters because of the problematic nature of the complex relationship between the public and the private self. In playing with the tension between performance and authenticity, observes Gabler, celebrity 'taps some of the deepest contradictions about who we are and who we would like to be. It simultaneously comforts us and disturbs us, celebrating the virtue of ordinariness while holding out something to which we can aspire' (2001: 15). The typical celebrity narrative invokes 'the story of the people who have been sprung from the pack in a kind of new Calvinism':

> We suspect that however much they may protest against the idea of their exceptionality, those who live celebrity are the sanctified, the best, the most deserving. And having conspired in the creation of this new art form as fans, we get the dispensation to watch them, to share them, to consume them, to enjoy them, to bask in their magnificence and to imagine that we might have a narrative of our own some day, allowing us to join them.

(p. 15)

For Gabler, then, a particular kind of Protestant ethic is at play, in which a theology is generated around one's predestination for an immortality derived from what fame was always concerned with – public visibility, recognition and permanent placement in social memory – but modified to include being experienced in one's own lifetime.

5 Celebrity in politics, diplomacy and development

> The quality . . . which most of all impresses the crowd is the prestige of celebrity . . . It is a point of honour with the masses to put the conduct of their affairs in the hands of a celebrity. The crowd always submits willingly to the control of distinguished individuals. The man who appears before them crowned with laurels is considered a priori to be a demi-god.
>
> (Michels 1911: 78–9)

> I ask myself if musicians should conduct themselves like politicians. They are only musicians. Where do they get the right to talk like that?
>
> (Eric Clapton, on Geldof's and Bono's interventions prior to the 2005 Gleneagles G8 summit)

In the 2008 US presidential campaign, Barack Obama visited Europe to the adulation of large crowds, especially in Berlin, in July. On his return to the United States on 29 July, the McCain campaign team ran a 30-second advertisement juxtaposing the coverage of his Berlin visit, accompanied by chants of 'Obama, Obama', with images of Paris Hilton and Britney Spears, and a female voice-over saying: 'He's the biggest celebrity in the world . . . but is he ready to lead?' The Republican strategist Steven Schmidt mobilized Boorstin's celebrity/hero distinction, saying 'Do the American people want to elect the world's biggest celebrity or do they want to elect an American hero?' (cited in Alexander 2010b: 414). As one Australian journalist put it, the 2008 election appeared to constitute 'the triumph of celebrity as the essential organizing principle of US politics', turning American politics into *American Idol*, with Bill Clinton as 'the critical transitional figure who morphed from a traditional politician into a pure soap opera celebrity'.[1]

At first the comparison seemed misplaced and a bit silly, but then it appeared to gain some traction in public discussions, and the Democratic campaign became worried, as the Republicans had hoped, that framing Obama as a celebrity would dominate the public perception of his speech accepting his nomination as the Democratic party's candidate for the presidency. In fact it did nothing of the sort, and it is hard to know how much damage it actually did to McCain, with

Paris Hilton producing some witty counter videos. Although it is true, as Jeffrey Alexander observes, that Americans are suspicious of celebrity (2010b: 415), they can also tell the difference between different foundations of celebrity. For Obama they include his skills as an orator and his capacity to connect emotionally with a sizable proportion of the American public. It was, after all, a bit rich for Ronald Reagan's and Arnold Schwarzenegger's party, not to mention Sarah Palin's, to be complaining about the role of celebrity in politics. The McCain campaign in fact drew on similar strategies, organizing itself around the presentation of McCain as a war hero rather than an experienced legislator, and the vice-presidential candidate Sarah Palin as a 'hockey-mom' and moose-hunter, rather than someone who could tell the difference between living in vague geographical proximity to a foreign country and actually having any diplomatic dealings with it.

For Jeffrey Alexander to suggest that Obama's acceptance speech projected 'sincere feelings and deeply patriotic principles, not artifice and celebrity' (2010b: 416), then, is to rely on a false distinction. Obama's celebrity, like that of John F. Kennedy and Ronald Reagan, rests precisely on his capacity to evoke sincerity and patriotism in a manner which large sections of the American, and indeed the world's, public can identify. That is why the Berlin crowds were chanting 'Obama, Obama' and seeking proximity to the man himself, and neither Paris Hilton nor Britney Spears would have been able to draw such a crowd or evoke such a response. Robert Michels (1911) noted around the turn of the twentieth century that a central feature of the mass psychology of all popular democracy is the tendency to frame political authority in terms of distinction and recognition achieved in a wide variety of fields by no means confined to politics itself. The 'suggestive influence' of a political leader, wrote Michels, is strongly influenced by 'the elevation to which he has climbed on the path leading to the Parnassus of celebrity' (1911: 78).

In addition to the question of how we should understand politicians as celebrities, there are also an increasing number of celebrities in non-political fields, especially music and film, who are taking on a role in the realms of politics and diplomacy, as well as social and political activism. The names that spring immediately to mind are Bono, Bob Geldof and Angelina Jolie, but the phenomenon is broader than that. Rather than treating these celebrity diplomats and politicians as imposing themselves on a reluctant political sphere, it is useful to be able to identify the processes and mechanisms by which they are socially produced.

Political celebrity and its close ally examined in the next chapter, celebrity in business and management, both pre-dates the kind of celebrity we now associate with sports, film, television and modelling stars and continues to operate alongside it. Prior to the emergence of film stars, political leaders were prominent in the field of celebrity, establishing intimate relations with their subjects/audience, projecting their private lives into the public arena, establishing themselves as ordinary human beings despite their extraordinary capacities, talents and social position (for Queen Victoria, Plunkett 2003; for Kaiser Wilhelm II, Kohlrausch 2010). Martin Kohlrausch refers to the 'dialectic between privacy and publicity' evident in Wilhelm II's regular holiday trips to Norway, where he restricted access by the media to selected photographers and film makers, 'to make exclusive short films and snapshots for public consumption, bringing the Kaiser right back into the homes of his subjects. Wilhelm II and his court thus increasingly stressed the private side of power through intimate pictures from the *Nordlandreisen*, while also appearing to show that he needed relaxation and an escape, only more so than everyone else' (2010: 61–2). Kohlrausch describes Wilhelm II as 'the first German movie star', by the turn of the century 'the most filmed person in the world' (p. 55). When Wilhelm II resigned in November 1918, his departure from the political stage in many respects helped create the conditions for the emergence of a new German political celebrity, and it was the media coverage of Adolf Hitler's 1924 trial following his failed putsch in 1923 which turned him a celebrity for the right-wing nationalists (Fulda 2009: 70).

When Leo Lowenthal (1984b [1944]) undertook his study of biographies in magazine and book form in 1941, he found both a significant increase in the sheer volume of biographical literature, which had increased four-fold between 1901 and 1941, and a shift in attention from political and business figures to the lives of entertainers and sports stars. 'In 1901', wrote Lowenthal, 'we are introduced to J.P. Morgan, the banker; his partner, George W. Perkins; James Hill, the railroad president'. In 1922, out of a total of 20 biographies in *Colliers*, there are 'only two entertainers, but eight professional and business men and ten politicians'. The explosion of contemporary interest in what Lowenthal called the 'idols of consumption' in the fields of entertainment, the arts and sport had been preceded by a focus on the 'idols of production', individuals active in 'the productive life, from industry, business, and natural sciences' (p. 206), in the 'vocations which serve society's basic needs' (p. 208). In fact, Lowenthal overlooks the much longer history of a culture of consumption, and underestimates the amount of interest that ordinary people had long had in idols of the theatre and the arts, an interest that might not have been evident in published biographies, but which manifested itself in newspapers, pamphlets and everyday public discussion. It is also a little odd, as Littler (2007) observes, for a Marxist cultural critic such as Lowenthal to valorize businessmen and the political managers of capitalist society. But the point about the centrality of political and business leaders in public consciousness remains salient, and highlights the need to grasp the partic-ular role of political and commercial prominence in celebrity society. This chapter examines the first, celebrity in political and diplomatic arenas, and the next chapter deals with business and management celebrity.

Celebrity politics, political celebrity

Francesco Alberoni once described celebrities as 'an elite of politically irrespon-sible stars' positioned alongside 'a political class considered as responsible for the results of its decisions on the collectivity' (1972: 97). Today one would be more inclined to say that this boundary has become blurred, at least, with the emergence and growth of the concept of political responsibility among high-profile musicians and actors, and the movement that appears to be possible between the realms of entertainment and politics, with Ronald Reagan and Arnold Schwarzenegger the leading examples (Street 2004). Barack Obama has been portrayed as a manifestation of a new kind of political celebrity, because he

> projected an image of himself as an inspiring political authority who does not expect a 'blind' or rationally motivated form of obedience (as do mainstream political leaders). He spoke about authority as a reciprocal and communicative, two-way power relationship that combines goals, tactics and ethos in order to get people with different, and sometimes even incompatible, identities and projects freely to accept that cooperation across all conventional boundaries may be the only way to resolve the common challenges and problems of the United States and the world in general.
>
> (Bang 2009: 133)

Celebrity clearly plays an important role in politics, both in the sense of politicians establishing linkages with celebrities in the more highly visible sectors of entertainment, music and sport and in terms of politicians constructing their speech, appearance, presentation of self, public relations techniques and strategies in terms of developing a distinct 'brand' (Needham 2005) or aesthetic style (Corner & Pels 2003a), on more or less the same lines as celebrities in other sectors, becoming that relatively rare creature, a powerful celebrity.

But to regard this as a particularly new development or ethos in politics, or to argue that celebrity politics 'may thus provide an unorthodox, but potentially effective, way of breaking the hold of established elites on political agendas and public discourse about policy' (Marsh et al. 2010: 333) is to overlook the extent to which a turn to both the celebrification of politicians and the active presence of celebrities in politics has been a central feature of political life in one way or another since the sixteenth century, for more or less the same reasons throughout that period. John Corner (2003: 68) points out that a concern with the role of the presentation of self is clearly visible in Machiavelli, so that what has changed is the variety of forms taken by political performance, not the centrality of political persona itself. As Peter Burke observes, 'contemporary politicians may be presented like products, but it might equally well be argued that contemporary products are eulogised in the manner once reserved for princes' (1992: 199).

For Richard Sennett, the line of development begins in the nineteenth century, which was when he observed the rise and spread of 'personality' in politics, a central part of what he diagnosed as the 'fall of public man' (2002). But the presence of a celebrity factor in political life can be traced further back, as celebrities in the fields of theatre, literature and art have long been capable of making their own contributions to both the consolidation and the undermining of political power. As David Kastan argues for England, the theatrical representation of history and politics 'nourished the cultural conditions that eventually permitted the nation to bring its King to trial' (1984: 460–1), generating a requirement for the powerful both to control the representation of power and to project their power into the realm of symbolism and representation. Because actors could 'be' kings, apparently often more effectively than real kings, kings also had to become actors.

Kevin Sharpe sees the roots of political celebrity as running still deeper, suggesting that political leaders have constructed themselves as celebrities in the constitution of their political power through processes of representation since Henry VIII. He argues in relation to English history that a key feature of Tudor rule was its capacity to secure the compliance of a sharply divided population through 'careful acts of representation – in words, images and spectacular perform-ances – that did not simply reflect or enact power but helped construct it' (2009: 6–7). The break with Rome made this all the more necessary, demanding from Henry VIII a corresponding capacity to capture his subjects' interior realms of conscience and spirituality – Henry needed to develop a hold their over minds and hearts which could match that of the Catholic Church and its armies of saints and bishops, rooted in 'an eroticization of power and manipulation of desire' (p. 70).

Henry VIII achieved this in ways that we can recognize today as constructing an action-man celebrity identity, a combination of swashbuckling movie idol, military hero and sports star. He was 'the jock who wanted to be a international sporting celebrity' (p. 158), which revolved at that time around jousting. Until he was 36, observes Sharpe, he took part in every major English tournament. In a well-known episode in 1524, 'when a lance splintered against his open helmet to the horror of all observers, the king, in Hollywood hero style, remounted and took the victory in all the ensuing contests' (p. 158). Added to jousting was tennis, archery, hawking and hunting. Another observer describes Henry's reign as resembling 'one endless sequence of tourneys, disguising, entertainments and pageants' (p. 159). Henry VIII's reign was an archetypal example of the need for kings not just to be kings, but to perform kingship.

This aspect of the exercise of political power can be seen even more clearly in the reign of Elizabeth I, whose iconic status, suggests Sharpe, 'owed less to a sanctity proclaimed by official scripts and images and more to a celebrity status granted by subjects' (p. 78). Through constant engagement with the public, frequent pageants and progresses, Elizabeth was able, argues Kastan, 'to transform her country into a theatre, and, in the absence of a standing army, create an audience, troops of loyal admirers, to guarantee her rule' (Kastan 1984: 466). This is why Ian Ward argues in his comparison of Elizabeth I with Princess Diana, that 'the greatest "Diana" in modern English history was Elizabeth I; the original Fairy Queen, and Gloriana, and Belphoebe and Sweet Cynthia and Deborah, the judge and restorer of Israel, and Astraea the "beauteous Queen of Second Troy" ' (2001: 6).

The same mechanisms and dynamics of power and rule can be seen in the reigns of other political leaders, with Louis XIV one of the leading examples and reference points. Peter Burke speaks of the 'fabrication' of Louis XIV; '[f]or his contemporaries as for posterity', notes Burke, 'the sun-king was a star' (1992: 1999). In his examination of Louis XIV, the sting in Burke's argumentative tail is the clear continuity between the nature of Louis XIV's symbolic penetration of French social and political life and those of his successors – not just Napoleon, Hitler, Mussolini and Stalin, but also French and American presidents.

A good illustration of the democratization of the logic of political celebrity beyond that of princes and monarchs was Benjamin Franklin's life and career, a striking example of the politician-as-celebrity, hitching the production of a particular kind of very public self to the pursuit of a wide range of political and scientific endeavours, from the discovery of electricity to the founding of the United States of America. His life captures nicely the connection between celebrity and individualism, since, as Braudy notes, 'to sell oneself is better than being sold by others . . . [and] to consider one's public image as something to be fashioned and sold may heighten the feeling of personal will, even though psychic alienation and the commodity self may loom in the future' (1986: 370–1). Franklin's experiments with electricity had made him a public celebrity before he embarked on his diplomatic ventures in France as America's 'Minister Plenipotentiary' (1776–78), and there were already portraits, engravings and busts circulating in French society, and by the 1760s he was instantly recognizable in caricatures (Braudy 1986: 452). In a letter to Sally, his daughter, on 3 June 1779, he expresses his astonishment at the 'incredible' number of medallions with his image being sold, 'some to be set in lids of snuff boxes, and some so small as to be worn in rings'. Combined with the pictures, busts and prints, his face had become 'as well known as that of the moon' (Franklin 1817: 42).

He was without a doubt to be included among the portrayals of 'illustrious moderns' that Josiah Wedgewood used to sell his plates, vases, figurines, teapots, busts and medallions. As Braudy observes, to those who portrayed Franklin, wore medallions or rings with his profile, or had his image in their homes in one form or another, he was more than an American diplomat, he represented a striking new human possibility, that of the New World itself (1986: 452). 'Wearing them on one's person or displaying them in one's home', notes Hershey, 'made a discreet statement of political inclination or intellectual pretension' (2005: 242). In that sense, Franklin's celebrity was tightly bound up with the process of democratization itself, replacing the portrayal of the monarch with the republican 'vir'. When he died, the snuffboxes produced subsequently portrayed him together with Rousseau and Voltaire, 'like a new "Holy Trinity" of the new republic of France' (p. 243)

In the 1784 English election campaign of the Whig politician Charles Fox against the Tory William Pitt (the younger), Fox utilized the canvassing support of a number of aristocratic women, led by Lady Georgina Cavendish, Duchess of Devonshire, the sculptor Ann Seymour Damer, friend of Horace Walpole, and the political hostess Lady Frances Crewe (Lana 2002: 49). He did so partly to draw on the involvement of women in his public life to underline his standpoint on a number of political issues, but to a large extent in order to benefit from their celebrity as beautiful, charming and witty women capable of attracting large crowds to any political meeting. The effect of the Foxite strategy, observes Renata Lana, was to increase significantly interest in the political function of women in the public sphere and to set a new benchmark for political responsiveness to women's voices and interests (p. 67). Since then, what has changed has been the nature and the extent of the celebrity being mobilized for political purposes – Sarah Palin is only one of the more recent examples – and if politicians have hesitated to make use of the logic of celebrity, this has generally been to their cost.

With the rapid population growth and the corresponding expansion of mass-circulation print and visual media in the nineteenth century discussed in Chapter 2, the production of political celebrity also came to be industrialized, extending the range of possibilities for the projection of political personality into the public sphere. A useful example of the utilization of contemporary forms of mass media, especially newspapers and photography, to create political celebrity is the career of Giuseppe Garibaldi, the nineteenth-century Italian military adventurer who came to embody the concept of a unified Italian nation. Born in 1807, in 1833 he joined Giuseppe Mazzini's revolutionary organization *Giovine Italia* (Young Italy), but after a failed insurrection and a death sentence hanging over him, he fled to Brazil and then Uruguay. In Uruguay, he formed an Italian legion which fought on the side of the Uruguayan nationalists. He returned to Italy in 1853, and led a successful expedition to pacify Sicily in 1860, the last step towards the unification of Italy. In the process, he achieved celebrity status as the father of a unified Italy not just domestically but also for an international audience.

At first glance, Garibaldi looks like a straightforward example of a 'hero', a talented soldier and politician, who drew on those talents to bring about significant political change. In fact, his image was highly constructed, meticulously crafted to make best use of the current developments in mass media technology and communications in the interests of assembling the embodiment of an emerging Italian national identity. Lucy Riall emphasizes that his speeches, his clothing, his novels and poetry, his photographs and engravings, his conduct in public and private, Mazzini's careful placement of stories about his military exploits along with refutations of criticisms, all indicate a well-organized public relations campaign (2007a: 13). As Riall puts it:

> the heroic cult of Garibaldi was used to represent and spread the Italian nationalist myth at home and abroad. The fame of Garibaldi brought material support – men and money – for the wars of Italian unification and helped make them victorious. So the cult served to focus, integrate and mobilize public support for the political myth of the Italian nation and to legitimize Italian nationalism as a political movement. As a symbol of the Italian nation, the cult of Garibaldi was supposed to transform the way people imagined their rulers and thought about politics; his heroic leadership was part of a broader attempt to create new rituals and promote a political language, and to make persuasive the nationalist vision of the future and the past.
>
> (p. 14)

Realizing immediately the potential of the new technology of photography, Mazzini commissioned portraits that were made into lithographs and sold in large numbers throughout Europe, because 'it will be useful to increase his fame'. In the 1860s, Gairbaldi was as good at selling newspapers and books in London, Paris and New York as Princess Diana would become more than a century later. In

London, more than 8000 *carte-de-visite* portraits were sold in ten days (Linkman 1993: 67). The new mass media and their audiences needed stories, and Mazzini and Garibaldi obliged with the narrative of Italian unification, so that the Italian conflict 'was re-narratavised as popular melodrama, and the main protagonists were recast to resemble the heroes and villains of historical and adventure novels' (Riall 2007a: 135).

When he visited London in 1864 to help swing English public opinion behind the nationalist cause, he succeeded beyond his supporters' wildest expectations. He was mobbed on arrival in Southampton on 3 April, and his visitors included Alfred Tennyson, with Mrs Tennyson most impressed by his appearance and demeanour (p. 331). On his first outing a crowd of 500,000 came out to see him, blocking roads, lining roofs and parapets, and perching in windows for five hours. He was mobbed by ecstatic women when he went to the opera, was invited to numerous receptions and met everyone who was anyone in London. Wedgewood china and Staffordshire figures were produced to commemorate the visit, streets and pubs were named after him, and men and women wore red shirts (pp. 331–4), piano sheet music about him proliferated, numerous formulaic biographies charting his revolutionary heroism were published. He exerted a powerful erotic effect on most women and some men as well, with a number of English ladies, married and single, falling head over heels in love with him. Much of his allure, observes Riall, was a product of the feeling produced by the prior circulation of newspaper stories, pamphlets, books and printed images of him, 'so that people felt as though they knew him personally, and identified emotionally with his life story' (p. 341). In many respects he was the nineteenth-century Che Guevara, projecting the same romantic revolutionary image and with the same charismatic effect on those he encountered.

Another manifestation of Garibaldi's international celebrity status was the moving panorama of Garibaldi's life and exploits made and shown from 1860, constructed in 1859 by J.J. Storey and Henry Selsun (Smith 2005: 2). Panoramas were large circular pictorial representations, sometimes stationary, sometimes moved on rollers, which viewers looked at from within a cylindrical structure, often accompanied by music, usually of cities, places or events, first used in London in 1788, which 'served as both newsreel and travelogue' (p. 6). The Garibaldi panorama portrayed all the events of his life, his military exploits in South America, including his torture in Uruguay, and it was viewed by thousands in Great Britain and then later in the United States, suggesting that he was among the earliest 'motion picture' stars, given the technology of the day.[2]

For Robert Michels (1911), it was clear that celebrity of all sorts was relatively easy to convert into political leadership, in socialist and social-democratic politics at any rate. He gives the examples of philosopher and lawyer Ferdinand Lassalle (1825–64) in Germany, Enrico Ferri (1856–1929) and Cesare Lombroso, both criminologists, in Italy, the philosopher Jean Jaures (1859–1914) in France, artist and writer William Morris (1834–96) in England, poet Herman Gorter (1864–1927) and writer Henriette Roland-Holst (1869–1952) in the Netherlands. In mass democracy, observed Michels, it was a widespread view that 'to bear a name which is already familiar in certain respects constitutes the best title to leadership' (p. 101).

The variety of public-relations mechanisms related to the production of celebrity continued to be developed throughout the nineteenth century. The American Whigs William Harrison and John Tyler made successful use of the song 'Tippecanoe and Tyler too' in their 1840 presidential campaign, and P.T. Barnum publically threw his support behind Lincoln in 1860, joining in his rallies and the Wide-Awake marches (Mansch 2005: 165). Lincoln did not miss the chance for a photo opportunity with two of Barnum's personalities, General Tom Thumb and his new wife (Charles S. Stratton and Livinia Warren), at a White House reception in 1863 (Kimmel 1957: 113).[3] For Queen Victoria, as for all forms of celebrity, the industrialization of the mass media demanded a similar industrialization of the production of royal authority, generating the same dangers faced by all celebrities, that the representation is seen as overshadowing, if not replacing, the 'reality' for which it is meant to stand (Plunkett 2003). Victoria was criticized along more or less along the same lines as the McCain campaign's attack on Obama-as-celebrity: Victoria-as-celebrity was perceived by many in nineteenth-century Britain as 'an invented figure without any material substance' (p. 10). The formation of nation-states in the nineteenth century was dependent on the construction of narratives organized around charismatic individuals which obeyed the central rules of the celebrity story, discursive rules that were in turn chained to the logic of the rapidly expanding mass-circulation press.

The expansion of the mass media came later in Germany, but Martin Kohlrausch (2010) argues that when it came, it unfolded more rapidly and with especially striking impact of the celebritization of political authority in Kaiser Wilhelm II. He was the subject of blanket media coverage, and his distinctive image made him ideally suited to the emerging technologies of photography and film. Kohlrausch estimates that he was possibly the first politician ever to be captured on film, opening the Kiel Canal in 1895, and he was always easily recognizable in his helmet and uniform. The leading German coffee merchant Ludwig Roselius is described by Kohlrausch as an advertising pioneer, and as referring to Wilhelm II as 'an impressive example of brand development' (p. 55).

In the US around the turn of the century, the response to partisan political debates was to portray politicians 'as "real men" whose temperaments, experience, and training were far more important for understanding their actions and assessing their merits as representatives of the public' (Ponce de Leon 2002: 173). This tendency was reinforced by rising advertising revenue, which made it possible for newspapers to become more independent from political parties. Dissatisfaction with both Democrats and Republicans, each with their own forms of corruption, generating a sense that the political parties were themselves 'part of the problem', underpinned the ideal of being non-partisan. An effective expression of that ideal became the concept of the 'real human being' behind the political front, in turn encouraging the construction of politicians as celebrities.

If corruption is framed as built into the system, observes Ponce de Leon (2002: 176), this leaves only the character of individual politicians as a bulwark against its effects. The figure which appeared as the remedy to systemic political corruption was that of the 'practical idealist', 'a virtuous foil to the professional politician, the demagogue, and the fanatic' (p. 183).

> Practical idealists were honest and public-spirited. Fired by a powerful sense of duty, they were devoted to public service, a trait that many journalists likened to the patriotism of the Founding Fathers. They were also courageous, willing to fight aggressively for right, regardless of the effect on their careers or personal fortunes.
>
> (p. 183)

A central part of this narrative was that 'practical idealists' were, by definition, ostracized by 'the organization' or the 'party machine', and needed to draw on the support of outsiders not corrupted by the machine. In the first quarter of the twentieth century, then, one can see in American politics the pursuit of a delicate balance between pragmatism and idealism, achieved only by a certain kind of individual character, with particular life experience, values and beliefs that needed to be demonstrated as being firm enough to withstand the corrosive effects of organized political life.

Later, as soon as there were movie stars they were being harnessed to political aims – Douglas Fairbanks, Charlie Chaplin and Mary Pickford were mobilized to sell war bonds during the First World War (Braudy 1986: 556–7), as was singer Kate Smith during the Second World War (Merton 1971). As Braudy observes:

> To a new generation of politicians, who were able to view their constituencies *as audiences* and themselves as necessarily in the spotlight, the rapidly expanding media of communication in the twentieth century presented the opportunity to assert their authority (and thereby power) in unprecedented ways.
>
> (1986: 557)

One of the key early figures in the increasingly organized use of celebrities in politics was Albert Lasker (1880–1952), often identified as the founding father of advertising (Cruikshank & Schultz 2010).[4] Lasker had come to the attention of the Republican Party because of his success with the California Fruit Growers Exchange (later Sunkist) and Van Camp's canned pork and beans, laying the foundations of the American obsessions with orange juice and canned food, not to mention the Lucky Strike 'It's toasted' slogan in 1917.

Lasker worked for the Republicans in the 1918 congressional elections, helping to reduce the Democratic majority in the House of Representatives and displace their control of the Senate, as well as attacking Woodrow Wilson's plans regarding the League of Nations. He then worked on Warren Harding's presidential election campaign in 1920, organizing media events, gathering numerous celebrities of the day into the Harding–Coolidge Theatrical League, including Al Jolson, Mary Pickford, Douglas Fairbanks, Lillian Russel, Lillian Gish, Ethyl Barrymore, Pearl White and Pauline Frederick. He helped to 'humanize' Harding, as John Morello observes, and 'took steps to manipulate events in Harding's life that most Americans could not relate to, that is, his marital infidelity, and allegations that he was part African-American' (2001: 2).

[M]any of the actors and actresses who joined the Harding-Coolidge Theatrical League were making the transition from vaudeville to the vinyl disc or the silver screen. They included Mary Pickford, Douglas Fairbanks, Lillian Russel, Lillian Gish, Ethyl Barrymore, Pearl White, and Pauline Frederick. Al Jolson served as the League's president. The group campaigned nationally on Harding's behalf and participated in one of the more memorable front-porch events. On August 24, trains carrying seventy League members arrived in Marion from Chicago and New York. They marched from the train station to Harding's home on Mount Vernon Avenue, now renamed Victory Way, escorted by a local band, Harding supporters, visitors, Marionites, and starstruck movie fans. When they reached Harding's home they posed for pictures on the porch with the candidate, including one of Al Jolson having a flower pinned to his lapel by Florence Harding. Finally, to crown the day's events, members of the Harding–Coolidge Theatrical League serenaded the Hardings with a song written by Jolson, a little number entitled 'Harding, You're the Man for Us' (Morello 2001: 54).[5]

When Harding died in 1923, the Republicans turned to Edward L. Bernays, Sigmund Freud's nephew and a founding father of the modern public relations industry – not to mention modern propaganda campaigns, the 'democratic engineering of consent', and the organized manipulation of public opinion by the state and business.[6] Bernays developed Lasker's technique and arranged for the public projection of President Calvin Coolidge's relatively unknown personality by shipping various actors and actresses, mostly Ziegfeld Follies stars at one point or another – Al Jolson (again), John Drew, Justine Johnstone, Ed Wynn and the Dolly Sisters, Charlotte Greenwood, and Raymond Hitchcock – from New York to Washington to have breakfast at the White House on 17 October 1924.[7] As Bernays observed, 'The country felt that a man in the White House who could laugh with Al Jolson and the Dolly sisters was not frigid and unsympathetic' (1928: 967). The newspaper headlines included 'Actor Eats Cake with the Coolidges . . . President Nearly Laughs'.

The underlying theme was established, and the role of celebrity in politics since has consisted of variations on it. John F. Kennedy's associations with Marilyn Monroe, Sammy Davis Jr and Frank Sinatra (West 2005) were an extension of Lasker's and Bernay's techniques, as was Ronald Reagan's and

Arnold Schwarzenegger's shift from entertainment to politics, and the efforts by Bill Clinton and Barack Obama to both construct themselves as celebrities and sustain that claim through association with a variety of other celebrity sectors.

The role of celebrity is not restricted to presidential campaigns, however, it permeates all political action. Like the Sorcerer's Apprentice, politicians and political movements can often find themselves overwhelmed by what they create in their utilization of the magic of celebrity, as Todd Gitlin (1980) shows in his study of the effect of the mass media on the US student anti-war movement in the 1960s. The price paid for the benefits of the increased visibility of the more prominent personalities who emerged as the movement's spokespersons was a conflict between their performance on the public stage and their responsiveness to their constituencies, who had not necessarily selected anyone to speak for them in public and resented the selective attention paid to these individuals. The effect was to alter the logic of the movement's composition, shifting emphasis from groups that met and shaped policy face to face, to virtual constituencies whose only link was their shared relationship to the mass media.[8] Nonetheless, these are cautionary tales rather than arguments against the reality that celebrity is an essential element of the focusing of public attention in a large-scale democratic society held together by lines of mass communication (Marks & Fischer 2002). Celebrity and politics are Siamese twins, for the simple reason that both are about visibility, recognition and esteem: where popular politics and any approximation of democracy was, there shall celebrity be.

Gitlin highlights a number of central features of the operation of celebrity in politics. First, the logic and mechanisms of the modern mass media themselves demand the production of celebrity-leaders for social and political movements, for a range of very simple reasons – interviews require individuals, and the more flamboyant and recognizable the individual, the more newsworthy the story. They included Jerry Rubin, Tom Hayden and Abbie Hoffman. As Gitlin observes, 'the media system acquired celebrities more regularly and more insistently than most leaders campaigned to be acquired' (1980: 153). This aspect of the mass media's logic can be seen most clearly when individuals attempt to refuse their political celebrity. Gitlin highlights the case of the People's Park movement, and its attempt to rotate speakers beyond their initial spokesman, Dan Siegal, to have more than one person interviewed. But, observes a CBS news cameraman who covered Bay Area politics, 'when it came right down to it, the media was either gonna interview its media-appointed leader, Dan Siegal, or nobody, and so he would go along with it.' The basic principle was that 'either you allow them to make certain people stars or you don't get your message out over the air' (p. 154).

Second, it became clear that celebrity was a resource which could be accumulated and translated into other forms of capital. As Gitlin puts it, 'after a point, celebrity can be parlayed – by celebrity and by media – into more celebrity: it is like money or a credit rating' (p. 147). Jerry Rubin rather gleefully observed the pleasures of just being 'Jerry Rubin':

Fame is an asset. I can call up practically anyone on the phone and get through. People respect famous people – they are automatically interested in what I have to say. Nobody knows exactly what I have done, but they know I'm *famous*.

(Rubin 1976: 93)

Gitlin notes that 'celebrity itself . . . is transferable', and he speaks of how political stars would 'pyramid' their celebrity, ' "investing" media attention to acquire more of the same' (1980: 166), and in that way convince themselves that they could, without any significant contradictions or conflicts, mesh the political aims of their group with their own ongoing accumulation of celebrity-capital.

Third, although the acquisition of celebrity leaders did have the effect of drawing more public attention to the movement's ideas and arguments, the highly individualized character of that process also had a corrosive effect which the anti-war and other New Left movements did not have the resources or experience to combat. Gitlin observes that 'the media were always searching for prominent personalities, attractive and articulate by media standards, and then, having made them prominent, continued to cover them *because* they were prominent, celebrity piled up for some leaders and eluded others' (p. 162). This generated enormous internal envy, rivalry, and gossip. Gitlin quotes Richard Flacks, a key member of the movement:

The media select leaders and the people believe them. The internal effect was the stimulation of competition and envy within the movement . . . that was one of the most destructive elements within the movement. Everyone secretly wanted the attention, and everyone could see that the people getting the attention were really no better qualified than anyone else. What an asshole X was, and how *he* should be the one to speak for the movement. Terrible.

(p. 162)

This focus on individuals also framed the political sphere in such a way that it encouraged certain kinds of political action – the dramatic symbolic event – and made it much harder for other, more collective forms – the critique of structures and mechanisms – to acquire public oxygen. Gitlin notes that attention focused on the individual 'leader-celebrities' whose constituencies were virtual, interconnected via the media rather than real political groups, engaging in 'extravagant, "incidental," expressive actions, actions which made 'good copy" because they generated sensational pictures rich in symbolism' (p. 176). The celebrity leaders became the story, at the expense of the movement's political aims and concerns.

Gitlin's account highlights the central aspects of the working of celebrity on a relatively naive and inexperienced group of political actors, and since that time these are all mechanisms that any political group or movement have learned to take into account and adjust their activities towards, with greater or lesser degrees of success. Celebrity as self-accumulating capital, celebrity as structuring the mechanisms of leadership, and celebrity as forcing an adjustment between one's political aims and the mass media's construction of 'news' and 'news as entertainment' – these are all concerns which political action today needs to take into account and manage, in ways which the 1960s New Left only slowly began to realize (for subsequent examples, see Meyer & Gamson 1995, on Walden Woods and Colorado's Amendment 2).

Those writers on celebrity and politics (Marshall 1997; Street 2003, 2004; Corner & Pels 2003a, b; Corner 2003; Pels 2003a; van Zoonen 2005) who go beyond the cultural pessimist construction of the relationship between celebrity and politics, as a doom-and-gloom scenario of decline and decay, portray the projection of a celebrity identity as a constituent element of all political activity, an essential element of the emotional dimensions of politics. Politicians constitute, structure and give shape to the emotional lives of their constituencies – or at least attempt to – in a very similar way, argues Marshall (1997: 203–14), to celebrities resonating with their audience's thoughts and feelings, so that politicians are in a structurally similar position to celebrities to the extent that they do more than give entirely rational expression to people's material interests. John Street (2003) and Dick Pels (2003a) go on to emphasize the aesthetic dimensions of politics and the importance of political style, highlighting the performative nature of all political action. Pels also notes the way in which politics operates as 'parasocial intimacy-at-a-distance' arguing that 'politicians increasingly share in the 'extraordinary ordinariness' which characterizes the modern democratic celebrity' (2003a: 59).

Liesbet van Zoonen (2005: 83) suggests a four-fold typology of the varying positions that politicians can adopt in relation to celebrity, either consistently or moving around them as strategic concerns demand. The two dimensions are whether one defines oneself and is perceived as insider or outsider to 'the political system', and whether one is an 'ordinary' celebrity, in the sense that any politician must be, or whether one makes a special claim to celebrity status – adopting a distinctive persona, drawing on attributes derived from outside the field of politics itself.

Celebrity: Politics:	Ordinary	Special
Insider	I	II
Outside	III	IV

Figure 5.1 Four-fold typology of the positions that politicians can adopt in relation to celebrity.

Source: Adapted from Liesbet van Zoonen (2005: 83).

Jimmy Carter, Al Gore and John Major are examples of Type I – political insiders with no special claim to celebrity status. Arnold Schwarzenegger and Sarah Palin are clearly Type IV – both political outsiders (or at least claiming to be), and with distinctive celebrity attributes. Bill Clinton and Barack Obama would be examples of Type II – insiders to politics, but with an extraordinary image based on specific charismatic characteristics. The only example van Zoonen can identity of Type III, an outsider with no celebrity identity, is Ross Perot, and it seems likely that this is the most difficult position to work from, perhaps impossible, having neither the resources of an insider position nor the claim on public attention generated by celebrity. In practice, political actors will move between the different positions – by definition outsider status, for example, is difficult to sustain over time, although it is possible that Ronald Reagan managed it.

There is likely to be a tendency to swing between the different positions, suggests van Zoonen, with the negative aspects of one being compensated for by the other, and then the same in reverse. So John Major was the antidote to Margaret Thatcher, and van Zoonen predicted in 2005 that Schwarzenegger's replacement as Governor of California was likely to be a Type I figure. Indeed, as it turned out, Jerry Brown clearly fits that categorization: having already served as governor between 1975 and 1983, being now the oldest serving governor in California and the United States, attempting and failing to be nominated as the Democratic presidential candidate in 1976, 1980 and 1992. It is said he once dated Linda Ronstadt. If there is a pendulum tendency, between Type I and II positions, with the occasional intrusion of a Type IV, then one would predict that the next president after Barack Obama is likely to be a Type I, an insider with a relatively low-key celebrity profile. It would also suggest that the strength of Type IV forces within the Republican Party are making Obama's second term more likely than not.

Celebrity diplomacy and philanthropy

The linkage of celebrity with political action has tightened in the subsequent period, with the involvement of actors and musicians becoming increasingly ubiquitous in arenas such as diplomacy, charity, environmentalism, inter-governmental dialogue and the ordinary work of the United Nations. The comedian Danny Kaye was the first United Nations Ambassador-at-Large (1954–87), with Audrey Hepburn taking over the role between 1988 and 1993. In addition to her genuine concern for the effects of poverty and war, especially for children, she had a clear sense of what she could bring to the task of attempting to support UNICEF's work: 'I'm glad I've got a name', she said, 'because I'm using it for what it's worth. It's like a bonus that my career has given to me.'[9] Kaye and Hepburn did not invent the idea of celebrity philanthropy and politics – Douglas Fairbanks and Mary Pickford gave public support to the Red Cross, and toured the United States promoting the sale of Liberty Bonds to finance American involvement in the First World War. The roots can be traced back further still, to interest in philanthropy displayed by Queen Victoria and Prince Albert, who made patronage of charities and other welfare initiatives a central aspect of their modernization of the monarchy in the face of radical and republican critiques. In addition to contributing 15 per cent of her income to charity, Victoria also lent her name to 150 different institutions (Plunkett 2003: 36).

But in many respects, argues Andrew Cooper, Hepburn set the basic template for celebrity involvement in contemporary diplomacy and philanthropic intervention (2008: 19–21), with every celebrity since – Sophie Loren, Liv Ullman, Richard Gere, Sharon Stone, David Beckham, Bono, Bob Geldoff, Angelina Jolie, George Clooney – either more or less replicating her working style, or producing variations on the underlying theme. She travelled to the locations of trauma, war, famine and natural disaster to draw public attention, functioned as a major fund-raiser, engaged in dialogue with major global political figures, was willing to express public emotion about failure to engage with issues of poverty, and constantly re-directed the interest in her as an iconic celebrity – as the star of *Breakfast at Tiffany's, Roman Holiday* and *My Fair Lady*, to the concrete political and moral issues surrounding global inequality.

Just a Warren Harding and Calvin Coolidge turned to actors and actresses to enhance their public profile, in relation to all forms of political action there are strong incentives for any social movement or cause to enlist the support of celebrities, to draw attention to their concerns and maximize their exposure (Meyer & Gamson 1995; West & Orman 2003: 74; West 2005). Kofi Annan explained the principle on 18 June 2002, in an address to a group of UN celebrity advocates:

> Whenever you put your name to a message, you raise awareness far and wide, among policy-makers and among the millions of people who elect them. In an age when the media tends to focus on issues they think of as more immediately accessible to the public, our chances of breaking through the barrier of indifference are vastly improved when we have people like you to plead our case. . . . You can help instil in young people the values of understanding, solidarity, respect and communication across cultures – the very ideals the United Nations stands for – so that those values come to them naturally for the rest of their lives.[10]

In relation to environmental politics, Boykoff and Goodman speak of celebrities as joining whales and polar bears in themselves being 'charismatic megafauna' occupying an expanding and increasingly central place in an 'emergent climate science–policy–celebrity complex' (2009: 396; also Boykoff et al. 2010). They highlight a radio interview with Fred Thompson, President of the Liver Foundation, where he is asked if it would be a good thing for the foundation's cause if Paris Hilton got hepatitis B. Thompson responds:

> Having a celebrity or somebody like a Paris Hilton, and she happened to have liver disease and we could get her as a spokesperson; that would be probably very helpful. We all know what Katie Couric did for colon cancer. So we are hoping to find some celebrities.
>
> (2009: 397, citing Garfield, Bob, 2007. On the Media:
> Interview with Fred Thompson. National Public Radio,
> Washington, DC, 16 March 2007)

Boykoff and Goodman (p. 398) observe that the extent of the linkage between celebrities and environmental politics is now 'unprecedented', with the involvement of celebrities of various sorts increasing dramatically since 2003. Key figures in the 'environmental celebretariat' (Boykoff et al. 2010: 3) today are Bono, Bob Geldoff, Angelina Jolie and Brad Pitt with their Jolie–Pitt Foundation, but also Scarlett Johansson and Helen Mirren as Oxfam Ambassadors, Emma Watson for People Tree, David Beckham for UNICEF and his own David and Victoria Beckham Charitable Trust. Others also include Jamie Oliver (in relation to British childhood nutrition through his school food television programme), Harrison Ford (Conservation International), Sting (Rainforest Alliance) and Jack Johnson 'All at Once' campaign (http://allatonce.org/, reducing plastics, organic food, growing own food, local produce, etc.). If one goes to the 'Look to the Stars: the World of Celebrity Giving' website, in the 'Environment' section, the top celebrities involved in this area of celebrity charity are Pierce Brosnan (13 charities), Daryl Hannah (10), Jack Johnson (9), Leonardo DiCaprio (8), Dave Matthews (6), Ed Begley Jr (6), Sting (5) and Annie Lennox (4). The list of causes with which the 2430 celebrities and 'personalities' listed on Look to the Stars are keen to associate themselves is endless: Joss Stone and bears, David Good (reality TV 'personality') and cancer prevention and treatment, Sean Penn and Haiti reconstruction, Tiger Woods and education, Cyndi Lauper and gay rights, Rachel Shenton (Hollyoaks star) and deaf children, and so on. Emma Watson's expression of global ethical responsibility is her support for the Fair Trade movement, through her involvement with People Tree's 'ethical' fashion line.

A measure of the impact that association with a celebrity's name can have is the fate of the novel *Anna Karenina* – in the 12 weeks prior to inclusion in Oprah Winfrey's Book Club, a little over 11,000 copies were sold. In the 12 weeks after, sales rose to over 643,000 copies (Garthwaite & Moore 2008: 8). Conversely, when Winfrey made an association between hamburgers and mad cow disease in 1996, cattle futures stocks fell 10 per cent, and a group of cattlemen sued her (unsuccessfully) for $12m.[11] Of course this also means that those wishing to influence public debates and perceptions, as always, have an interest in allying themselves with celebrities. In the field of celebrity diplomacy, it is not always clear exactly whose ideas are being put forward, so that celebrities can function as Trojan Horses for particular positions in the debates. Bono and Jolie, for example, are aligned with Columbia University's Jeffrey Sachs, himself a celebrity economist; as Dieter observes, 'Bono and Sachs have become something of a double act, with the professor providing the intellectual message and the rock star bringing it to large audiences' (Dieter & Kumar 2008: 261).

That constitutes the pull side, on the 'push' side, celebrities themselves have an equally powerful interest in devoting themselves to the right kind of causes quite apart from their actual concern for the particular issue at stake, making it increasingly difficult to disentangle the different motivations – to soften the critical edge of the popular response to celebrities, but also quite simply to further maximize their capacity to attract attention and to cross-fertilize with their other roles in the public imagination. In that sense it looks at first glance as thought there is a mutual 'everybody wins' effect, in that the cause gets more attention and public profile, and so too does the celebrity.

The reservation is that critics also argue that celebrities and their sponsors get much more out of support for charities and causes than they give, given the enormous commercial value of their increased visibility, and the facilitation of the celebrities own global identity and visibility (Goodman & Barnes 2011: 77). In relation to Product RED, set up by Bono and Bobby Shriver, Armani, Apple and Amex produce RED versions of their products and donate roughly 1 per cent of their earnings to The Global Fund, to combat AIDS in Africa, but this is a trivial amount compared to the improved visibility of their brand and their product. Celebrity diplomacy is vulnerable to the criticism surrounding its agenda-setting effects, so that global economic issues are defined as single, containable issues that can be dealt with by donations, overlooking less 'saleable' and media-friendly concerns, and without significant changes in the underlying politico-economic relations between the core and the periphery, the North and the South (Stole 2006, cited in Littler 2008: 243; Goodman & Barnes 2011: 72). Indeed, often the effect is to improve the overall profitability of the corporations concerned (Littler 2008: 244). Littler notes, drawing on Luc Boltanski's (1999) *Distant Suffering*, celebrity philanthropy constitutes a politics of pity rather than justice, more hand-wringing and adjusted consumption patterns than real social and political adjustment.

Boycoff and his colleagues also argue that the particular contribution of the celebrification of environmentalism is the creation of a kind of environmental concern that meshes with the very consumption patterns that some would regard as far more central to the underlying problem. In this way, they argue, 'the global "climate change" citizen can seemingly be created, fostered and furthered through a simple trip to the shopping mall, local store and/or supermarket, attendance at a football game, or by just flicking off (or on as the case may be) the television or movie screen' (2010: 9). Consumer choice becomes the core concern – this car instead of that one, this cleanser instead of that one – without any impact on the overall volume of consumption. This does not mean, though, that celebrity advocacy necessarily realizes its aims. Thrall and his colleagues (2008) argue, on the contrary, that when one looks at a broader range of celebrity advocacy, not just the high profile examples, the increased utilization of celebrity 'star power' in social movements is accompanied, paradoxically, by a relatively weak impact on the direction taken by the public debate. Their impact appears to be confined to getting issues on the political agenda, without then being able to shape their subsequent development.

Nonetheless, the overall effect of the ever-tightening linkages between individualism, democracy and celebrity remains that celebrities function as important 'vehicles for the simulation of political consent' (Marks & Fisher 2002: 372). Democratic political leaders rely on the bonding effect of broad public recognition, but this then works in the opposite direction as well, so that universal recognition itself comes to be granted political authority (pp. 393–4). It may be pushing the argument too far to suggest, as Michael Marks and Zachary Fisher do, that under democratic conditions people 'may be willing to accept the authority of celebrities because, in the end, one set of charismatic individuals may be as good as another in providing a sense of common purpose to those who follow them' (p. 392), but the instability of the boundary between different forms of authority and charisma remains a central feature of the role of celebrity in politics. Celebrities are today experienced by their audiences in many respects as being their own creation – despite the reality of the celebrity production process – and thus in some respects they are 'representatives' in ways that parallel that of their elected politicians (p. 384). Stephen Hatch observed this dynamic in relation to the British monarchy in 1960:

> As power becomes more and more remote, and the understanding of society increasingly difficult, so it appears to be closer to us than ever before, its personalities and processes displayed before us in ever increasing abundance, generating a 'spurious egalitarianism' which serves only to thwart a desire for equality, and conceals the extent to which the practice of government departs from its democratic ideal.
>
> (1960: 65)

This is why, as John Street argues, the celebrity politician is 'characteristic of the nature of political representation generally' (2004: 449), rather than an anomaly deviating from or diverting 'normal' political processes.

Edgar Grande (2000) has taken the argument further by emphasizing the changing role that charisma and personality play as the political sphere becomes increasingly complex and subjected to contradictory tendencies. Grande begins with Schelsky's (1983) discussion of Carl Schmitt in relation to contemporary political conditions, and his distinction between two levels of reality within 'the political'. First, the level of 'Realpolitik', of 'negotiating democracy', of long tedious meetings consisting of laborious negotiations and above all compromises that remain anonymous, with no winners or losers. Here the fundamental principle, says Grande, is: 'The larger the problem, the smaller the circle of actors taking part in the negotiations' (2000: 127). Schumpeter and most political theorists after the Second World War saw the average citizen as poorly informed, emotional and inclined to hysteria, with Hitler and Stalin precisely what one got when the 'masses' took control, so that their goal was to reduce popular participation to its absolute minimum, voting in elections, and this remains a powerful concern in all democratic polities, restricted only by the population's preparedness to be contained within existing political parameters.

How effectively this level of democratic politics operates depends on Schelsky's second level of political reality, that of politics in the public sphere, what he called 'media democracy'. Here Schelsky is referring to what would today be called political 'spin', the interaction of politicians and government officials with the mass media, each attempting to manipulate and outwit the other. As Grande observes, here the ground rule is: 'The smaller the problem, the more elaborate the attempts to seek public attention' (2000: 128). Here politics is organized around individual personalities about whom as much as possible needs to be known to ascertain and assess their motives, and there is a clear distinction between winners and losers.

If one had recently read Erving Goffman (1959), one might see the distinction as similar to that between the back stage and the front stage. The problem then becomes, argues Grande, that as the operations of 'negotiation democracy' becomes increasingly complex, unwieldy and opaque, citizens find it more and more difficult to reduce political complexity to a manageable and understandable level, and increasingly demand mechanisms for such complexity reduction. Grande outlines three such complexity-reduction mechanisms identified in the literature: (a) use of procedure for political legitimation, (b) mobilization of religious and political images of the world and (c) reliance on the persuasion of expertise (2000: 132). The first is only of limited utility, the second has lost much of its effect with the decline of the salience of the distinction between left and right, and the dissolution of party allegiances, and the third is undermined by the contradictory nature of expert knowledge and the critique of expertise itself.

As these mechanisms fail, a new one has emerged – or rather, new life has been given to the old political function of charisma – charismatic and publically persuasive leaders become increasingly significant as a means of restoring political comprehension and coherence. While Weber thought that the role of charisma would recede in the face of bureaucratization, rational–legal authority and the disenchantment of the world, in fact it retains a central significance in its capacity to make sense of an increasingly contingent, complex and unpredictable world. Given this demand for charisma, in situations of short supply of natural charm and persuasiveness, the next step is clearly simply to manufacture the required resource, and this then links up with two parallel developments, the expanding role of the electronic mass media, and its increasing commercialization (Grande 2000: 136).

These developments combined create specific possibilities for particular kinds of charismatic celebrity politicians, and one can see different but fundamentally related strategies being pursued over recent years in democratic political systems. As Grande observes:

> Political actors can use the public sphere not just to improve their personal profile and popularity, but also to mobilize it strategically to improve their chances of success in negotiation democracy. In this way they can seek to improve their negotiation position or weaken that of other actors with targeted leaking of information (or disinformation). Or they can mobilize the media to create and re-work political landscapes so as to create a need for negotiation, to define the goals of negotiation, and to intensify the compulsion to come to agreement.
>
> (p. 138)

This is essentially the script informing the political career of politicians such as Geert Wilders in the Netherlands or Jörg Haider in Austria, spelling out the central role that the personalization of politics and its organization about 'celebrified' political figures plays in democratic politics. This connection between complexity and celebrity need not be framed in quite the evolutionary terms suggested by Grande's terminology; although the communication technology has clearly changed, it is unlikely that the average inhabitant of any European city, town or village in the fifteenth or sixteenth century felt that they had any more insight into the machinery of government than the democratic citizen of the twenty-first century, and one could say that this goes a large way to explaining the representational practices of projecting political power adopted by absolutist monarchs (Burke 1992; Sharpe 2009).

6 Business and management celebrity

In the realm of business and management, the functioning of commercial organizations today is also marked by the central role that celebrity CEOs play in establishing a firm's success, and firms themselves will often achieve success by attained celebrity status, in the sense of being known for being well known – Walt Disney, Coca-Cola and Nike are just some examples. The whole point of branding is precisely to establish a celebrity status for a name, a face, a word, an object or an image. Many leading corporations are closely identified with their CEOs. As Jo Littler (2007) and Guthey et al. (2009) observe, most of the scholarly accounts of celebrity, especially in cultural and media studies, tend to overlook business celebrities, focusing instead on entertainment and sports stars. However, before Hollywood took its central position in the public imagination in relation to celebrity, entrepreneurs such as Rockefeller, Carnegie, J.P. Morgan, Edison and Ford 'became highly visible repositories of the tensions and debates generated by social, commercial, and technological changes that contributed to the development of the Hollywood film industry itself'. For Guthey and his colleagues, commercial and financial celebrities 'helped make up the rules of the game in the first place' (2009: 8–9).

A CEO becomes a celebrity CEO, suggest Hayward et al. (2004), when a firm's positive performance is attributed to that CEO, at the expense of consideration of other possible factors, including luck, the firm's changing environment, or lower-placed members of the firm. Jo Littler has a more restrictive definition, proposing that we should see celebrity CEOs in addition as those 'whose profiles extend *beyond* the financial or business sectors of the media' (2007: 233). For Littler, the straddling of multiples media sites and genres is the key to their celebrity status, and many of the elements of basic pattern of CEO celebrity production were laid down in the course of the nineteenth century.

A central part of the explosion of the scope and volume of the mass-circulation print media from the middle of the nineteenth century was increased attention being paid to the world of commerce and finance, and the wealthy and 'captains of industry' were frequent topics of press coverage and public discussion. Charles Ponce de Leon points out that in the face of attacks on their role in society, particular when economic conditions were poor and their wealthy lifestyles contrasted most sharply with the poverty and misery of the bulk of the population, leading entrepreneurs increased their philanthropic endeavours to help transform the public perception of their contributions to the community (2002: 142). But these efforts were only marginally successful in the face of the far more numerous stories of financial and personal scandals, partly driven by the media interest in addressing the concerns and orientations of an expanding working- and middle-class readership.

The nature of capitalist enterprise had shifted towards large corporations and banks, and the owners and managers of the large and ever-expanding enterprises characterizing an emerging monopoly capitalism constituted a new business elite possessing levels of wealth and power familiar enough to Europeans, but relatively new to American society. The central figures are well known – J.P. Morgan, John D. Rockefeller, Andrew Carnegie, William K. Vanderbilt, Jay Gould – and they pursued a lifestyle which clearly established them as an elite. As Ponce de Leon puts it, 'the late-nineteenth-century rich showed a new determination to set themselves apart from the rest of society and establish a world of their own' (2002: 143). By the early years of the twentieth century, there was a widespread perception of the business elite as 'robber barons' who were parasitic on the rest of society, a decadent aristocracy as foreign to real American values of modesty, frugality, hard work and ordinary respectability as the old European aristocracy. For large parts of the American press, 'the robber baron was a destructive force in American society, a throwback to an earlier era when men, unrestrained by morality or religious faith, freely indulged their desires for wealth and power, creating an environment where chicanery and cutthroat struggle were widespread' (p. 147).

Leading businessmen were seen as wholly immoral, unprincipled monsters, concerned only to accumulate infinite wealth on the back of ruthless exploitation and the outright fraud of ordinary, hard-working Americans, no matter what the destructive effects on the world beyond their own mansions and playgrounds. Even worse, the robber baron had political power as well, and individuals such as J.P. Morgan – 'Owners of America' – exercised a sinister control over the whole political process to protect and further expand to an unfathomable extent their wealth, luxury and privilege. The media largely portrayed the 'rich and famous' as 'dissolute and parasitic, a class of Americans who lived amid grotesque opulence and were completely removed from the virtuous mainstream of society' (p. 149).

It has become a standard formula in public relations and advertising that 'if you don't like what is being said about you, change the conversation'. This is exactly what the American business elite did, transforming the discourse of the 'robber baron' into that of the 'industrial statesman', which, beginning early in the twentieth century and certainly by the 1920s, had become 'the primary archetype around which press depictions of capitalists, financiers, and corporate executives revolved', consigning the robber baron to the dustbin of history (p. 152). This shift from 'robber baron' to 'industrial statesman'/'progressive philanthropist' was driven by a particular kind of celebrification of the entrepreneur which remains central to the representation of the business world today, with a number of key elements that remain central to the construction of celebrity CEOs today.

First, you distinguish one entrepreneur from another, cordon off the 'bad apples' and emphasis the individual character of corporate transgression, rather than its systemic nature. Then you emphasize the construction that accompanies destruction, stressing the future direction of society rather than obsession with the past. In a variant of Robespierre's 'Omelettes are not made without breaking eggs', Rockefeller was quoted in a profile of him by F.N. Doubleday in 1908 as stressing that 'no order of new things can go into effect without bringing antagonism into being' (Ponce de Leon 2002: 152). An emphasis is placed on the risk-taking, boldness and inventiveness of leading entrepreneurs, and an opposition is constructed between large-scale capitalist enterprise as 'order' on the one hand, and 'chaos' on the other. As Ponce de Leon observes, in countering the widespread perception of businessmen as faceless bureaucrats, 'celebrity profiles of businessmen in the 1920s and early 1930s offered readers a very different picture, one that endowed the industrial statesman with the aura of a virile, swashbuckling adventurer' (p. 156).

The negative effects of capitalist enterprise are re-conceptualized as 'incidental' – in today's language, as collateral damage. The motivations of entrepreneurs are re-framed as focused not on wealth – which is just a happy side-effect of their efforts – but primarily on order, efficiency and progress. The claim is made that they could have been much richer if they'd been *really* ruthless and less public-spirited. To drive this point home, as much philanthropy is to be pursued as possible, building museums, colleges, universities, medical centre, concert halls, despite the criticism that the amounts given were paltry, they were designed to draw attention away from business practices, they were directed at symptoms rather than causes and they often exacerbated problems they were meant to solve (p. 158).

Above all, you construct a behind-the-scenes portrayal of a firm's and a CEO's operations. One of Ponce de Leon's examples is the portrait of P.D. Armour, the meatpacking magnate, in *McClure's*, which 'described in laborious detail how he directed his industrial "empire" from a plain desk in the middle of a large room filled with his lieutenants and a small army of clerks' (p. 154). The core theme to be developed as much as possible is the rags-to-riches trajectory, that the system is meritocratic and that these are self-made men. These types of treatments of the private lives of business leaders provide the opportunity to reveal how 'gratifying' philanthropy is and to emphasize its effectiveness. They also make it possible to draw wives and children keen to be useful (and possibly compensate for their husband's and father's capitalist excesses) into the picture being painted of social responsibility (p. 161), in the process linking the world of business with the women's movement.

The real human being behind the tycoon was often portrayed as leading a simple life – eating plain diets, getting plenty of sleep, taking lots of wholesome exercise (golf, horse-riding) (not just accumulating money), engaging in small social gatherings with family and friends (not sumptuous parties), associating with ordinary folk who lived nearby, and utilizing a simple child-rearing regime. This shifted in 1920s and 1930s to a more consumerist model with a greater acceptance of a luxurious lifestyle, but excessive consumption was framed as 'eccentricity' rather than as moral turpitude, and today one will often see attempts to somehow combine the two models in the representation of the private lives of high profile CEOs. Today Richard Branson, for example, takes the edge off his wealth with casual dress, a modest, hesitant and reserved manner in the appropriate settings (in front of the cameras, but not in the boardroom), and the emphasis on his humble beginnings, leaving school at 15 and so on (McCarthy & Hatcher 2005).

Rakesh Khurana (2002) connects the rise of the celebrity CEO since the late 1970s with a tendency towards constructing business success as being primarily about having the 'right' CEO, of appointing CEOs from outside the firm or organization, according to criteria to do with their charisma and supposed leadership qualities, their capacity to charm shareholders and 'the market' into thinking that their unique personality will make all the difference to the firm's or the organization's success.

He attributes this, first, to the decline of managerial capitalism and the corresponding development of 'institutional investor capitalism' since the 1970s. Davis and Steil define institutional investors as 'specialized financial institutions that manage savings collectively on behalf of small investors toward a specific objective in terms of acceptable risk, maximum return maximization, and maturity of claims' (2001: 12). The category includes pension funds, life assurance companies, mutual funds, personal trusts, retirement and superannuation funds. The proportion of shares held by institutional shareholders has increased dramatically since the 1970s, from around 10 per cent in the 1960s to around 60 per cent in the late 1990s (p. 57). In 2010, institutional investors hold 62 per cent of the shares in the largest 25 US corporations – 63.7 per cent of Microsoft, 70.8 per cent of Apple, 73.4 per cent of Cisco Systems, 77.4 per cent of Hewlett-Packard, 79.6 per cent of Google (Tonello & Rabimov, 2010).

The willingness of such investors to intervene into the appointment of CEOs has correspondingly increased, partly because the large number of shares they hold undermined the usual expression of shareholder preference – exit – because, argues Khurana, it tends to be difficult to unload a large number of shares at one time, leading to increasing use of 'voice', that is, direct involvement in the processes of CEO appointment. The concern by powerful institutional investors to 'turn around' underperforming firms has in turn led to a preference for outsiders, because insiders were seen as having gone native within the existing, poorly performing firm. Insiders are regarded as 'having too much baggage', with their existing social and emotional ties to the organization and its current inhabitants making it harder for them to make difficult decisions that may involve job losses and shifts in status. Khurana quotes one observer expressing it this way: 'You don't see many examples of internal candidates getting to the top of the system and then laying waste to the existing culture' (2002: 65). The career of GE's Jack Welch, 'manager of the century', which indicates precisely that having come through the ranks need not be seen as an obstacle to the capacity to make hard-headed choices, appears to be treated as the exception which proves the rule, and the narrative of the unaligned ruthless outsider thus manages to resist the intrusion

Table 6.1 Institutional ownership in the 26 largest US corporations (by market value, as at 26 March 2010)

		Market value ($m)	% total shares outstanding held by institutions
1	Exxon Mobil Corp	314,153.50	48.2
2	Microsoft Corp	260,131.90	63.7
3	Apple Inc	209,379.00	70.8
4	Walmart Stories Inc	208,662.50	35.9
5	Berkshire Hathaway Inc	200,900.50	25.0
6	General Electric Co	195,740.50	49.4
7	Procter & Gamble C	184,993.50	58.0
8	Bank of America Corp	179,572.90	54.9
9	Google Inc	179,104.10	79.6
10	JP Morgan Chase & Co	178,865.00	73.3
11	Johnson & Johnson	177,169.10	63.9
12	IBM Corp	167,909.10	61.3
13	Wells Fargo & Co	161,742.30	75.2
14	AT&T Inc	154,870.40	55.1
15	Cisco Systems Inc	151,500.30	73.4
16	Chevron Corp	149,481.70	62.2
17	Pfizer Inc	138,285.20	69.7
18	Oracle Inc	128,940.40	60.8
19	Coca-Cola Enterprises Inc	125,975.00	63.5
20	Hewlett-Packard Co	125,274.90	77.4
21	Citigroup Inc	123,088.90	37.8
22	Intel Corp	122,853.80	63.2
23	Merck & Co Inc	116,606.30	73.4
24	PepsiCo Inc	110,052.60	66.2
25	Phillip Morris International Inc	97,215.10	71.7
26	Goldman Sachs Group	91,077.10	54.9

Source: Adapted from Tonello & Rahm, *The 2010 Institutional Investment Report: Trends in Asset Allocation and Portfolio Composition* (2010: 29)

of uncomfortable contrary experiences. As Khurana puts it, 'choosing an outsider became a way of demonstrating to Wall Street the board's commitment to change' (p. 65).

Second, this emphasis on outsiders' powers of swift organizational transformation correspondingly generated an increased focus on dramatic personalities who could claim to make an immediate and striking difference to the firm's performance – so the mechanisms encourage glamour and distinction. One useful indication of this is the way in which an aspiring CEO who is in fact an insider can nonetheless succeed if they can somehow frame themselves as 'really' an outsider – Jack Welch in GE – Khurana speaks of other 'faux' outsiders such as Jacques Nasser in Ford and American Express's Harvey Golub (p. 61). The drift towards an emphasis on charismatic leadership was also related to changes in the structure of firms and the workplace, and the nature of work. The increased deregulation of business made commercial survival and success more volatile and dependent on increasing worker productivity to compete with the expanding new economies, which in turn demanded a firm's capacity to inspire and motivate its workforce, to do more for less (Rose 1999: 114–16).

The structure of working life described in William Whyte's 1956 *The Organization Man* demanded a subordination of individual identity to the requirements of the organization as a whole, and this remains true of organizations today, but the nature of that subordination and those requirements have changed, certainly for CEOs for whom, in Khurana's words, life 'is now about communicating an essential optimism, confidence and can-do attitude', so that 'individuality has become a desired attribute, not a liability' (2002: 71). Khurana suggests that the birth of this new CEO figure can probably be traced to the emergence of Lee Iacocca as chairman and CEO of Chrysler Corporation in September 1979, who became adept not just a being a good manager, but also at projecting a charismatic identity as a leader in the public domain, so that there were attempts to persuade him to run for president (p. 72).

Another factor underpinning the celebrification of the CEO appointment is the expansion of the business media, accelerating since the 1980s (Chen & Meindl 1991), along with the ever-growing army of business analysts, and their role in informing the market. Constance Hays, for example, observed that the 1980s was characterized by a rapid growth in the 'information industry' concerning the business world, more people paid more attention to business ups and downs, and 'CEOs who posted superb results lost their facelessness and became celebrities' (2005: 146–7), appearing on magazine covers and being interviewed on television chat shows. If nothing else, the celebrification of a CEO is an effective way to gain relatively cheap publicity for the firm, across a variety of media outlets (Littler 2007: 233).

The preference in the business information industry is for narratives about individual trials and triumphs over adversity, for explanations of business success in terms of individual character and personality (Meindl et al. 1985; Hayward et al. 2004: 638), which further encourages a celebrification of CEOs. Chen and Meindl (1991) refer to the contrast between a *determinist* perspective on organizational functioning and change, which explains a firm's performance in terms of environmental and structural features of its operations and sees leadership as largely symbolic, and an *antideterminist* perspective, which suggests that firm performance is better explained in terms of the personal characteristics of its leader(s). The mass media in the West generally display a strong preference for an antideterminist perspective, consistent with the emphasis in Western social and political thought on individual free will and agency. A central element of the appeal of what Meindl and colleagues (1985) call the 'romance of leadership', or what in other contexts would be called the 'great man' view of history, is also, of course, complexity-reduction. It is just a lot easier to explain highly complex situations and organizations in terms of key individual actors than to comprehend the interaction of an array of cross-cutting processes and mechanisms operating 'together in highly intricate and overlapping networks, complete with multiple inputs and outcomes, numerous feedback loops, and all existing in some dynamic state of flux' (p. 80).

Instead of focusing on the complex and messy details of management practice, observes Khurana, business journalists will instead concentrate on the psychological attributes and habits of key actors, so that 'the press has thereby turned CEOs – once as unknown to the American public as their secretaries, chauffers, and shoe-shiners – into a new category of American celebrity' (2002: 74). For investors it is a seductive means of reducing complexity to understand a firm primarily in terms of its CEO. As Gideon Haigh observes about the 1990s, 'it was the essence of the boom that it thrust individuals into the limelight, not only because the modern cult of celebrity demanded superstars, but because personalizing a company, concept or creation was often the only way to nail it down'. No wonder, continues Haigh, that one survey found that 95 per cent of its respondents looked to CEO profiles in selecting stock, 'at what else could one look?' (2003: 55).

The result is that celebrity, the 'ability to command attention from the media and stock market analysts in a way that will establish credibility for the firm and inspire confidence in both investors and others' (Khurana 2002: 78), is central to CEO success. As Ernest Sternberg explains in relation to the operation of the labour market more broadly,

> Within any industry, corporation or profession, the aspirant reaches the economic apex when she becomes a celebrity, a human icon. Now colleagues cite her name with awe or jealousy when she is not present; subordinates show deference as a matter of course; her ideas are respected by the very fact that they arose from her; even to meet her is an honor; and all long to hire her, work with her, and gain her counsel, were she only available. Now lifted above the usual competitive anonymity, the performer can use her hard-won iconicity to assert advantages over competitors and to command for her services a market premium.
>
> (1998: 6)

More than that, once the media have constructed a CEO as a celebrity, this perception will also be resistant to subsequent evidence to the contrary (Chen & Meindl 1991). This results in turn in a greater inclination towards mergers and acquisitions, and inflates the price that CEOs are willing to pay for new acquisitions, because CEOs end up believing their own press, and the resultant CEO hubris (Roll 1986; Hayward & Hambrick 1997) inflates a CEO's assessment of their ability to recoup their outlays.

Littler (2007) highlights the way in which these tendencies constitute a central paradox of the post-Fordist commercial enterprise – the combination of this demand for greater public visibility for firms in the form of a superhero CEO with the parallel demand for increased worker productivity. That increased productivity was to be secured by moving away from the centralized, authoritarian and top-down structures of the Fordist era to post-Fordist flexibility, flat organizational structure, encouragement of worker entrepreneurialism, and the construction of the 'enterprising self' (Rose 1999). The celebrity CEO is a means of reconciling these twin imperatives as well as deflecting the charges of CEO greed surrounding the astronomical salaries commanded by celebrity CEOs, turning, as Littler puts it, 'the despised figure of the "fat cat" into a media-friendly "cool cat" ' (2007: 238).

Guthey et al. (2009) have argued more broadly that business celebrity is also a product of the cultural contradictions and tensions generated by the particular role of commercial enterprises in contemporary capitalist society, as well as the complexities of individuals' relationship to large-scale organizations. It is not their expression, but their argument could be characterized as suggesting that CEO celebrity is a central characteristic of Organization Man 2.0. For example, the individuals who attract attention as business celebrities are in many respects models or at least reference points for how it is possible to achieve distinction and upward social mobility in an otherwise increasingly competitive work environment, where it is not enough to have skills and capacities, one needs to also have some sort of 'x-factor' (hence the attraction of that TV programme) which will enable one to stand out from the crowd and foreground oneself in relation to vast, anonymous business and government organizations seemingly beyond any individual's control. Littler notes how particular celebrity CEOs, such as Dov Charney of American Apparel and *The Apprentice*'s Alan Sugar offer support for the aspiration towards upward social mobility, and the more engaging a rags-to-riches narrative one can provide, the more successful and effective one is likely to be as a celebrity CEO.

As Guthey and his colleagues argue, a central feature of celebrity is the framing of human action in highly individualized ways, at the expense of a perception of the social, collective, organized and structured nature of the human world:

> Celebrities depend for their status as such on the activities of a complex network of individuals, organizations, commercial forces, and cultural dynamics, but in the process of celebrification and mediation these various activities are folded into or overshadowed by the personalities and actions of the celebrities themselves.
>
> (2009: 12)

Celebrities can thus be seen as embodying the aspiration towards the very idea of individual agency, influence and capacity to make a difference in a highly structured world apparently structured by forces beyond individual control. The realm of business celebrity constitutes the mobilization of this aspiration in relation to economic action, driven by a complex network of activities engaged in the production of celebrity CEOs and celebrity firms. Guthey et al. emphasize the importance, too, of thinking in terms of a production process and not individual personalities such as Jack Welch, Donald Trump or Richard Branson, suggesting that business celebrities are best understood, not as particular individuals, but as

> clusters of promotional activities, representational practices, and cultural dynamics that revolve around different types of exemplary business

personalities – corporate leaders, entrepreneurs, management gurus, investment bankers, traders, marketers, Hollywood agents and producers, and so on.
(2009: 36)

The production of business celebrity concerns 'the orchestrated co-production, cross-promotion, and circulation of images, narratives, and personal appearances of such figures via a wide range of medial platforms and channels' (p. 36).

It is not obvious, one should add, that the celebrification of CEOs is necessarily consistent with success, productivity and effectiveness in firm performance – CEO celebrity is essentially a highly volatile substance that can significantly improve a firm's commercial success, or blow up in its collective face. Hayward et al., for example point out that firms with celebrity CEOs are likely to over-rely on the strategies that have brought success in the past, making them in fact less adaptable to changing conditions (2004: 638). Celebrity CEOs, they go on to note, are more likely to underestimate the quality of competitors' actions, overestimate the returns likely to accrue to their own strategies, underestimate the potential impact of factors other than their own actions (changed legislation, cultural shifts, technological change), all of which can increase the strategic intertia in the firm (p. 646).

Celebrity CEOs also play a particular role in acting as models in the formation of particular social identities suited to the dominant cultural and political context. This aspect of celebrity entrepreneurship is less clearly defined in Western countries because of the parallel, ongoing critiques of capitalism, and because it is market-driven, and thus subject to contradictory forces and tendencies. However, it can be clearly seen in its state-driven form in China today. David Davies looks at a number of popular television programmes in China, including *Fortune Time* and *Boss Town*, which present the individual life stories of successful entrepreneurs in more or less the same pedagogic way that they were put forward under Mao-Tse Tung (1949–76):

> An individual is marketed as an 'example' (*bangyang*) for others to encounter and emulate and this is 'staged' in a way that they then might be invited, compelled or challenged to speak about the details of his or her life. Exemplary models are presented and structured as a method of self-cultivation, whereby encounters with such models are intended to elicit a comparision and a subsequent struggle to improve oneself.
>
> (2011: 198)

In the Maoist period, the models turned into China-wide celebrities would be heroic soldiers, model workers, exemplary commune workers and so on. Such models were, as Davies emphasizes, 'in effect, "mass celebrities" – the state-sponsored equivalent of the market-driven celebrities of the capitalist West' (p. 198). Their contemporary heirs are the reform-era entrepreneurs, creative and inspired 'entrepreneurial heroes' representing the success of the Chinese nation and national character, rather than the exploitation of the proletariat. The property developer Wang Shi, for example, owner of China's largest real estate development company

Vanke, has an especially heightened celebrity status, having climbing the highest mountains on all seven continents, constructing the accumulation of enormous wealth into a lifelong 'adventure'. In this sense, Chinese celerity entrepreneurs constitute the reference points for a particular narrative of the ideal self suited to the nation's competitive requirements in an increasingly globalized world economy, and although the operation of this logic is less orchestrated, in market-oriented societies, too, the construction of key entrepreneurs as celebrities plays a very similar role.

Virtual CEOs

David Boje and Carl Rhodes (2005) have also highlighted the ways in which celebrity CEOs need not be actual human beings, and can often operate as 'virtual leaders', developing a variety of substitutes for real, embodied leadership. Their account of the 'virtual leader construct' (VLC) provides a useful illustration of how CEOs are transformed into celebrities. Boje and Rhodes see virtual leadership as operating across three orders of virtuality: a real person becoming an imitation of him or herself; a representation of a real person; and a completely fictional construct. The first order VLC is related to how celebrity CEOs generally function, in that a particular narrative is assembled about an individual which glosses over the inconsistencies and contradictions, making it consistent with a heroic but homely struggle from ordinary beginnings to ultimate triumph and commercial success. They give the example of Dave Thomas, founder of Wendy's Old Fashioned Hamburgers in 1969, identified by the Guinness Book of Records as the star of the largest number of corporate advertisements (roughly 800) featuring one of the corporation's executives.

Thomas had ceased his day-to-day management activities in 1982, and took on the role of starring in the TV commercials in 1989, where he turned into an image of himself, 'an imitation or counterfeit of his alter ego as a corporate leader' (2005: 414). Although the boardroom Thomas and the TV Thomas were one and the same person, the celebrity CEO attracting the public attention was the TV Thomas, constructed as a regular guy with a rags-to-riches biography and old-fashioned values – 'quality is our recipe', 'do the right thing', 'treat people with respect', 'profit is a not a dirty word' and 'give something back' – that could somehow be transmitted and sustained by eating Wendy's hamburgers. 'Quality is our recipe' is registered as a trademark and used as Wendy's marketing slogan. On their website today, Dave Thomas's life story is featured as conveying the ethos of the firm and its products.

The key example of a second-order VLC is Colonel Sanders, the cartoon Colonel Sanders. The real Harland Sanders started off as a first-order VLC like Dave Thomas – after selling Kentucky Fried Chicken in 1964, Sanders came out of retirement and became a paid corporate spokesman, appearing in advertisements much as Thomas had for Wendy's, as well as on talk shows. Thomas was the regular guy, while Sanders was the eccentric Southern gentleman. Sanders died in 1980, and in 1990 the company tried to revive his VLC character with look-alikes, unsuccessfully, shifting in 1993 to an animation with Randy McQuaid's voice, together with changing the name to KFC. As such, suggest Boje and Rhodes, Sanders remained reasonably effective as a marketing device, but lost all authority as a CEO.

More effective as a celebrity CEO was the example of the third-order VLC, Ronald McDonald, a completely imaginary character. When the new McDonalds CEO, Jim Cantalupo, died in 2004, shortly after beginning to turn the firm's fortunes around with a new orientation to fitness and nutrition, Charlie Bell was declared the new CEO within the hour, but it was Ronald who appeared in full-page advertisements saying 'we miss you Jim' with a tear running down his cheek. Ronald's character had been transformed in the late 1990s from a mere figure of entertainment into a creative, adventurous and heroic risk-taker, one who was also fit and healthy. As Boje and Rhodes put it, 'Ronald had the charismatic influence to appeal to people around the world, and to meet the strategic goal of sustaining corporate image cohesion in a time of crisis' (2005: 418). Following on from that turning point, Ronald (via all the actors playing him and animated Ronalds) is playing a key role in representing McDonalds to its customers, especially in holding together continuity with McDonalds as an established firm with also representing a break with its unhealthy past. He does, write Boje and Rhodes, what all transformational leaders do: 'espousing the company's vision, influencing outsiders to have a favorable impression of the corporation, showing determination and confidence, setting an example, and communicating enthusiasm and inspiration' (p. 418).

Firm celebrity

The construction of CEOs as celebrities is in practice often difficult to disentangle from the very similar dynamics which can be observed in relation to firms themselves as 'actors'. Rindova et al. define celebrity firms as 'those firms that attract a high level of public attention and generate positive emotional responses from stakeholder audiences' (2006: 51), and this often takes place alongside the CEO attracting attention to themselves – Dov Charney and American Apparel, Anita Roddick and The Body Shop, Richard Branson and Virgin, Steve Jobs and Apple. The core aspirations of all branding revolve around name recognition – McDonalds, Walt Disney Corporation, IBM, Microsoft, Coca-Cola, Nike, the Body Shop – that is, around firm celebrity, often, but not always, in conjunction with a celebrity CEO. Just as the business media organize their analysis of changes and future directions in the commercial world around narratives of the distinctiveness of individuals, the same applies to firms as business actors, and the future of whole industries is often attributed to the actions of key leading firms. Rindova et al. see celebrity as an intangible asset for any firm, akin to reputation, status and legitimacy, playing a particular role in the construction of the firm's image, and therefore stakeholders' responses to that firm, in the marketplace.

Like CEO celebrity, firm celebrity is a product of the inclination in the mass media towards dramatic narratives: stories of conflicts, the firm as a protagonist undergoing character development, laced with new and 'confidential' insights into its real nature. Rindova et al. cite the example of a journalist's revelation of the culture and work routines at Yahoo!:

> Despite Yahoo!'s meteoric ascent, Edwards [VP of marketing at the time] and her colleagues continue to exude an air of humility. The company has moved out of its initial headquarters, a nondescript building that resembled a distribution warehouse, to a more modern structure. Even by Silicon Valley standards, the office climate at Yahoo! is relaxed yet scarily efficient. While Yahoo! staffers typically work sweatshop hours, the buzz of activity resembles a frat house more than an office building. Visitors tell stories of staffers busily working at monitors decked out in shorts and T-shirts, and sometimes shoes. Workers typically wear competitors' T-shirts and decorate their work space with their ads, Edwards said. One notorious story is that a senior producer of the Yahoo! financial pages tattooed the company logo on his buttocks to make good on a promise he made should the stock price hit $50.
>
> (B. Warner cited in Rindova et al. 2006: 59)

The focus details of personal life in a celebrity individual has its parallel in revelations about a firm's culture, orientation, actions 'behind the scenes' and the personal characteristics of its staff, especially its leaders.

Firm celebrity is centrally organized around the construction of 'novelty', because actions which deviate from expectations stand out and are perceived as having greater salience, making such actions a key way to establish a firm as proactive and to capture media and market attention. It is almost always the result of highly organized efforts to construct the firm as a celebrity actor standing at the heart of an engaging dramatic commercial narrative, channelling information to the media, organizing events, setting up stories about the firm's culture and activities. Yahoo!, for example, employed two PR firms to place stories in the media about the firm, its origins and development, and its founders – Dave Filo and Jerry Yang – placed quirky advertisements and offered free paint jobs to employees who carried the company's logo, so that 'many small yet powerfully distinctive details traveled from the private life of the firm into the public domain of its celebrity persona' (Rindova et al. 2006: 62).

Rinodova et al. distinguish between two types of firm novelty: under-conforming 'rebels' and over-conforming 'market-leaders', both of which will enhance the celebrity of a firm if the non-conforming behaviour can be evaluated positively by a large enough proportion of a firm's market. The example they give of the 'rebel' firm is Southwest Airlines in 1971, which was the first airline to adopt the strategy now so familiar to us in airlines such as Ryanair and Easyjet, of underconforming to accepted industry norms of seat allocation, differing ticket classes, flight routes, and provision of in-flight meals (p. 60). The Ritz-Carlton, on the other hand, provides service beyond normal expectations by attempting to ascertain and reflect the personal tastes and preferences of guests in the more luxurious rooms.

There are two pathways which can be followed by a 'rebel' firm. After initially attracting attention as a 'rebel', a firm can then move to consolidate its position by establishing itself as a market leader if its innovations shift the industry norms. The Southwest Airlines business model is now widespread through the airlines industry, and Rindova et al. note the example of Nike, beginning its life in the 1970s and 1980s as a 'rebel' firm with non-conforming colours and designs for its sports shoes, which in turn became the industry design norm, so that it is now a market leader. Once a firm has gained market attention and is thus less dependent on its non-conforming behaviour to sustain its visibility, either the industry's norms will have shifted in response, or it can afford to become more conformist and expand its legitimacy in a larger market, losing its celebrity status but gaining profitability. The other pathway, in the absence of matching shifts in industry norms, is to sustain and even amplify the firm's non-conforming behaviour, with the usual outcome being that its actions will become evaluated negatively, becoming an 'outlaw' firm, and its market share will decline. The example Rindova et al. give here is of Enron, which 'took its nonconformist behaviors in an increasingly extreme direction, with devastating results' (p. 62).

A final theme running through Rindova et al.'s analysis is the essential volatility of celebrity as an intangible asset for a firm. They refer to research on cognition which emphasizes the unstable nature of attention and positive emotional responses, and observe that celebrity may be inherently transitory (p. 66). How well celebrity works for a firm will be related to the evolution of the relevant industry norms, and exactly how strategic the firm's placement of itself in relation to those norms – whether they stay stable, change, or the direction in which they change. Although firm celebrity can be a useful means of achieving distinction in a crowded, competitive field, making the pursuit of celebrity 'a highly rational and beneficial strategic choice for a firm' (p. 68), making it an end in itself almost always weakens rather than strengthens firm performance.

7 Celebrity's futures

15 minutes of fame, or fame in 15 minutes

Proliferation, differentiation, amplification

In the frontispiece to the catalogue for his exhibition at the *Moderna Museet* in Stockholm between 10 February and 17 March 1968, Andy Warhol observed that: 'In the future everybody will be world famous for fifteen minutes.' In 1979, he added: 'I'm bored with that line. I never use it anymore. My new line is, "In fifteen minutes everybody will be famous" ' (Warhol & Colacello 1979: 48).

Warhol may here have been simply saying what he knew would attract our attention. It is also equally possible that he was making a perceptive observation on the overall direction that celebrity is moving – towards a shorter pathway to celebrity, along with its greater distribution among a larger number of people, but for shorter periods of time, taking up a larger proportion of our attention. One of the more obvious recent developments in the production of celebrity has been the sheer proliferation of numbers of recognizable individuals jostling for public recognition, the variety of arenas in which high visibility might be achieved, and the diversity of routes which can be followed to becoming well known to smaller or larger audiences. Since the expansion of the Internet in the 1990s, there has been a never-ending flow of new, often short-lived, rapid-rise celebrity identities. In 2000, Joshua Gamson mentioned among the earlier examples, Mahir Çağrı, a Turkish musician and journalist, whose goofy web page, *IKissyou.org*,[1] peppered with broken English and displaying much of the comic style of Sacha Cohen's character Borat, generated a snowball of attention-accumulation, including derision and parody, which took him to number 100 on the Forbes Celebrity 100, and emails from Bill Clinton and Bill Gates. 'Like any good celebrity', wrote Gamson, 'he is working on a film deal and has announced plans to use his fame to promote World Peace and help The Children' (2000: 40).

The capacity of the Internet to deliver an enormous global audience at very high speed is clearly demonstrated by YouTube and its powerful ability to capture the attention of large numbers of viewers, captured with the concept of a video 'going viral', for a variety of reasons that are not restricted to the usual ones of talent and ability, in ways that Andy Warhol would be delighted with. Joshua Gamson points out that a central driving force remains ever-increasing competition in the mass media, generating a constantly increasing requirement to organize the delivery of media products – news, films, television programmes and so on – in ways that will stand out from the crowd, which has meant 'a need for more subject matter, and more opportunities for recognition: literally more editorial space for those aspiring to fame or to regain faded recognition, for star-for-a-day ordinary people, and for celebrities from untapped fields' (1994: 149). Chris Rojek has suggested the term 'celetoid' to capture this kind of phenomenon, referring to 'any form of compressed, concentrated, attributed celebrity' (2001: 20). He sees celetoids as the 'accessories of cultures organized around mass communication and staged authenticity' (pp. 20–1), including examples such as 'lottery winners, one-hit wonders, stalkers, whistle-blowers, sports arena streakers, have-a-go heroes, mistresses of public figures' (p. 21), along with anyone on whom media attention gets focused intensely for brief periods. On the whole, celetoids are by definition short-lived, although there are some exceptions – Rojek gives the example of the Californian woman Angelyne, whose appeal to 'kitsch culture' seems to have allowed her career as a celebrity to extend beyond that of most celetoids.

The term has not really caught on in the analysis of celebrity, but the basic point about the possibility of celebrity status being generated more quickly, often for shorter periods of time, remains salient. How long a celetoid lasts ends up being a question of strategy and the capacity for status-conversion, *translating* 'celetoid' status, to stick with Rojek's term, into a more lasting celebrity identity. In 2011, Rebecca Black, for example, ended up drawing 167 million viewers to the video of her singing the simulacrum of a pop song, 'Friday', originally a vanity music video made by Ark Music Factory for $4000, a gift from her mother. The attention it received was primarily negative, the discussion was about whether it really was the 'worst song ever' – as one comment on the YouTube site wrote, 'you're not hated because you're famous, you're famous because you're hated'. It contained inspired lines like 'Tomorrow is Saturday And Sunday comes after . . . wards', provoking a variety of parodies on other days of the week.

Becoming such a significant attention-trap has its payoffs if the established machinery of celebrity-production is cranked up[2] – Black has subsequently been included in Katie Perry's music video 'Friday night', in a sense the 'real' version of the song that Black performed, and the Australian telecommunications firm Telstra has used her to launch their 4G phones. The song itself was reported in March 2011 as earning more than $24,000 a week through iTunes, and her net worth in June 2011 has been estimated at $1.2 million.[3] Lady Gaga (Stefani Germanotta), unsurprisingly, understands the dynamics of attention-capital; in response to a question about the role of YouTube in the production of Internet fame, she said 'I think it's fantastic. I say Rebecca Black is a genius, and anyone who's telling her she's cheesy is full of shit.'[4] This was after confessing that she had not actually seen the video, but it doesn't really matter. Similarly Simon Cowell, who also has a clear grasp of the mechanics of attention-capture, identified the song as 'a "hair-dryer song," a song girls sing into their hair dryers as they're getting ready to go out'. For Cowell, 'the fact that it's making people so angry is brilliant'.[5]

> Julia Allison, journalist: 'I saw how hard it was to work your way up [in the media]. The work was badly paid . . . But I saw a short cut. If I become famous, I will never have a problem getting my work published' (Wilson 2008: 28).

Social media such as Twitter also make an enormous difference to the capacity of an expanding range of individuals to either enhance existing celebrity status, or acquire it via a new route (Marwick & Boyd 2011). In relation to Stephen Fry, for example, one journalist has noted that his tweets are read 'by more people than the printed copies of the Times, the Telegraph, the Financial Times, the Guardian and the Independent combined' (Bendedictus 2011). On Fry's website there is a warning which reads 'like something you'd see stencilled on a reactor':

> WARNING: When Stephen tweets a URL to a given website, up to 3000–500,000 people will attempt to visit that website within one hour. Very few websites can manage that intense traffic. Your website, it must be able to capable of taking 1200+ calls per second to the website's server in order to be able to stay live once Stephen's Tweeted. . . . There are three waves of capacity within that hour with the 2nd wave of retweeting generally as strong as the first original Tweet.[6]

But in October 2011 Fry had only a mere three million followers: the *Twitaholic* rankings had Fry at 68th in the world, with Lady Gaga coming in first with over 15 million, followed by Justin Bieber (14 million), Katy Perry (11 million), and Kim Kardashian, Barack Obama, and Britney Spears clustering around ten million.[7] The Chinese actress Yao Chen's microblogging site does not appear in Twitaholic's listing, but in September 2011 her fans on Sina Weibo, the Chinese version of Twitter, reached 12 million – Taiwanese actress Dee Hsu is up there with Obama on ten million. This kind of attention-capital is of course easily converted to various other forms of capital, such as old-fashioned cash – Kim Kardashian is reported as being paid $10,000 per tweet promoting a product or service – or political capital, in Obama's case.

The impact of the Internet and ever-expanding forms of computer-mediated social interaction has been to enable the construction of very large audiences at high speed. But it has also meant an increasing number of celebrity characters, along with a far more differentiated assemblage of smaller, niche audiences for a wider range of localized or smaller-scale celebrities. As Ferris puts it, Internet technology has created 'more opportunities for celebrity, with smaller, more segmented and specialized audiences, and the prospect of more open awareness contexts' (2010: 393). Local newspapers, blogs, Facebook and Twitter all construct an expanding variety of locally visible and recognizable individuals with their own audience of fans or followers, but with different types of interactions – possibly more mutually interactive – with that audience because they operate on a lower scale (pp. 393–4). This is why commercial activity seems increasingly likely to be framed as 'social business': the structuring of economic (and educational, political and scientific) action around ongoing conversations with consumers, followers, fans, audiences, students, and constituencies, multiplying the value of attention-capital, increasing the important of branding and 'meta-branding' – the provision of models for how to brand oneself.

The proliferation and expansion of the field of celebrity (Turner 2006) itself makes celebrity's role as an attention-trap even more significant and increases its commercial value. Rather than *displacing* the mega-celebrities – and, as Sconce refers to Paris Hilton, the meta/meta-celebrities – the increasing range and variety of the celebrity field, including the bloggers, reality TV personalities and the YouTube video stars, makes those who can stand above this growing crowd even more strategically important, and valuable, as guides to where one can and should direct one's attention in an increasingly crowded celebrity scene. The likely outcome, if we learn from the history, is a proliferation of alliances across celebrity fields, so that value of mega-celebrities increases as a mechanism for improving the visibility of anyone seeking a public profile at a lower level of attention-circulation. This has been a central element of the operation of celebrity society and the circulation of attention-capital since the eighteenth century at least, with a great deal of celebrity status being generated through the leveraging of attention-gathering potential on a smaller scale – in the French salons, for example, the aristocrat would leverage the well knownness of the currently fashionable musician, poet, explorer or writer, essentially gathering together their attention-capital and snowballing it with their own.

This is the mechanism lying behind a great deal of the success of figures such as Oprah Winfrey, Kim Kardashian and so on. The larger, more diverse and more differentiated the field of celebrity is, the greater the capacity of those higher up the scale of visibility to use it as a springboard for their own visibility and recognition. As the base of the pyramid expands, in other words, the higher its peak will rise. The more sociologists there are in the world, to give another example, the more books and journal articles there are likely to be about Max Weber, Pierre Bourdieu, Michel Foucault, Emile Durkheim and so on, not just because there are so many more interesting things to say about them, but because of the constantly increasing importance of their role as attention-traps. And of course there will always be interest in identifying new celebrity sociologists which can be used as attention-springboards – Slavoj Žižek is an obvious candidate at the moment, himself very skilled at the accumulation of attention-capital.

Globalization

The account of celebrity society I have developed here has been very much concentrated on Western Europe and North America, as well as related countries such as Australia and New Zealand. This is true of most of the literature on celebrity as well, although there is a slowly growing body of studies of celebrity in other parts of the world (Nayar 2008; Bolagnani 2011). But it is clear that processes of globalization are as important to take into consideration as they are in any other field of enquiry, and this will be an increasingly important aspect of the analysis of celebrity society. In 1986, Braudy wrote:

> as the international order becomes more prominent in the way individuals situate themselves in the world . . . then media fame, with its comparative lack of national specificity and its appeal to what is 'common' in human nature has become the standard of all fame, and saints, sports figures, and movie stars cross national boundaries with equal felicity and ease.
>
> (1986: 593)

There are two ways in which the concept 'globalization' can be applied to the continuing analysis of celebrity society, in relation to *universalizing* (in Braudy's sense) and also *localizing* tendencies, which in practice are intertwined with each other. I will use the development of celebrity society in China as an example of both. The first concerns the ways in which the mechanisms of celebrity-production increasingly spread from the West – Western Europe, Britain and Ireland, North America, Australia and New Zealand – throughout the rest of the world, and celebrities, as Braudy observes, can be global actors, as well known in Japan and Korea as they are in California. The technological means by which celebrity is produced has a lot to do with this dynamic, with American and European films and television programmes traversing the globe.

The techniques of celebrity production are themselves also subject to processes of globalization, spreading 'like a virus' around the world. Jeffreys and Edwards highlight the Chinese version of the *Pop Idol* talent competitions, the *Mongolian Cow Yoghurt Super Girl Contest* (now known as the BBK Music Phone Super Girl Contest), the ranking of top celebrities on various media portals, including Forbes itself, and the enthusiasm displayed for sports stars (2011: 2), the proliferation of television programmes organized around high-profile individuals in a variety of arenas, and the appearance of Internet-based celetoids including the blogger Furong Jiejie, who attracts attention to a large extent because of her misplaced self-confidence in her appearance as well as her writing and performing abilities (Roberts 2011). Until the late 1990s, the mass media were controlled by the state and engaged in the production of celebrity 'either by deifying political leaders such as Chairman Mao Zedong or by holding up idealized representations of socialist citizens (workers, soldiers, and peasants) as role models for public emulation' (p. 3). The emergence of a new kind of celebrity production can be understood in terms of the marketization of the media and a resultant shifting economics of attention. Newspapers were required to earn more of their income through subscription, new regulations introduced greater competition into television broadcasting, both linked to the growing purchasing power and numbers of consumers.

At the same time, Chinese celebrity society also has a number of very distinctive characteristics that are rooted in China's particular history, culture and institutional structures. The ongoing central role of the Chinese Communist Party

(CCP) and its associated government apparatus places the publicity spotlight more on some types of celebrities than others, and affects how the celebrity production process operates in ways which remain continuous with China's pre-reform, Maoist period. Military celebrities, for example, play a more central role in China than they do in most other parts of the world, to a large extent flowing from the close relationship between the People's Liberation Army (PLA) and the CCP (Edwards 2011: 25), and the long history of the PLA's involvement in a variety of social and political functions beyond the purely military. Edwards points out that the PLA's propaganda function has had the effect of also making it a central site for a variety of types of artistic musical and literary production, so that many celebrities receive their initial training during their time in the PLA.

Celebrity 'heroic and model servicemen' occupy a central place in the CCP's organization of popular consciousness and self-formation around particular moral and psychological characteristics: loyalty to the party, selfless service to the people, ordinariness, an activist and collectivist orientation. The earlier figures who were the focus of 'Learn from . . .' campaigns in the 1960s were Lei Feng, Ouyang Hai and Wang Jie, but interestingly relatively little was said about their activities as soldiers – the emphasis was on noble deeds and dedication to the collective good, aiming to 'reaffirm the political links between the Party, the army and the people rather than for the purposes of warfare' (Edwards 2011: 29). The more recent military celebrities, including Xu Honggang and Ye Aiqun, have their public profile organized not around any military skill or bravery in battle, but in chasing robbers and muggers. Changes in technology have intensified the celebrity production process, involving frequent television appearances and interactions with viewers, rolling speaking tours and award ceremonies, Internet videos and interviews.

This is not to say that there have not also been significant changes in the construction of the military celebrity. Since the 1990s, noble deeds having increasingly become organized around the defence of private property, and cash has become part of their reward. As Edwards notes, 'when the political catch-cry is "to get rich is glorious" celebrities must engage with the cash economy to be credible' (p. 36), although the tension with the rhetoric of self-sacrifice is often resolved with donations to charity. The mechanisms by which celebrities are identified and promoted have also shifted, from awards clearly provided by the CCP, to quasi-governmental foundations which appear to operate at arm's length from the CCP (p. 37). The military celebrity is also now more likely to come from the officer ranks, when under Mao they would always have been drawn from the ranks of regular soldiers. Edwards argues that this is part of a strategy both to exert more influence on the behavioural codes of individuals in positions of authority and responsibility and to encourage a perception of people in elite positions as being just as dedicated, hard working and socially responsible as ordinary workers (p. 39). But the underlying distinctiveness of the Chinese construction of military celebrities alongside film and music stars continues to give celebrity in China a different flavour and tone from the form it takes in Western societies.

Towards a critical account

> The apparent rulers of the English nation are like the most imposing person-
> ages of a splendid procession: it is by them the mob are influenced; it is they
> whom the spectators cheer. The real rulers are secreted in second rate
> carriages; no one cares for them or asks about them, but they are obeyed
> implicitly and unconsciously by reason of the splendour of those who eclipsed
> and preceded them.
>
> (Bagehot 1867: 53)

So far I have skirted around the question of a critique of celebrity society because
the critical stance towards celebrity has been so strongly organized around the
hero/celebrity opposition. Critical accounts tend to revolve around the idea that
celebrity is an unfortunate affliction that ought to somehow just go away. The
proliferation of celebrities tends to be bemoaned as the 'cult of celebrity', an
'obsession' that distracts people from more noble and virtuous concerns. However,
I have argued that this type of cultural pessimism about celebrity betrays a poor
sense of the social, political, economic and technological underpinnings of celebrity society. We can no more do without celebrity in contemporary society than
we can dispense with electricity or democracy. The 'celebritization of society',
which has been a long-term process tied to the increased differentiation of the
division of labour, the emergence of mass society and its globalization, has generated ever-longer and more-complex 'chains of interdependence', to use Elias's
term. As social life becomes denser, more competitive, more highly differentiated
and more dependent on a variety of means of indirect communication, visibility
beyond one's immediate circle of face-to-face contacts becomes increasingly
significant and also increasingly lucrative, with the rewards attached to the accumulation of attention-capital expanding as the economic significance of attention-
capital increases in a post-industrial knowledge and information society.

Ever since the emergence of the 'Gutenberg galaxy', the historical tendency has
been towards a 'city' organized not just around physical relations, but also around
intangible relationships based on the flow of information and on the structuring of
human attention. The rise of post-industrial society, focusing on the production
and distribution of knowledge and information, and the shift in communicative
infrastructure brought about by the Internet, have accelerated this tendency to the
point where some observers will claim that the significance of the intangible
circulation of information now outweighs that of tangible, real objects, and that
the virtual community has a similar status to the real community. This increases
the significance of the gatekeepers and switching points for the distribution
of attention, 'the subway stations attention must pass through to get where it
ultimately goes' (Rötzer & Goldhaber 1998), and celebrities are leading examples
of such 'attention traps'.

The complaint about the 'superficiality' of modern culture lies at the heart of
the concept of 'celebrity culture', and extends beyond that topic to be deeply
embedded in social theory more broadly. Richard Sennett's widely read book, *The*

Fall of Public Man, for example, operates with a similar distinction, presenting the 'fall' of a serious, thoughtful and reflective approach to public life as lying in the 'corruption' of political and social life by 'personality', the intrusion of a concern with the personal lives of public figures, a central feature of the logic of celebrity. A measure of how 'fallen' public life had become was, for Sennett, the French writer and politician Alphonse de Lamartine's (1790–1869) envy of Franz Liszt's capacity to generate public enthusiasm. The result, like Boorstin's society of pseudo-events, is that 'a believable public event is created by a believable public person rather than a believable action . . . what remains is only the obscurantist, paralyzing effect of a "politics of personality"' (2002: 237). Throughout this book I have argued that this is not a useful way to approach celebrity, that such an analysis misperceives the nature and dynamics of celebrity society.

As Bruno Latour (2004) has remarked about the critical spirit more generally, generals are often accused of being one war behind, using the weapons honed to perfection in the previous battles, and it is worth considering whether much of the critique of celebrity may also be one war too late. This does not mean that there is no longer any value in a critical analysis of celebrity society, it simply means that it is possible to change the terms and concepts with which it works, and there are a number of areas where it is indeed worthwhile to develop and deepen a critical perspective. To the extent that is true, as Walter Bagehot said, that 'the few rule by their hold, not over the reason of the multitude, but over their imaginations, and their habits; over their fancies as to distant things they do not know at all, over their customs as to near things which they know very well' (1867: 55), this can be approached as a fact demanding analysis that requires constant updating, rather than an unfortunate popular proclivity, and there remains no reason why 'the multitude' might not reflect on how this mode of governance works, and on how its operation might be questioned and perhaps altered. As Latour puts it, 'history changes quickly and . . . there is no greater intellectual crime than to address with the equipment of an older period the challenges of the present one' (2004: 231).

For example, although Sennett's overall account of 'cultural decline' has its problems, he makes an important set of points about the dynamics of what Richard Lanham called the 'centripetal gaze', and what Sennett calls the 'star system'. Sennett was referring to the tendency for public attention not just to concentrate on a selected elite in any area – his example is concert pianists – but to concentrate to such an extent that everyone below the level of celebrity or star risks disappearing from view altogether. Not only does adding a recognizable name to an enjoyable musical performance increase the audience, it becomes a necessary condition for there to be a viable audience at all. The result is a monopolization and centralization process a lot like state-formation; a large number of smaller units gradually reduce to a small number of very large units, where here the units are audiences and concert venues. Sennett describes how this worked in nineteenth-century Vienna:

> Between 1830 and 1870 the size of the average Vienna piano recital audience increased by 35 percent, often overcrowding the available halls, while the

number of piano concerts fell sharply. One estimate is that the proportion of musicians able to earn a living full-time by performing fell by half during these years . . . above all, public interest in music shifted to hearing those pianists who had more than Viennese reputations, who were international celebrities – and that usually meant that they had been heralded in Paris, London, and Berlin. The result was massive concert audiences, and fewer and fewer pianists at work.

(2002: 290)

The overall effect is to accentuate inequality, since celebrity by definition puts the majority of non-celebrities into the shade, and the attention paid to celebrities will tend to crowd out the attention able to be paid to the full range of 'performers' in any given field. The economics of attention becomes, as Sennett puts it, an all-or-nothing exercise, which is 'coupled to a sense that you aren't any good at all unless you are very special' (p. 291).

Sennett went on to apply this analysis to the realm of politics, and identified three principles at work in the celebritization of political life. He argued, first, that there is a shift from attending to the relationships between the political party and its membership to the promotion of a smaller number of highly visible political personalities – 'all the sponsors' efforts go into building a "product" which is distributable, a saleable candidate, rather than building and controlling the system of distribution itself, the party' (p. 292). Second, he highlighted the emergence of the question of 'overexposure', suggesting that the value of a political personality increases the more special and select their public appearances are. Third, he believed that politics also becomes a 'winner-takes-all' game, in which the attention focused on celebrity, 'personality' politicians detracts from the political influence of every other political actor. He concludes that charisma no longer attaches to 'titans or devils, neither Weber's ancient kings nor Freud's father subduing the unruly passions of his children'. Instead, it is 'the little man who is now the hero to other little men. He is a star; neatly packaged, underexposed, and so very straightforward about what he feels, he rules over a domain in which nothing much changes until it becomes an insoluble crisis' (pp. 292–3).

It is certainly true that the operation of the star system is problematic in a variety of ways, so that understanding the logic of celebrity can establish the value of at least some degree of resistance to the centripetal gaze. One can also choose to look away, to the side, or further afield, sometimes at least. But Sennett was also putting the argument too strongly and negatively, in that there are also a variety of countervailing tendencies – the question of public exposure, for example, is more a matter of how it is managed than simply its 'volume', as we can see today with exposure of high-profile political figures in the mass media and via the Internet. How political parties operate on the ground in relation to their potential constituencies remains as important as how their leading candidates perform in the public arenas, and the new social media have accentuated this aspect of political action, reinforcing the tendencies towards the plebiscitary character of contemporary politics (Pels 2011).

One can simply push the observation that society and politics have become increasingly subjected to a process of celebrification in directions other than Sennett's cultural pessimism, and reflect instead on what changes could be encouraged in the way celebrity is conceived and acted upon. Pels and others (van Zoonen 2005) have argued, for example, in favour of promoting a more informed and nuanced celebrity 'literacy', in which the operation of celebrity society is understood more clearly and related to in ways that link up with people's concerns and aspirations, instead of passively remaining at the mercy of celebrity rationality. As Pels argues, contrary to Sennett's dark vision of the corruption of politics by personality:

> The infiltration of the 'star system' into political culture does not constitute an absolute threat to democracy, but suggests new forms of political identification, citizenship, trust and representation. In contrast to the 'old' politics, the relation between political star and political fan revolves less around reasonable agreement and more around affective recognition of style and taste: around the impact of visual personalities who speak to the public imagination. Both the politics of stars and fan democracy thus imply a critique of the political rationalism of the prioritisation of a reasonable culture of democratic dialogue.
>
> (Pels 2011: 120)

Rather than fussing about whether it is a good or bad thing that relations between politician and citizen have become constituted along similar lines to the celebrity–fan relationship, the question for a critique of celebrity society becomes how that shift in the nature of political life can and should be approached, depending on what one's vision of democratic politics looks like (Corner & Pels 2003a).

Other analyses of contemporary democratic politics have attempted to pinpoint the specificity of contemporary modes of governance by developing the concept of 'cultural governance' (Bang 2004), in which increasing complexity is addressed by incorporating more mechanisms by which individuals develop self-reflexive autonomous identities, as a more workable alternative to hierarchical top-down forms of government and administration. Given the role that the cognitive orientation towards celebrities play in self-formation, this also suggests that the practice and dynamics of democratic politics in increasingly complex, globalizing societies is likely to continue to be closely bound up with particular form taken by celebrity.

When one looks closely at how celebrity society has evolved over time, the way in which celebrity configures inequality in particular ways also deserves closer scrutiny. A large part of the seductiveness of celebrity is the promise of a fast route to success, a means of circumventing the usual highly complex, often arduous but also unpredictable avenues to social advancement. In a 'risk society', it seems a good way to reduce risk as well as complexity, if only one can hit upon the right 'x-factor', much like the right Lotto number. When Michael Young wrote his satire *The Rise of the Meritocracy* (1959), his underlying argument was that the downsides of meritocracy included its legitimation of inequality, reducing large sections of the population to mere 'casualties of progress'. Anticipating Sennett's point, Young's narrator admits that 'Every selection of one is a rejection of many' (p. 12). Later his son, Toby Young (2008), reflected on how celebrity and the emergence of a 'celebritariat' relate to these arguments, suggesting that celebrity provides a means of smoothing over what Michael Young saw as the likely discontent among the majority of the population with meritocracy. Toby Young argued that celebrity can help secure popular support for the concept of a winner-takes-all society, because 'the entry requirements are so low'.

> If people believe there is a genuine chance they might be catapulted to the top, they're more likely to endorse a system in which success is so highly rewarded. To paraphrase the advertising slogan for the National Lottery, it could be them. As with the lottery, people may know that the actual chances of winning are low but the selection mechanism itself is fair – a level playing field. After that, their 'specialness' will take care of the rest.
>
> (2008)

In this sense the hero/celebrity distinction operates precisely to cement in place, entirely uncritically, the *appeal* of an unreflective relationship to the logic of celebrity society, because it suggests the possibility of overcoming complexity and risk in a relatively easy, albeit 'magical' way.

One of the more important useful aspects of thinking in terms of celebrity society as a particular type of rationality in the structuring and organization of social relations is that it makes it more possible to see how a celebrity logic can *migrate* across enormous social distances, appearing in places where one would not expect it, establishing connections between 'Paris Hilton' as a figure, social type or even social location, and interactions normally regarded as having a quite different quality. Robert Merton's original analysis of the Matthew effect was focused on the conduct of science and the practices of scientists, and the question of the celebrity dimensions of the knowledge-production process remain important. A central measure of scholarly 'value' is the citation index, that is, how much attention a scholar's work receives, or how much of a celebrity they are. This is why Georg Franck (1993, 1998, 1999) likes to use science as a key example of his arguments about celebrity as the accumulation and circulation of attention-capital, defining scientists as 'entrepreneurs who allocate time and effort so as to maximize the attention received from other scientists' (2002: 9). These tendencies have only been accentuated with the emergence of ranking systems and regimes of evaluation of university performance. The tendency in the process of academic appointments has been towards the organization of the discursive construction of the process around how 'exciting' the candidate is, and how impressed other parts of the university world – ideally the world beyond as well – will be that one has secured their services. In other words, how much of a scholarly celebrity they are is as much of a concern as how they actually perform.

The way in which this tendency has played itself out in different national higher education systems has varied over time. It probably first characterized the practices in elite US universities and spread in fits and starts from there around the world – but if the fact that a balance is being struck between these two questions remains implicit, there will always be the possibility that the former is in fact outweighing the latter. This has always been the critique of what is called 'post-modernity', the tendency towards representation becoming more important than what is being representing, the symbol taking over from the symbolized, or the imaginary from the real. Central to a critical approach to celebrity, then, is a sense of how different kinds of celebrity rationality play their particular role in all parts of social, political and economic life, and to identify the implications, analytical and practical, of their interconnections.

Just as the process of civilization can be seen as having a 'dark side' (van Krieken 1999), the same can be said about the celebritization process, leading at least to some degree of reserve about how celebrity society frames one's cognition and structures the process of self-formation. The power dynamics of synopticism and the logic of the 'viewer society' are important to highlight and analyse, at least to provide some conceptual resources for a more considered and critical relationship for the price one pays for being seduced by the centripetal gaze. It is worth taking more seriously than has been the case in both the scholarly and the public discussions of celebrity so far, the extent to which the dynamics of celeb-rity society produces a very particular kind of political regime, a specific mode of governance, but operating under the radar and escaping any degree of critical questioning and analysis. The task then becomes one of moving beyond observing that celebrity support is an important element of political mobilization, or that the conduct of politicians is required to conform to the same logic as that of celebri-ties, to identifying what impact these tendencies have, and how they relate to other aspects of structures of governance. The jury is still out on how the increasing 'personalization' of politics should be assessed and responded to, and engaging with this question is one of the central, still unfinished, tasks of the analysis of political celebrity.

The connections between the organization of our identity, conversations and perceptions around celebrity, to a greater or lesser extent, and other aspects of the ordering of social life, between techniques of the self and techniques of govern-ance with respect to celebrity, are worth examining and unravelling. Against the background of the increasing significance of self-branding (Sternberg 1998; Hearn 2008) in the post-Fordist 'new spirit of capitalism' (Boltanski & Chiapello 2006), the way in which self-formation modelled on celebrity figures has moved beyond mimicking clothing, gesture, character, movement and hairstyles to reshaping one's body through increasingly invasive cosmetic surgery (Elliott 2008, 2011) raises a number of questions about how exactly deeply into our souls as well as our bodies it is sensible to allow the cognitive orientation to celebrity to reach. In *Brave New World*, Aldous Huxley (1932) warned of the ways in which pleasure and desire can be mobilized to seduce people into subjection to particular power structures, and this is a concern that is worth taking seriously in relation to celebrity. The critics of the role of celebrity in relation to the public understanding of central issues of concern such as global warming, human rights, and world poverty and hunger, for example, emphasize how particular ways of thinking are pushed into the foreground, and others not given the consideration they deserve.

It is true that celebrity solves particular kinds of problems at a variety of levels – social and cultural coordination, shared cognition, a model or reference point for self-formation, a means of attracting attention – but this does not exclude the possibility of finding other ways of responding to those problems. It will always be a good idea to be at least a little reflective about exactly how celebrity society manufactures particular kinds of human beings, with specific ways of seeing and thinking about the world, just in case we might be, as Neil Postman (1985) once put it, amusing ourselves to death.

Notes

Introduction: understanding celebrity society

1 Joshua Gamson (1994) and Chris Rojek (2001) outline earlier discussions of the celebrification process. Jessica Evans (2005: 12) means something different: the process by which an individual becomes a celebrity.
2 The literature informing my account includes: Alberoni 1972; Elliott 1998; Evans 2005; Ferris 2007; Gabler 2001; Gamson 1994; Keller 1963, 1983; Kurzman et al. 2007; Marshall 1997; Mills 1957; Milner Jr 2005; Peters 1996; Rojek 2001, 2006; Turner 2004; Wenzel 2000.

1 From fame to celebrity: the celebritization of society

1 Himself, in a sense, a celebrity of the Anglican Reformation – there is a collective portrait of Jewel, Hugh Latimer, Sir Nicholas Bacon, Sir Francis Walsingham and William Cecil.
2 Jewel, Iohn (Bishoppe of Sarisburie), *A replie vnto M. Hardinges ansvveare by perusinge whereof the discrete, and diligent reader may easily see, the weake, and vnstable groundes of the Romaine religion, whiche of late hath beene accompted Catholique.* Imprinted at London: In Fleetestreate, at the signe of the Blacke Oliphante, by Henry VVykes, 1565, p. 114.
3 Bridges, John, *A defence of the gouernment established in the Church of Englande for ecclesiasticall matters.* London: Printed by Iohn VVindet [and T. Orwin], for Thomas Chard, 1587, p. 343.
4 *The Oxford English Dictionary* (2nd edn, 1989).
5 For France, see Giesen (1998) on the absolutist state's recruitment of an educated elite of civil servants and office holders as the 'new aristocracy'.
6 For a twenty-first-century observer, it's hard not to notice the parallel with the projection of the private sphere into public life in phenomena such as Big Brother, confessional television suchnas Dr Phil, Oprah Winfrey, or Judge Judy.
7 Revel (1997) provides a useful account of the mechanisms used in the court of Louis XIV to manage ranked distinctions and create new ones to suit the king's strategic purposes.
8 (1561) Plowden 223; (1562) 75 ER 339.
9 *Willion v. Berkley* (1561) Plowden 223 at 233a.
10 Similar positions are adopted by Dena Goodman (1989, 1992), Daniel Gordon (1989) and Roger Chartier (1991).
11 For example, in *The Second Shepherds' Play* (1500), the story concentrates on a comic character trying to hide a sheep he has stolen from the other shepherds on the night of the birth of Christ.
12 *Acte for the punishement of Vacabondes and for the Releif of the Poore & Impotent* (1572).

13 *An Act for the Encouragement of Learning, by vesting the Copies of Printed Books in the Authors or purchasers of such Copies, during the Times therein mentioned.*

2 Producing celebrity and the economics of attention

1 See the wonderful collection at: www.facesoftheconfederacy.com/art_carte_home. html.
2 Forbes Celebrity 100, available at: www.forbes.com/wealth/celebritieslist. Rankings result from a combination of earnings with web mentions on Google press clips compiled by LexisNexis; TV/radio mentions by Factiva; Twitter followers and Facebook fans; and number of times a celebrity's face appeared on the cover of 32 major consumer magazines. In practice, few top celebrities remain entirely confined to only one celebrity sector.
3 For analyses of the mechanics of academic celebrity, see Lamont (1987) and Clegg (1992).
4 www.portfolio.com/culture-lifestyle/culture-inc/arts/2008/01/14/Britney-Spears-Career-Analysis/.
5 www.forbes.com/2009/10/27/top-earning-dead-celebrities-list-dead-celebs-09-entertainment_land.html.
6 Merton later noted the various arguments that can be mounted about designating it the 'Matthew effect': Matthew probably did not write that Gospel, Mark and Luke probably said it first, if Jesus was being quoted, then one might as well call it the Jesus effect, and it was probably a folk saying in general circulation in any case, but he nonetheless stuck with Matthew (Merton 1988: 609). The parable is generally read as meaning 'the rich get richer and the poor get poorer', but in relation to the story itself, this is a misinterpretation, albeit one that the wording encourages. The parable runs as follows: three servants get differing amounts of money or 'talents' – one gets five, the other two, and the third only one. The first two put their money to good use and multiply it, but the third just buries it. When the master returns, he is pleased with the first two, but cross with the third for having made no effort. It is supposed to be more about the importance of attempting to make best productive use of one's resources, no matter what they are, and the misery likely to attend the failure to do so, even though one would have to be sceptical about the likelihood of the one-talent man ever being able to please his master. The story would have been more interesting, looked a little less like proto-capitalist ideology, and been more persuasive about its moral point if it had been the bloke with the five talents who made no effort and just sat on his wealth, and the servant with one who managed, with the help of micro-finance perhaps, to increase his holdings.

3 Celebrity as a social form: status, charisma and power

1 'The popularity of the term, it must be admitted, is due in a great part to Lucius Beebe, who started using it often in writing his weekly pillar in the *Herald Tribune* on cooking, drinking and the best place to buy mauve garters. . . . when, in 1938, Paramount Pictures set about making their epic called "Cafe Society," that organization paid $5,000 merely for the use of the title, but not to Maury Paul. They paid it to Lucius Beebe. This sent Maury into what amounted to a purple rage' (Brown 1947: 279). Elsa Maxwell defined cafe society as 'people who don't get invited to homes'.
2 *Haelan Laboratories v. Topps Chewing Gum*, 202 F. 2d 866 (2d Cir 1953).
3 Attorney-General v Guardian Newspapers Ltd (No 2) [1990] 1 AC 109 at 282, per Lord Goff of Chieveley.
4 Campbell v MGN [2004] 2 All ER 995 at 1010.
5 *Von Hannover* (2005) 40 EHRR 1 at 74.
6 Deutsche Welle 20.7.2006 – www.dw-world.de/dw/article/0,,2104577,00.html.

5 Celebrity in politics, diplomacy and development

1 Greg Sheridan, 'Politics of celebrity takes over', *The Australian*, 1 November 2008.
2 'The Garibaldi Panorama: Visualizing the Risorgimento': http://dl.lib.brown.edu/garibaldi/panorama.php.
3 www.mrlincolnswhitehouse.org/inside.asp?ID=210&subjectID=3.
4 www.anbhf.org/laureates/lasker.html. Many of the themes of the TV series *Mad Men* can be seen as reworkings of elements of Lasker's career in advertising, being the first to employ copy writers on a regular basis for advertising campaigns, beginning with John E. Kennedy. The model for the Don Draper character is meant to be Rosser Reeves (1910–1984), but the character also draws on Lasker and his second hire in 1908, Charles C. Hopkins, who came up with 'It's toasted' for Lucky Strike in 1917.
5 *We need a man to guide us, Who'll always stand beside us, One who is a fighter through and through, A man who'll make the White House, Shine out just like a lighthouse, And Mister Harding, we've selected you. Harding, lead the G.O.P. Harding, on to Victory! We're here to make a fuss! Mister Harding, you're the man for us! We know we'll always find him, With Coolidge right behind him, And Coolidge never fails, you must agree, We know he will be guarding, The Nation just like Harding, When they are both in Washington, D.C. Harding, Coolidge is your mate, Harding, lead the ship of state, You'll get the people's vote, And you'll also get the Donkey's goat!*
6 Bernays was in turn influenced by Gabriel Tarde's (1890) *Laws of Imitation*, Gustave Le Bon's (1897) *The Crowd: A Study of the Popular Mind, and* Wilfred Trotter's (1921) *Instincts of the Herd in Peace and War*. He also has the distinction of inspiring Joseph Goebbels, and selling the 1954 military coup in Guatemala to the Eisenhower administration and the American public (Tye 1998).
7 Again Jolson had a song: *The race is now begun, and Coolidge is the one, the one to fill the Presidential chair. Without a lot of fuss, he did a lot for us, So let's reciprocate and keep him there! Keep Coolidge! Keep Coolidge! And have no fears for four more years! Keep Coolidge! Keep Coolidge! For he will right our wrongs. He's never asleep, still water runs deep. So keep Coolidge! Keep Coolidge! He's right where he belongs!* Coolidge did not sing along. http://kaiology.wordpress.com/2010/09/29/breakfast-with-president-coolidge/.
8 The culmination of the development towards publicity and celebrity for its own sake was the murder of a California school superintendent, the kidnapping of publishing heiress Patty Hearst, and a bank robbery by the 'Symbionese Liberation Army', a group with no constituency at all and no political programme or ideology to speak of (Gitlin 1980: 176).
9 www.audrey1.org/biography/21/audrey-hepburn-unicef-overview.
10 www.un.org/apps/news/story.asp?newsid=3960&cr=&cr1.
11 Under the provisions of Chapter 96 of the Texas Civil Practice and Remedies Code 'False Disparagement of Perishable Food Products', a person is liable if: '(1) The person disseminates in any manner information relating to a perishable food product to the public; (2) the person knows the information is false; and (3) the information states or implies that the perishable food product is not safe for consumption by the public.' In determining whether the information is false, 'the trier of fact shall consider whether the information was based on reasonable and reliable scientific inquiry, facts, or data' (www.cspinet.org/foodspeak/laws/states/texas.htm).

7 Celebrity's futures: 15 minutes of fame, or fame in 15 minutes

1 www.istanbul.tc/mahir/mahir/.
2 But not if it isn't – Ghyslian Raza, the 'Star Wars kid', now a law student in Montreal, was one of the earliest Internet crazes, with more than 900 million views in 2006, but

the video had been posted by classmates at his school without this knowledge, and the ridicule merely made him depressed – his parents sued the families of the classmates who released the video, reportedly settling out of court.

3 www.therichest.org/celebnetworth/celeb/singer/rebecca-black-net-worth/.
4 www.youtube.com/watch?v=-dOlqZSdeyY.
5 www.hollywoodreporter.com/news/simon-cowell-rebecca-black-is-169331.
6 www.stephenfry.com/misc/contacts/.
7 http://twitaholic.com/.

Bibliography

Abercrombie, Nicholas, & Longhurst, Brian (1998) *Audiences: A Sociological Theory of Performance and Imagination*. London: Sage.

Abril, Patricia Sánchez (2011) 'The evolution of business celebrity in American law and society', *American Business Law Journal*, 48(2): 177–225.

Adair-Toteff, Christopher (2005) 'Max Weber's charisma', *Journal of Classical Sociology*, 5(2): 189–204.

Adams, John (1805) *Discourses on Davila: a series of papers on political history* (NY: De Capo Press, 1973 edn). Boston: Russell & Cutler.

Adams-Price, C., & Greene, A.L. (1990) 'Secondary attachments and adolescent self-concept', *Sex Roles*, 22(3/4): 187–198.

Adler, Patricia A., & Adler, Peter (1969) 'The gloried self: the aggrandisement and the construction of self', *Social Psychology Quarterly*, 52(4): 299–310.

Adonis, Andrew, & Pollard, Stephen (1997) *A Class Act: The Myth of Britain's Classless Society*. London: Penguin.

Adorno, Theodor W., & Horkheimer, Max (1979 [1944]) *Dialectic of Enlightenment*. London: Verso.

Agrawal, Jagdish, & Kamakura, Wagner A. (1995) 'The economic worth of celebrity endorsers: an event study analysis', *Journal of Marketing*, 59(3): 56–62.

Alberoni, Francesco (1972) 'The powerless "elite": theory and sociological research on the phenomenon of the stars', in D. McQuail (ed.), *Sociology of Mass Communications*. Harmondsworth: Penguin. pp. 75–98.

Alexander, Jeffrey (2010a) 'The celebrity-icon', *Cultural Sociology*, 4(3): 323–336.

—— (2010b) 'Barack Obama meets celebrity metaphor', *Society*, 47(5): 410–418.

Allen, Katie (2010) 'From crematorium to cashpoint: the delebs who carry on earning from beyond the grave', *The Guardian*, 29 October.

Allen, Woody (Director and writer) (1998) *Celebrity* (Film). (Sweetland Films & Magnolia Productions).

Allen-Mills, T. (2008) 'Sarah Palin's failure set to reap her $7m book deal'. *Sunday Times*, 16 November.

Alperstein, Neil M. (1991) 'Imaginary social relationships with celebrities appearing in television commercials', *Journal of Broadcasting & Electronic Media*, 35(1): 43–58.

Altimore, M. (1999) ' "Gentleman athlete": Joe DiMaggio and the celebration and submergence of ethnicity', *International Review for the Sociology of Sport*, 3(4): 359–368.

Amos, Amanda, & Haglund, Margaretha (2000) 'From social taboo to "Torch of Freedom": the marketing of cigarettes to women', *Tobacco Control*, 9(1): 3–8.

Anderson, Benedict R. O'G. (1983) *Imagined Communities: Reflections on the Origin and Spread of Nationalism*. London: Verso.

—— (1992) *Long-Distance Nationalism: World Capitalism and the Rise of Identity Politics*. Amsterdam: Centre for Asian Studies Amsterdam.

Anderson, Joel (1995) 'Translator's introduction', in A. Honneth (ed.), *The Struggle for Recognition: The Moral Grammer of Social Conflicts*. Cambridge: Polity. pp. x–xxi.

Andrews, David L., & Jackson, Steven J. (2001) 'Sport celebrities, public culture, and private experience', in D.L. Andrews & S.J. Jackson (eds), *Sport Stars: the Cultural Politics of Sporting Celebrity*. London: Routledge. p. 6.

—— (eds) (2001) *Sport Stars: the Cultural Politics of Sporting Celebrity*. London: Routledge.

Anker, Kirsten J. (2002) 'Possessing star qualities: celebrity identity as property', *Griffith Law Review*, 11(1): 147–168.

Archer, Ian W. (2008) 'City and court connected: the material dimensions of royal ceremonial, ca. 1480–1625', *Huntington Library Quarterly*, 71(1): 157–179.

Armstrong, Nancy (2001) 'Monarchy in the age of mechanical reproduction', *Nineteenth-Century Contexts*, 22(4): 495–536.

Asch, Ronald G. (1991) 'Court and household from the fifteenth to the seventeenth centuries', in R.G. Asch & A.M. Birke (eds), *Princes, Patronage, and the Nobility: the Court at the beginning of the Modern Age, c.1450–1650*. Oxford: Oxford University Press.

—— (2003) *Nobilities in Transition, 1550–1700: Courtiers and Rebels in Britain and Europe*. London: Arnold.

Asch, Ronald G., & Birke, Adolf M. (eds) (1991) *Princes, Patronage, and the Nobility: the Court at the beginning of the Modern Age, c.1450–1650*. Oxford: Oxford University Press.

Aston, Margaret (1968) *The Fifteenth Century: the Prospect of Europe*. London: Thames & Hudson.

Auchter, Dorothy (2001) *Dictionary of Literary and Dramatic Censorship in Tudor and Stuart England*. Westport, Conn.: Greenwood Press.

Bagehot, Walter (1867) *The English Constitution*. London: Chapman & Hall.

Bang, Henrik P. (2004) 'Culture governance: governing self-reflexive modernity', *Public Administration*, 82(1): 157–190.

—— (2009) ' "Yes we can": Identity politics and project politics for the later-modern world', *Urban Research & Practice*, 2(2): 1–21.

Barme, Geremie R. (1999) 'UniversityCCPTM and ADCULT PRC', *The China Journal*, 41: 1–23.

Barrell, John (2000) *Imagining the King's Death: Figurative Treason, Fantasies of Regicide 1793–1796*. Oxford: Oxford University Press.

Barro, Robert J., McCleary, Rachel M., & McQuoid, Alexander (2010) 'Economics of Sainthood (a preliminary investigation)'. Online: www.economics.harvard.edu/faculty/barro/files/Saints%2Bpaper%2B020910.pdf.

Barron, Lee (2009) 'An actress compelled to act: Angelina Jolie's Notes from My Travels as celebrity activist/travel narrative', *Postcolonial Studies*, 12(2): 211–228.

Barry, Elizabeth (2008a) 'Celebrity, cultural production and public life', *International Journal of Cultural Studies*, 11(3): 251–258.

—— (2008b) 'From epitaph to obituary: death and celebrity in eighteenth-century British culture', *International Journal of Cultural Studies*, 11(3): 259–275.

Bartholomew, Richard (2006) 'Publishing, celebrity, and the globalisation of conservative Protestantism', *Journal of Contemporary Religion*, 21(1): 1–13.

Bartlett, Robert (1999) 'Cults of Irish, Scottish and Welsh saints in twelfth-century England', in B. Smith (ed.), *Britain and Ireland 900–1300: Insular Responses to Medieval European Change*. Cambridge: Cambridge University Press. pp. 67–86.

Baudrillard, Jean (1983) *Simulation*. New York: Semiotext(e).

—— (1988) *Jean Baudrillard, Selected Writings, ed. Mark Poster* (Mark Poster ed.). Stanford: Stanford University Press.

Bauman, Zygmunt (2005) *Liquid Life*. Cambridge: Polity.

Baumeister, Roy F., Zhang, Liqing, & Vohs, Kathleen D. (2004) 'Gossip as cultural learning', *Review of General Psychology*, 8(2): 111–121.

Beer, David, & Penfold-Mounce, Ruth (2009) 'Celebrity gossip and the new melodramatic imagination', *Sociological Research Online*, 14(2).

—— (2011) 'Researching glossy topics: the case of the academic study of celebrity', *Celebrity Studies*, 1(3): 360–365.

Bell, Daniel (1972) 'On meritocracy and equality', *The Public Interest*, 29: 29–68.

Bellany, Alastair (2008) 'The murder of John Lambe: crowd violence, court scandal and popular politics in early seventeenth-century England', *Past & Present*, 200: 37–76.

Beller, Jonathan (2006) *The Cinematic Mode of Production: Attention Economy and the Society of the Spectacle*. Hanover, NH: Dartmouth College Press.

Benedictus, Leo. (2011) 'From Stephen Fry to Hugh Grant: the rise of the celebrity activist', *The Guardian*, 16 April.

Benezra, Karen, & Gilbert, Jennifer (2002) 'The CEO as brand: their names are synonymous with their companies' products – and that presents a slew of unique challenges'. Online: www.allbusiness.com/business-planning-structures/business-structures/105010-1.html.

Beniger, James R. (1987) 'Personalization of mass media and the growth of pseudo-community', *Communication Research*, 14(3): 352–371.

Bennett, Tony (1988) 'The exhibtionary complex', *New Formations*, 4: 73–102.

Benson, John (2009) 'Calculation, celebrity and scandal: the provincial press in Edwardian England', *Journalism Studies*, 10(6): 837–850.

Berenson, E. & Giloi, E. (eds) (2010) *Constructing Charisma: Celebrity, Fame, and Power in Nineteenth-Century Europe*. New York: Berghahn.

Berlanstein, Lenard R. (2004) 'Historicizing and gendering celebrity culture: famous women in nineteenth-century France', *Journal of Womens History*, 16(4): 65–91.

Bernays, Edward L. (1928) 'Manipulating public opinion: the why and the how', *American Journal of Sociology*, 33(6): 958–971.

—— (1947) 'The engineering of consent', *The ANNALS of the American Academy of Political & Social Science*, 250(1): 113–120.

—— (1971) 'Emergence of the public relations counsel: principles and recollections', *Business History Review*, 45(3): 296–316.

Bird, S. Elisabeth (1992) *For Enquiring Minds: A Cultural Study of Supermarket Tabloids*. Knoxville: University of Tennessee Press.

Biressi, Anita, & Nunn, Heather (2004) 'The especially remarkable: celebrity and social mobility in Reality TV', *Mediactive*, 2: 44–58.

Blake, David Haven (2006) *Walt Whitman and the Culture of American Celebrity*. New Haven: Yale University Press.

Böhme-Dürr, Karin (2001) 'Die Währung "Aufmerksamkeit" ', in K. Böhme-Dürr & T. Sudholt (eds), *Hundert Tage Aufmerksamkeit: Das Zusammenspiel von Medien,*

Menschen und Märkten bei 'Big Brother'. Konstanz: Universitätsverlag Konstanz. pp. 11–33.

Boje, David M., & Rhodes, Carl (2005) 'The virtual leader construct: the mass mediatization and simulation of transformational leadership', *Leadership*, 1(4): 407–428.

Bolognani, Marta (2011) 'Star fission: Shoaib Akhtar and fragmentation as transnational celebrity strategy', *Celebrity Studies*, 2(1): 31–43.

Boltanski, Luc (1999) *Distant Suffering: Morality, Media and Politics*. Cambridge: Cambridge University Press.

Boltanski, Luc, & Chiapello, Ève (2006) *The New Spirit of Capitalism*. London: Verso.

Boltanski, Luc, & Thevenot, Laurent (2006) *On Justification: Economies of Worth*. Princeton: Princeton University Press.

Boorstin, Daniel J. (1962) *The Image, or What Happened to the American Dream*. Harmondsworth: Penguin.

Bourdieu, Pierre (1984) *Distinction: A Social Critique of the Judgement of Taste*. London: Routledge & Kegan Paul.

—— (1987) 'Legitimation and structured interests in Weber's sociology of religion', in S. Lash & S. Whimster (eds), *Marx Weber: Rationality and Modernity*. London: Allen & Unwin. pp. 119–136.

Boykoff, Max, Goodman, Mike, & Littler, Jo (2010) *'Charismatic megafauna': the growing power of celebrities and pop culture in climate change campaigns*. London: Dept of Geography, University College London.

Boykoff, Maxwell T., & Goodman, Michael K. (2009) 'Conspicuous redemption? Reflections on the promise and perils of the "celebretization" of climate change', *Geoforum*, 40(3): 395–406.

Boyle, Ellexis (2010) 'The intertextual terminator: the role of film in branding "Arnold Schwarzenegger" ', *Journal of Communication Inquiry*, 34(1): 42–60.

Boyle, Raymond, & Kelly, Lisa W. (2010) 'The celebrity entrepreneur on television: profile, politics and power', *Celebrity Studies*, 1(3): 334–350.

Boyt, Susie (2008) *My Judy Garland Life*. London: Virago.

Braudy, Leo (1986) *The Frenzy of Renown: Fame and its History*. New York: Oxford University Press.

—— (2010) 'Secular anointings: fame, celebrity, and charisma in the first century of mass culture', in E. Berenson & E. Giloi (eds), *Constructing Charisma: Celebrity, Fame, and Power in Nineteenth-Century Europe*. New York: Berghahn. pp. 165–182.

Breese, Elizabeth Butler (2010a) 'Meaning, celebrity, and the underage pregnancy of Jamie Lynn Spears', *Cultural Sociology*, 4(3): 337–355.

—— (2010b) 'Reports from "Backstage" in Entertainment News', *Society*, 47(5): 396–402.

Briggs, Peter M. (1991) 'Laurence Sterne and literary celebrity in 1760', *The Age of Johnson*, 4: 251–273.

Brigham, John, & Meyers, Jill (2005) 'Celebrity as authority in law', *Contemporary Issues in the Semiotics of Law*: 95–113.

Brock, Claire (2006) *The Feminization of Fame, 1750–1830*. New York: Palgrave Macmillan.

Brockington, Dan (2008) 'Powerful environmentalisms: conservation, celebrity and captialism', *Media, Culture & Society*, 30(4): 551–568.

Brody, E.W. (2001) 'The "attention" economy', *Public Relations Quarterly*, 46(3): 18–21.

Brookhiser, Richard (1998) 'Celebrity conquers America', *American Heritage Magazine*, 49(4).

Brown, Eve (1947) *Champagne Cholly: The Life and Times of Maury Paul*. New York: E.P. Dutton & Company.

Brown, Gregory (2002) 'Social encounters and self-image in the Age of Enlightenment: Norbert Elias in eighteenth-century French cultural historiography', *Journal of Early Modern History*, 6(1): 24–51.

Brown, Peter (1981) *The Cult of the Saints: its Rise and Function in Latin Christianity*. Chicago: University of Chicago Press.

—— (1983) 'The saint as exemplar in late antiquity', *Representations*, 2: 1–28.

Browne, Janet (2003) 'Charles Darwin as a celebrity', *Science in Context*, 16(1–2): 175–194.

Burckhardt, Jacob (2004 [1860]) *The Civilization of the Renaissance in Italy*. Harmondsworth: Penguin.

Burke, Kenneth (1941 [1938]) 'Literature as equipment for living', in *Philosophy of Literary Form: Studies in Symbolic Action*. Baton Rouge: Louisiana State University Press. pp. 293–304.

Burke, Peter (1992) *The Fabrication of Louis XIV*. New Haven: Yale University Press.

—— (1997) 'Representations of the self from Petrarch to Descartes', in R. Porter (ed.), *Rewriting the Self: Histories from the Renaissance to the Present*. London: Routledge. pp. 17–28.

Butterfield, L. (1950) 'B. Franklin's Epitaph', *New Colophon*, 3: 9–39.

Callinan, Ian (2007) 'Privacy, confidence, celebrity and spectacle', *Oxford University Commonwealth Law Journal*, 7(1): 1–22.

Camic, Charles (1980) 'Charisma: its varieties, preconditions and consequences', *Sociological Inquiry*, 50(1): 5–23.

Carlson, Peter (2009) 'P.T. Barnum Meets Queen Victoria', *American History*, 44(1): 24–25.

Carroll, John (2010) 'The tragicomedy of celebrity', *Society*, 47(6): 489–492.

Carsch, Henry (1968) 'The protestant ethic and the popular idol in America. A case study', *Social Compass*, 15(1): 45–69.

Cashmore, Ellis (2008) 'Tiger Woods and the New Racial Order', *Current Sociology*, 56(4): 621–634.

Cashmore, Ernest Ellis (2002) *Beckham*. Cambridge: Polity.

—— (2006) *Celebrity/Culture*. Abingdon: Routledge.

Cassirer, Ernst (1963[1927]) *The Individual and the Cosmos in Renaissance Philosophy*. New York: Barnes & Noble.

Cathcart, Robert S. (1994) 'From hero to celebrity: the media connection', in S.J. Drucker & R.S. Cathcart (eds), *American Heroes in a Media Age*. Cresskill, NJ: Hampton Press. pp. 36–48.

Caudill, D. (2004) 'Once more into the breach: contrasting US and Australian rights of publicity', *Media & Arts Law Review*, 9: 263.

Caughey, John L. (1978) 'Artificial social relations in modern America', *American Quarterly*, 30(1): 70–89.

—— (1984) *Imaginary Social Worlds: A Cultural Approach*. Lincoln: University of Nebraska Press.

—— (1988) 'Masking the self: fictional identities and the construction of self in adolescence', *Adolescent Psychiatry*, 14: 319–322.

Chaney, David (1995) 'The spectacle of honour: the changing dramatization of status', *Theory, Culture & Society*, 12(3): 147–167.

Chartier, Roger (1989) 'The practical impact of writing', in R. Chartier (ed.), *A History of Private Life, Vol. III: Passions of the Renaissance*. Cambridge, Mass.: Harvard University Press. pp. 111–159.

—— (1991) *The Cultural Origins of the French Revolution, trans. Lydia G. Cochrane.* Durham, NC: Duke University Press.

Chaussinand-Nogaret, Guy (1985) *The French Nobility in the Eighteenth Century: From Feudalism to Enlightenment.* Cambridge: Cambridge University Press.

Chen, Chao C., & Meindl, James R. (1991) 'The construction of leadership images in the popular press: the case of Donald Burr and People Express', *Administrative Science Quarterly*, 36(4): 521–555.

Chenu, Alain (2010) 'From paths of glory to celebrity boulevards: sociology of *Paris match* covers, 1949–2005', *Revue française de sociologie*, 51(5).

Cherry, Mark, & Wajnryb, Ruth (2004) 'Celebrating "selfebrity" ', *Griffith Review*, 5: 29–35.

Chin, Bertha, & Hills, Matt (2008) 'Restricted confessions? Blogging, subcultural celebrity and the management of producer-fan proximity', *Social Semiotics*, 18(2): 253–272.

Clark, C. Robert, Clark, Samuel, & Polborn, Mattias K. (2006) 'Coordination and status influence', *Rationality & Society*, 18(3): 367–391.

Clark, Timothy, & Salaman, Graeme (1998) 'Telling tales: management gurus' narratives and the construction of managerial identity', *Journal of Management Studies*, 35(2): 137–161.

Clarke, Robert (ed.) (2009a) *Celebrity Colonialism: Fame, Power and Representation in Colonial and Postcolonial Cultures.* Newcastle: Cambridge Scholars Publishing.

—— (2009b) 'Star traveller: celebrity, Aboriginality and Bruce Chatwin's The Songlines', *Postcolonial Studies*, 12(2): 229–246.

—— (2009c) 'Travel and celebrity culture: an introduction', *Postcolonial Studies*, 12(2): 145–152.

Clayton, Tim (2005) ' "Figures of Fame": Reynolds and the printed image', in M. Postle (ed.), *Joshua Reynolds: The Creation of Celebrity*. London: Tate Publishing. pp. 49–59.

Clegg, Stewart (1992) 'How to become an internationally famous British social theorist', *Sociological Review*, 40(3): 576–598.

Clegg, Stewart R. (2005) 'Puritans, visionaries, and Survivors', *Organization Studies*, 26(4): 527–546.

Clegg, Stewart R., & van Iterson, Ad (2009) 'Dishing the dirt: gossiping in organizations', *Culture & Organization*, 15(3/4): 275–289.

Cogswell, Thomas (2004) ' "Published by authoritie": newsbooks and the Duke of Buckingham's EXpedition to the Île de Ré', *Huntington Library Quarterly*, 67(1): 1–25.

Cohen, Jonathan (2006) 'Audience identification with media characters', in J. Bryant & P. Vorderer (eds), *Psychology of Entertainment*: Lawrence Erlbaum Associates. pp. 183–197.

Cole, C.J., & Hribar, A.S. (1995) 'Celebrity feminism – *Nike Style* – post-Fordism, transcendence, and consumer power', *Sociology of Sport Journal*, 12(4): 347–369.

Collins, Sue (2008) 'Making the most out of 15 minutes: reality TV's dispensable celebrity', *Television & New Media*, 9(2): 87–110.

Connell, Ian (1992) 'Personalities in the popular media', in P. Dahlgren & C. Sparks (eds), *Journalism and Popular Culture*. London: Sage. pp. 64–83.

Coombe, Rosemary J. (1992a) 'Publicity rights and political aspiration: mass culture, gender identity, and democracy', *New England Law Review*, 26(4): 1221–1280.

—— (1992b) 'The celebrity image and cultural identity: publicity rights and the subaltern politics of gender', *Discourse*, 14: 59–88.

Cooper, Andrew F. (2008) 'Beyond one image fits all: Bono and the complexity of celebrity diplomacy', *Global Governance*, 14(3): 265–272.

—— (2008) *Celebrity Diplomacy*. Boulder: Paradigm Publishers.

Corner, John (2003) 'Mediated persona and political culture', in J. Corner & D. Pels (eds), *Media and the Restyling of Politics: Consumerism, Celebrity and Cynicism*. London: Sage. pp. 67–84.

Corner, John, & Pels, Dick (eds) (2003a) *Media and the Restyling of Politics: Consumerism, Celebrity and Cynicism*. London: Sage.

—— (2003b) 'The re-styling of politics', in J. Corner & D. Pels (eds), *Media and the Restyling of Politics: Consumerism, Celebrity and Cynicism*. London: Sage. pp. 1–18.

Corrigan, Philip, & Sayer, Derek (1985) *The Great Arch: English State Formation as Cultural Revolution*. Oxford: Basil Blackwell.

Couldry, Nick (2001) 'The umbrella man: crossing a landscape of speech and silence', *European Journal of Cultural Studies*, 4(2): 131–152.

—— (2003) 'Media meta-capital: extending the range of Bourdieu's field theory', *Theory & Society*, 32(5–6): 653–677.

—— (2008) 'Reality TV or the Secret Theatre of Neoliberalism', *The Review of Education, Pedagogy, & Cultural Studies*, 30: 3–13.

—— (2010) *Why Voice Matters: Culture and Politics after Neoliberalism*. London: Sage.

Couldry, Nick, & Markham, Tim (2007) 'Celebrity culture and public connection: Bridge or chasm?', *International Journal of Cultural Studies*, 10(4): 403–421.

Cowen, Tyler (2000) *What Price Fame?* Cambridge, Mass.: Harvard University Press.

Cross, Steve, & Littler, Jo (2010) 'Celebrity and *Schadenfreude*', *Cultural Studies*, 24(3): 395–417.

Cruikshank, Jeffrey L., & Schultz, Arthur W. (2010) *The Man who Sold America: The Amazing (but True!) Story of Albert D. Lasker and the Creation of the Advertising Century*. Cambridge, Mass.: Harvard Business Press.

Davenport, T., & Beck, J. (2002) 'The strategy and structure of firms in the attention economy', *Ivey Business Journal*, 66(4): 49–55.

Davenport, Thomas H., & Beck, John C. (2000) 'Getting the attention you need', *Harvard Business Review*, 78(5): 118–126.

—— (2001) *The Attention Economy: Understanding the New Currency of Business*. Cambridge, Mass.: Harvard Business School Press.

Davies, David J. (2011) 'China's celebrity entrepreneurs: business models of "success" ', in L. Edwards & E. Jeffreys (eds), *Celebrity in China*. Hong Kong: Hong Kong University Press. pp. 193–216.

Davis, E. Philip, & Steil, Benn (2001) *Institutional Investors*. Cambridge, Mass.: MIT Press.

Davis, Lennard J. (2009). 'In academe, once a star, always a star', *The Chronicle of Higher Education*, 26 June.

Davis, Natalie Zemon (1983) *The Return of Martin Guerre*. Cambridge, Mass.: Harvard University Press.

De Backer, Charlotte J.S., Nelissen, Mark, Vyncke, Patrick, Braeckman, Johan, & McAndrew, Francis T. (2007) 'Celebrities: from teachers to friends – a test of two hypotheses on the adaptiveness of celebrity gossip', *Human Nature*, 18(4): 334–354.

De Carvalho, Mário Vieira (1995) 'From opera to "soap opera": on civilizing processes, the dialectic of Enlightenment and Postmodernity', *Theory, Culture & Society*, 12(2): 41–61.

de Swaan, Abram (1999 [1969]) 'Waarom roem?', in J. Heilbron & G. de Vries (eds), *De draagbare De Swaan*. Amsterdam: Prometheus. pp. 252–254.

Debord, Guy (1994) *Society of the Spectacle*. New York: Zone Books.

deCordova, Richard (2007) 'The emergence of the star system in America', in S. Redmond & S. Holmes (eds), *Stardom and Celebrity: A Reader*. London: Sage. pp. 132–140.

Deleuze, Gilles (1983) 'Plato and the simulacrum', *October*, 27: 45–56.

Denner, Michael (2009) ' "Be not afraid of greatness . . .": Leo Tolstoy and celebrity', *Journal of Popular Culture*, 42(4): 614–645.

Derrick, Jaye L., Gabriel, Shira, & Tippin, Brooke (2008) 'Parasocial relationships and self-discrepancies: faux relationships have benefits for low self-esteem individuals', *Personal Relationships*, 15(2): 261–280.

Deuchar, Stephen, & Buzzoni, Andrea (2005) 'Foreword', in M. Postle (ed.), *Joshua Reynolds: The Creation of Celebrity*. London: Tate Publishing. p. 9.

Dewald, Jonathan (2008) 'Crisis, chronology, and the shape of European social history', *American Historical Review*, 113(4): 1031–1052.

Dickens, Arthur Geoffrey (1966) *Reformation and Society in Sixteenth-century Europe*. London: Thames and Hudson.

Dickinson, Kay (2004) 'Pop stars who can't act: The limits of celebrity "multi-tasking" ', *Mediactive*, 2: 74–85.

Dieter, H., & Kumar, R. (2008) 'The downside of celebrity diplomacy: the neglected complexity of development', *Global Governance*, 14(3): 259–264.

Dietz, P., Matthews, D., van Duyne, C., Martell, D., Parry, C., Stewart, T., et al. (1991) 'Threatening and otherwise inappropriate letters to Hollywood celebrities', *Journal of Forensic Sciences*, 36(1): 185–209.

DiFonzo, N., & Bordia, P. (2007) *Rumor Psychology: Social and Organizational Approaches*. Washington, DC: American Psychological Association.

Dolar, Mladen (2008) 'Freud and the political', *Unbound*, 4: 15–29.

Doyle, Judith (2000) *New Community or New Slavery? The Emotional Division of Labour*. London: Industrial Society.

Drake, Philip, & Miah, Andy (2010) 'The cultural politics of celebrity', *Cultural Politics: An International Journal*, 6(1): 49–64.

Drucker, Susan J. (1994) 'The mediated sports hero', in S.J. Drucker & R.S. Cathcart (eds), *American Heroes in a Media Age*. Cresskill, NJ: Hampton Press. pp. 82–93.

Drucker, Susan J., & Cathcart, Robert S. (1994a) 'The celebrity and the fan: a media relationship', in S.J. Drucker & R.S. Cathcart (eds), *American Heroes in a Media Age*. Cresskill, NJ: Hampton Press. pp. 260–269.

—— (1994b) 'The hero as a communication phenomenon', in S.J. Drucker & R.S. Cathcart (eds), *American Heroes in a Media Age*. Cresskill, NJ: Hampton Press. pp. 1–11.

du Gay, Paul (1996a) *Consumption and Identity at Work*. London: Sage.

—— (1996b) 'Organizing identity: entrepreneurial governance and public management', in S. Hall & P. du Gay (eds), *Questions of Cultural Identity*. London: Sage. pp. 151–169.

du Gay, Paul, & Salaman, Graeme (1996) 'The conduct of management and the management of conduct', *Journal of Management Studies*, 33(3): 263–283.

Dugdale, Timothy (2000) 'The fan and (auto)biography: writing the self in the stars', *Journal of Mundane Behavior*, 1(2).

Duindam, Jeroen (1994) *Myths of Power: Norbert Elias and the Early Modern European Court*. Amsterdam: Amsterdam University Press.

Dyer, Richard (1979) *Stars*. London: BFI Publishing.

—— (1987) *Heavenly Bodies: Film Stars and Society*. Houndmills: Macmillan.

Edwards, Louise (2011) 'Military celebrity in China: the evolution of "heroic and model servicemen" ', in L. Edwards & E. Jeffreys (eds), *Celebrity in China*. Hong Kong: Hong Kong University Press. pp. 21–43.

Eggins, Suzanne, & Slade, Diane (1997) *Analyzing Casual Conversation*. London: Cassell.

Ehrenreich, Barbara, Hess, Elizabeth, & Jacobs, Gloria (1992) 'Beatlemania: girls just want to have fun', in L.A. Lewis (ed.), *The Adoring Audience: Fan Culture and Popular Media*. London: Routledge. pp. 84–106.

Eisenstein, Elizabeth L. (1968) 'Some conjectures about the impact of printing on Western society and thought: a preliminary report', *Journal of Modern History*, 40(1): 1–56.

—— (1969) 'The advent of printing and the problem of the Renaissance', *Past & Present*, 45: 19–89.

—— (1979) *The Printing Press as an Agent of Change: Communications and Cultural Transformations in Early Modern Europe*. Cambridge: Cambridge University Press.

—— (2002) 'An unacknowledged revolution revisited', *American Historical Review*, 107(1): 87–105.

—— (2005 [1983]) *The Printing Revolution in Early Modern Europe* (2nd edn). Cambridge: Cambridge University Press.

Elias, Norbert (2000) *The Civilizing Process: Sociogenetic and Psychogenetic Investigations* (revised edn). Oxford: Blackwell.

—— (2006) *The Court Society. The Collected Works of Norbert Elias, Vol. 2. Edited by Stephen Mennell*. Dublin: UCD Press.

Elliott, Anthony (1998) 'Celebrity and political psychology: remembering Lennon', *Political Psychology*, 19(4): 833–852.

—— (1999) *The Mourning of John Lennon*. Berkeley: University of California Press.

—— (2008) *Making the Cut: How Cosmetic Surgery is Transforming our Lives*. London: Reakton.

—— (2011) ' "I want to look like that!": Cosmetic surgery and celebrity culture', *Cultural Sociology*, 5(4): 463–477.

Eltis, Sos (2005) 'Private lives and public spaces: reputation, celebrity and the late Victorian actress', in M. Luckhurst & J. Moody (eds), *Theatre and Celebrity in Britain, 1660–2000*. Basingstoke: Palgrave Macmillan. pp. 169–188.

Emerson, Ralph Waldo (19– [1848]) *English Traits*. Hoboken, NJ: BiblioBytes.

Emler, N. (1994) 'Gossip, reputation, and social adaptation', in R.F. Goodman & A. Ben-Ze'ev (eds), *Good Gossip*. Lawrence: University Press of Kansas. pp. 117–138.

Epstein, Joseph (2005) 'Celebrity culture', *Hedgehog Review*, 7(1): 7–20.

Erasmus, Desiderius (1516) *The Education of a Christian Prince*. Translated by Lester K. Born [*c*.1936]. New York: Octagon Books, 1963.

Evans, Jessica (2005) 'Celebrity, media and history', in J. Evans & D. Hesmondhalgh (eds), *Understanding Media: Inside Celebrity*. Maidenhead: Open University Press. pp. 11–55.

—— (2009) ' "As if" intimacy? Mediated persona, politics and gender', in S. Day-Schlater, D. Jones W., H. Price & C. Yates (eds), *Emotion: New Psychosocial Perspectives*. Basingstoke: Palgrave. pp. 72–84.

Evans, Jessica, & Hesmondhalgh, David (eds) (2005) *Understanding Media: Inside Celebrity*. Maidenhead: Open University Press.

Fairchild, Charles (2007) 'Building the authentic celebrity: the "idol" phenomenon in the attention economy', *Popular Music & Society*, 30(3): 355–375.

Feasey, Rebecca (2008) 'Reading heat: the meanings and pleasures of star fashions and celebrity gossip', *Continuum*, 22(5): 687–699.

Featherstone, Mike (1992) 'The heroic life and everyday life', *Theory, Culture & Society*, 9: 159–182.

Ferri, Anthony J. (2010) 'Emergence of the entertainment age?', *Society*, 47(5): 403–409.

Ferris, Kerry O. (2001) 'Through a glass, darkly: the dynamics of fan-celebrity encounters', *Symbolic Interaction*, 24(1): 25–47.

—— (2007) 'The sociology of celebrity', *Sociology Compass*, 1(1): 371–384.

—— (2010) 'The next big thing: local celebrity', *Society*, 47(5): 392–395.

Ferris, Kerry O., & Harris, Scott R. (2011) *Stargazing: Celebrity, Fame, and Social Interaction*. London: Routledge.

Fishman, Jay E. (2004) 'Celebrity as a business and its role in matrimonial cases', *American Journal of Family Law*, 17(4): 203–211.

Fogo, F. (1994) *I Read the News Today: The Social Drama of John Lennon's Death*. Maryland: Rowman & Littlefield.

Foucault, Michel (1977) *Discipline and Punish*. London: Allen & Unwin.

Fowles, Jib (1992) *Star Struck: Celebrity Performers and the American Public*. Washington, DC: Smithsonian.

Franck, Dora, & Franck, Georg. (1995). Discussion: The economy of attention. Online: www.alamut.com/subj/economics/attention/frank_discussion.html.

Franck, Egon, & Nuesch, Stephan (2007) 'Avoiding "Star Wars" – celebrity creation as media strategy', *Kyklos*, 60(2): 211–230.

Franck, Georg (1989) 'Die neue Währung: Aufmerksamkeit. Zum Einfluß der Hochtechnik auf Zeit und Geld', *Merkur*, 486: 688–701.

—— (1993) 'Ökonomie der Aufmerksamkeit', *Merkur*, 47(9/10): 748–761.

—— (1998) *Ökonomie der Aufmerksamkeit. Ein Entwurf*. Munich: Carl Hanser.

—— (1999) 'Scientific communication – A vanity fair?', *Science*, 286(5437): 53–55.

—— (2000) 'Prominenz und Populismus: Zu Pierre Bourdieus Ökonomie des immateriellen Reichtums', *Berliner Debatte Iinitial*, 11(1): 19–28.

—— (2002) 'The scientific economy of attention: A novel approach to the collective rationality of science', *Scientometrics*, 55(1): 3–26.

—— (2005) 'Mental capitalism', in W.P.W.P.i.A.a. Design (ed.), *Michael Shamiyeh DOM Research Laboratory*. Basel: Birkhäuser. pp. 98–115.

—— (2007) 'Jenseits von Geld und Information – Zur Oekonomie der Aufmerksamkeit', in M. Piwinger & A. Zerfass (eds), *Handbuch Unternehmenskommunikation*. Wiesbaden: Gabler. pp. 159–169.

—— (2010) 'Kapitalismus Zweipunktnull', in S. Neckel (ed.), *Kapitalistischer Realismus*. Frankfurt: Campus. pp. 217–223.

—— (2011) 'Celebrities: Elite der Mediangesellschaft?', *Merkur*, 65(4): 300–310.

Frankenberg, Ronald (1957) *Village on the Border*. London: Cohen & West.

Franklin, Benjamin (1817) *The Private Correspondence of Benjamin Franklin, Vol. 1*. London: Henry Colburn.

Fraser, Benson P., & Brown, William J. (2002) 'Media, celebrities and social influence: identification with Elvis Presley', *Mass Communication & Society*, 5(2): 183–206.

Freud, Sigmund (2004 [1921]) 'Mass psychology and the analysis of the "I" ', in *Mass Psychology and Other Writings*. Harmondsworth: Penguin.

Friedersdorf, Conner (2011), 'Sarah Palin's legacy: politics as a path to celebrity and riches', *The Atlantic*, 6 October. Online: www.theatlantic.com/politics/archive/2011/10/sarah-palins-legacy-politics-as-a-path-to-celebrity-and-riches/246243/ (accessed 9 November 2011).

Friedland, William H. (1964) 'For a sociological concept of charisma', *Social Forces*, 43(1): 18–26.

Friedman, Lawrence M. (1999) *The Horizontal Society*. New Haven: Yale University Press.

Friedrich, Jonahton (2007) 'Glamour trials: the creation of rights and the celebrity industry in *Douglas v Hello!*', *Media & Arts Law Review*, 12(4).

Fulda, Bernhard (2009) 'Media personalities, 1918–24', in *Press and Politics in the Weimar Republic*. Oxford: Oxford University Press. pp. 45–75.

Furedi, Frank (2010) 'Celebrity culture', *Society*, 47(6): 493–497.

Gabler, Neal (1998) *Life: The Movie*. New York: Knopf.

—— (2001) *Towards a New Definition of Celebrity*. Los Angeles: Normal Lea Center, University of Southern California, Annenberg School for Communication.

—— (2003) *Walter Winchell: Gossip, Power and the Culture of Celebrity*. New York: Vintage.

Gamson, Joshua (1992) 'The assembly line of greatness: celebrity in twentieth-century America', *Critical Studies in Mass Communication*, 9(1): 1–24.

—— (1994) *Claims to Fame: Celebrity in Contemporary America*. Berkeley: University of California Press.

—— (1999) 'Taking the talk show challenge: television, emotion, and public spheres', *Constellations*, 6(2): 190–205.

—— (2000) 'The web of celebrity', *American Prospect*, 11(20): 40–51.

—— (2001) 'Jessica Hahn, media whore: sex scandals and female publicity', *Critical Studies in Media Communication*, 18(2): 157–173.

—— (2007) 'The assembly line of greatness: celebrity in twentieth-century America', in S. Redmond & S. Holmes (eds), *Stardom and Celebrity: A Reader*. London: Sage. pp. 141–155.

Garland, Robert (2010) 'Celebrity ancient and modern', *Society*, 47(6): 484–488.

Garner, Roberta (1990) 'Jacob Burckhardt as a theorist of modernity: reading the civilization of the Renaissance in Italy', *Sociological Theory*, 8(1): 48–57.

Garratt, Sheryl (1984) 'All of us love all of you', in S. Steward & S. Garratt (eds), *Signed, Sealed and Delivered: True Life Stories of Women in Pop*. Boston: South End Press. pp. 138–150.

Garthwaite, Craig, & Moore, Timothy J. (2008) The Role of Celebrity Endorsements in Politics: Oprah, Obama, and the 2008 Democratic Primary. Online: www.stat.columbia.edu/~gelman/stuff_for_blog/celebrityendorsements_garthwaitemoore.pdf.

Geertz, Clifford (1977) 'Centers, kings, and charisma: reflections on the symbolics of power', in J. Ben-David & T. Nichols (eds), *Culture and its Creators: Essays in Honor of Edward Shils*. Chicago: University of Chicago Press.

Giesen, Bernhard (1998) 'Cosmopolitans, patriots, Jacobins, and romantics', *Daedalus*, 127(3): 221–250.

Gilbert, Jeremy (2004) 'Small faces: the tyranny of celebrity in post-Oedipal culture', *Mediactive*, 2: 86–109.

Giles, David (2000) *Illusions of Immortality: A Psychology of Fame and Celebrity*. Houndmills: Macmillan.

Giles, David C. (2002) 'Parasocial interaction: a review of the literature and a model for future research', *Media Psychology*, 4(3): 279–305.

—— (2010) 'Parasocial relationships', in J. Eder, F. Jannidis & R. Schneider (eds), *Characters in Fictional Worlds: Understanding Imaginary Beings in Literature, Film, and Other Media*. Berlin: De Gruyter.

Gitlin, Todd (1980) *The Whole World is Watching: Mass Media in the Making and Unmaking of the New Left*. Berkeley: University of California Press.

—— (1998) 'The culture of celebrity', *Dissent*, 45(3): 81–83.

Glover, Brian (2002) 'Nobility, visibility, and publicity in Colley Cibber's apology', *Studies in English Literature 1500–1900*, 42(3): 523–539.

Gluckman, Max (1963) 'Gossip and scandal', *Current Anthropology*, 4(3): 307–316.

Goffman, Erving (1959) *The Presentation of Self in Everyday Life*. New York: Anchor Books.

Goldhaber, Michael H. (1997) 'Attention shoppers!', *Wired*, 5(12).

Goldsmith, Jason (2009) 'Celebrity and the specactacle of nation', in T. Mole (ed.), *Romanticism and Celebrity Culture, 1750–1850*. Cambridge: Cambridge University Press. pp. 21–40.

Gomes, Rita Costa (2003) *The Making of a Court Society: Kings and Nobles in Late Medieval Portugal*. Cambridge: Cambridge University Press.

Goode, William J. (1978) *The Celebration of Heroes: Prestige as a Social Control System*. Berkeley: University of California Press.

Goodman, Dena (1989) 'Enlightenment salons: the convergence of female and philosophic ambitions', *Eighteenth-Century Studies*, 22(3): 329–350.

—— (1992) 'Public sphere and private life: toward a synthesis of current historiographical approaches to the Old Regime', *History & Theory*, 31: 8–14.

—— (1994) *The Republic of Letters: A Cultural History of the French Enlightenment*. Ithaca, NY: Cornell University Press.

Goodman, Lenn E. (2010) 'Supernovas: the dialectic of celebrity in society', *Society*, 47(5).

Goodman, Michael K. (2010) 'The mirror of consumption: celebritisation, developmental consumption and the shifting cultural politics of fair trade', *Geoforum*, 41(1): 104–116.

Goodman, Michael K., & Barnes, Christine (2011) 'Star/poverty space: the making of the "development celebrity" ', *Celebrity Studies*, 2(1): 69–85.

Goodman, Robert F., & Ben Ze'ev, Aaron (eds) (1994) *Good Gossip*. Lawrence: University Press of Kansas.

Gooley, Dana (2010) 'From the top: Liszt's aristocratic airs', in E. Berenson & E. Giloi (eds), *Constructing Charisma: Celebrity, Fame, and Power in Nineteenth-Century Europe*. New York: Berghahn. pp. 69–85.

Gordon, Daniel (1989) ' "Public opinion" and the civilizing process in France: the example of Morellet', *Eighteenth-Century Studies*, 22: 302–328.

Gott, Richard. (2006) 'The story of the iconic image of Che Guevara', *The Hindu*, 5 June.

Graffin, S.D., Wade, J.B., Porac, J.F., & McNamee, R.C. (2008) 'The impact of CEO status diffusion on the economic outcomes of other senior managers', *Organization Science*, 19(3): 457–474.

Grande, Edgar (2000) 'Charisma und Komplexitaet: Verhandlungsdemokratie, Mediendemokratie und der Fuhrungswandel politischer Eliten', *Leviathan*, 28(1): 122–141.

Granovetter, Mark (1973) 'The strength of weak ties', *American Journal of Sociology*, 78(6): 1360–1380.

—— (1983) 'The strength of the weak tie: revisited', *Sociological Theory*, 1: 201–233.

Gray, Jonathan, Sandvoss, Cornel, & Harrington, C. Lee (eds) (2007) *Fandom: Identities and Communities in a Mediated World*. New York: New York University Press.

—— (2007) 'Introduction: Why study fans!', in J. Gray, C. Sandvoss & C.L. Harrington (eds), *Fandom: Identities and Communities in a Mediated World*. New York: New York University Press. pp. 1–16.

Greenblatt, Stephen (1980) *Renaissance Self-Fashioning: From More to Shakespeare*. Chicago: University of Chicago Press.

Greenfeld, Liah (1985) 'Reflections on two charismas', *British Journal of Sociology*, 36(1): 117–132.

Greer, Germaine (2001) 'Watch with brother', *The Observer*, 24 June.

Guo, Yingje (2011) 'China's celebrity mothers: female virtues, patriotism and social harmony', in L. Edwards & E. Jeffreys (eds), *Celebrity in China*. Hong Kong: Hong Kong University Press. pp. 45–66.

Gurevich, Aaron J. (1995) *The Origins of European Individualism*. Oxford: Blackwell.

Guthey, Eric, Clark, Timothy, & Jackson, Brad (2009) *Demystifying Business Celebrity*. London: Routledge.

Habermas, Jürgen (1974) 'The public sphere: an encyclopedia article', *New German Critique*, 3: 49–55.

—— (1989) *The Structural Transformation of the Public Sphere*. Cambridge: Polity Press.

Haigh, Gideon (2003) 'Bad company: the cult of the CEO', *Quarterly Essay*, 10: 1–97.

—— (2004) *Bad Company: The Strange Cult of the CEO*. London: Aurum Press.

Hallett, Mark (2005) 'Reynolds, celebrity and the Exhibition space', in M. Postle (ed.), *Joshua Reynolds: The Creation of Celebrity*. London: Tate Publishing. pp. 35–47.

Harrington, C. Lee, & Bielby, Denise D. (1995) 'Where did you here that? Technology and the social organization of gossip', *Sociological Quarterly*, 36(3): 607–628.

—— (2010) 'A life-course perspective on fandom', *International Journal of Cultural Studies*, 13(5): 429.

Harrington, C. Lee, Bielby, Denise D., & Bardo, Anthony R. (2011) 'Life course transitions and the future of fandom', *International Journal of Cultural Studies*, 14(6): 567–590.

Harris, John (2007) 'The first metrosexual rugby star: rugby union, masculinity, and celebrity in contemporary Wales', *Sociology of Sport Journal*, 24(2): 145–164.

Harriss, G.L. (1963) 'Medieval government and statecraft', *Past & Present*, 25: 8–39.

Harvey, David (1990) *The Condition of Postmodernity*. Oxford: Basil Blackwell.

Hatch, Stephen (1960) 'Religion of the celebrity', *New Left Review*, 1(3): 64–65.

Hauch, Jeanne M. (1994) 'Protecting private facts in France: the Warren and Brandeis Tort is alive and well and flourishing in Paris', *Tulane Law Review*, 68(5): 1219–1302.

Hays, Constance L. (2005) *Pop: Truth and Power at the Coca-Cola Company*. London: Arrow.

Hayward, Mathew L.A., & Hambrick, Donald C. (1997) 'Explaining the premiums paid for large acquisitions: evidence of CEO hubris', *Administrative Science Quarterly*, 42(1): 103–127.

Hayward, Mathew L.A., Rindova, Violina P., & Pollock, Timothy G (2004) 'Believing one's own press: the causes and consequences of CEO celebrity', *Strategic Management Journal*, 25: 637–653.

Hearn, Alison (2006) ' "John, a 20-year-old Boston native with a great sense of humour": on the spectacularization of the "self" and the incorporation of identity in the age of reality television', *International Journal of Media & Cultural Politics*, 2(2): 131–147.

—— (2008) ' "Meat, mask, burden": probing the contours of the branded "self" ', *Journal of Consumer Culture*, 8(2): 197–217.

Heisch, Allison (1975) 'Queen Elizabeth I: parliamentary rhetoric and the exercise of power', *Signs*, 1(1): 31–55.

Henderson, Amy (1992) 'Media and the rise of celebrity culture', *OAH Magazine of History*, 6.

Herbst, Susan (2003) 'Political authority in a mediated age', *Theory & Society*, 32: 481–503.

Herman, Gabriel (1997) 'The court society of the Hellenistic Age', in P. Cartledge, P. Garnsey & E. Gruen (eds), *Hellenistic Constructs: Essays in Culture, History, and Historiography*. Berkeley: University of California Press. pp. 199–224.

Hermes, Joke (1995) *Reading Women's Magazines: An Analysis of Everyday Media Use*. Cambridge: Polity Press.

—— (1999) 'Media figures in identity construction', in P. Alusuutari (ed.), *Rethinking the Media Audience: The New Agenda*. London: Sage.

Hershey, Constance V. (2005) 'Benjamin Franklin: portrait of the statesman as a rock star', *Antiques & Fine Art*: 239–243.

Hesmondhaigh, David (2005) 'Producing celebrity', in J. Evans & D. Hesmondhalgh (eds), *Understanding Media: Inside Celebrity*. Maidenhead: Open University Press. pp. 97–134.

Higgins, Michael (2010) 'The "public inquisitor" as media celebrity', *Cultural Politics: an International Journal*, 6(1): 93–109.

Hills, Matt (2002) *Fan Cultures*. London: Routledge.

Hinerman, Stephen (1992) ' "I'll be here with you": fans, fantasy and the figure of Elvis', in L.A. Lewis (ed.), *The Adoring Audience: Fan Culture and Popular Media*. London: Routledge. pp. 107–134.

Hollander, Paul (2010a) 'Michael Jackson, the celebrity cult, and popular culture', *Society*, 47(2): 147–151.

—— (2010b) 'Slavoj Zizek and the rise of the celebrity intellectual', *Society*, 47(4): 358–360.

—— (2010c) 'Why the celebrity cult?', *Society*, 47(5): 388–391.

Holmes, Oliver Wendell (1863) 'Doings of the sunbeam', *Atlantic Monthly*, 12(69): 1–15.

Holmes, Su, & Jermyn, Deborah (eds) (2004) *Understanding Reality Television*. London: Routledge.

Honneth, Axel (1995) *The Struggle for Recognition: The Moral Grammar of Social Conflicts* (J. Anderson, trans.). Cambridge: Polity.

Horton, Donald, & Strauss, Anselm (1957) 'Interaction in audience-participation shows', *American Journal of Sociology*, 62(6): 579–587.

Horton, Donald, & Wohl, R. Richard (1956) 'Mass communication and para-social interaction: observations on intimacy at a distance', *Psychiatry*, 19(3): 215–229.

Houlberg, R. (1984) 'Local television news audiences and the para-social interaction', *Journal of Broadcasting* 28: 423–429.

Howe, Elizabeth (1992) *The First English Actresses: Women and Drama 1660–1700*. Cambridge: Cambridge University Press.

Howells, Richard (2011) 'Heroes, saints and celebrities: the photograph as holy relic', *Celebrity Studies*, 2(2): 112–130.

Hudson, Alan (2003) 'Intellectuals for our times', *Critical Review of International Social & Political Philosophy*, 6(4): 33–50.

Hughes, P.L., & Larkin, J.F. (eds) (1969) *Tudor Royal Proclamations, Vol. 2*. New Haven: Yale University Press.

Hughes-Freeland, Felicia (2007) 'Charisma and celebrity in Indonesian politics', *Anthropological Theory*, 7(2): 177–200.

Hunt, Lynn Avery (1992) *The Family Romance of the French Revolution*. Berkeley: University of California Press.

Huxley, Aldous (1932) *Brave New World: A Novel*. London: Chatto & Windus.

Inglis, Fred (2010) *A Short History of Celebrity*. Princeton: Princeton University Press.

Jackson, Bradley G. (1996) 'Re-engineering the sense of self: the manager and the management guru', *Journal of Management Studies*, 33(5): 571–590.

Jacoby, Melissa B., & Zimmerman, Diane Leenhher (2002) 'Foreclosing on fame: exploring the unchartered boundaries of the right of publicity', *NYU Law Review*, 77(5): 1322–1368.

Jaffe, Aaron (2005) *Modernism and the Culture of Celebrity*. Cambridge: Cambridge University Press.

James, Kyle (2006) 'Royalty very much in vogue in Republican Germany', *Deutsche Welle*, 20 July. Online: www.dw-world.de/dw/article/0,,2104577,00.html (accessed 9 November 2011).

James, Clive (1993) *Fame in the 20th Century*. New York: Random House.

Jeffreys, Elaine (2011) 'Accidental celebrities: China's chastity heroines and charity', in L. Edwards & E. Jeffreys (eds), *Celebrity in China*. Hong Kong: Hong Kong University Press. pp. 67–84.

Jeffreys, Elaine, & Edwards, Louise (2011) 'Celebrity/China', in L. Edwards & E. Jeffreys (eds), *Celebrity in China*. Hong Kong: Hong Kong University Press. pp. 1–20.

Jenkins, Henry (1992) *Textual Poachers: Television Fans & Participatory Culture*. New York: Routledge.

—— (2006) *Fans, Blogger and Gamers*. New York: New York University Press.

Jenks, Chris, & Lorentzen, Justin J. (1997) 'The Kray fascination', *Theory, Culture & Society*, 14(3): 87–107.

Jenson, Joli (1992) 'Fandom as pathology: the consequences of characterization', in L.A. Lewis (ed.), *The Adoring Audience: Fan Culture and Popular Media*. London: Routledge. pp. 9–29.

Jinda, Michael (1994) 'Star Trek fandom as a religious phenomenon', *Sociology of Religion*, 55(1): 27–51.

Johansson, Sofia (2006) ' "Sometimes you wanna hate celebrities": tabloid readers and celebrity coverage', in S. Holmes & S. Redmond (eds), *Framing Celebrity: New Directions in Celebrity Culture*. London: Routledge. pp. 343–358.

Johnston, Anna (2009) 'George Augustus Robinson, the "Great Conciliator": colonial celebrity and its postcolonial aftermath', *Postcolonial Studies*, 12(2): 153–172.

Jones, Deborah (1980) 'Gossip: notes on women's oral culture', *Women's Studies International Quarterly*, 3(2–3): 193–198.

Jones, Peter (2006) 'Equality, recognition and difference', *Critical Review of International Social & Political Philosophy*, 9(1): 23–46.

Kahan, Jeffrey (2010) *Bettymania and the Birth of Celebrity Culture*. Bethlehem, USA: Lehigh University Press.

Kale, Steven D. (2002a) 'Women, salons, and the state in the aftermath of the French Revolution', *Journal of Women's History*, 13(4): 54–80.

—— (2002b) 'Women, the public sphere, and the persistence of salons', *French Historical Studies*, 25(1): 115–148.

—— (2004) *French Salons: High Society and Political Sociability from the Old Regime to the Revolution of 1848*. Baltimore: Johns Hopkins University Press.

Kaminer, Wendy (2005) 'Get a life: illusions of self-invention', *Hedgehog Review*, 7(1): 47–58.

Kanter, Rosabeth M. (1977) *Men and Women of the Corporation*. New York: Basic Books.

Kaplan, Benjamin (1967) *An Unhurried View of Copyright*. New York: Columbia University Press.

Kastan, David Scott (1984) 'Proud majesty made a subject: Shakespeare and the spectacle of rule', *Shakespeare Quarterly*, 37(4): 459–475.

Keller, Suzanne (1963) *Beyond the Ruling Class: Strategic Elites in Modern Society*. New York: Random House.

—— (1983) 'Celebrities as a national elite', in M.M. Czudnowski (ed.), *Political Elites and Social Change*. DeKalb: Northern Illinois University Press. pp. 3–14.

Kellner, Douglas (2001) 'Nike's America/America's Michael Jordan', in D.L. Andrews (ed.), *Michael Jordan, Inc.: Corporate Sport, Media Culture, and Late Modern America*. Albany: State University of New York Press. pp. 37–63.

—— (2009) 'Barack Obama and celebrity spectacle', *International Journal of Communication*, 3: 715–741.

Kenyon, Andrew T., & Milne, Esther (2005) 'Images of celebrity: publicity, privacy, law', *Media & Arts Law Review*, 10(4).

Keohane, Nannerl 0. (1977) 'Montaigne's individualism', *Political Theory*, 5(3): 363–390.

Kessler, Randall M., & McCormack, Sarah (2005) 'Representing "high profile" clients in family law cases', *American Journal of Family Law*, 19(1): 12–14.

Ketchen Jr, David J., Adams, Garry L., & Shook, Christopher L. (2008) 'Understanding and managing CEO celebrity', *Business Horizons*, 51(6): 529–534.

Khurana, Rakesh (2002) *Searching for a Corporate Saviour: the Irrational Quest for Charismatic CEOs*. Princeton: Princeton University Press.

Kimmel, Stanley Preston (1957) *Mr. Lincoln's Washington*. New York: Coward-McCann.

King, Barry (1992) 'Stardom and symbolic degeneracy: television and the transformation of the stars as public symbols', *Semiotica*, 92(1/2): 1–48.

—— (2008) 'Stardom, celebrity and the para-confession', *Social Semiotics*, 18(2): 115–132.

—— (2010) 'Stardom, celebrity, and the money form', *The Velvet Light Trap*, 65: 7–19.

Kirby, David (2006) 'Celebrities R Us', *American Interest Online*, 1(3).

Kirby, Mark (1998) 'Death of a princess', *Capital & Class*, 64: 29–41.

Kjus, Yngvar (2009) 'Idolizing and monetizing the public: the production of celebrities and fans, representatives and citizens in reality TV', *International Journal of Communication*, 3: 277–300.

Klaprat, Cathy (1985) 'The star as market strategy: Bette Davis in another light', in T. Balio (ed.), *The American Film Industry*. Madison: University of Wisconsin Press. pp. 351–376.

Klein, Lawrence E. (1996) 'Coffeehouse civility, 1660–1714: an aspect of post-courtly culture in England', *The Huntington Library Quarterly*, 59(1): 30–51.

Kniffin, Kevin M., & Wilson, David Sloan (2005) 'Utilities of gossip across organizational levels', *Human Nature*, 16(3): 278–292.

—— (2010) 'Evolutionary perspectives on workplace gossip: why and how gossip can serve groups', *Group & Organization Management*, 35(2): 150–117.

Koch, Gertrud (1999) 'From kingdom to stardom', *Constellations*, 6(2): 206–215.

Kohlrausch, Martin (2010) 'The workings of royal celebrity: Wilhelm II as Media Emperor', in E. Berenson & E. Giloi (eds), *Constructing Charisma: Celebrity, Fame, and Power in Nineteenth-Century Europe*. New York: Berghahn. pp. 52–66.

Kurzman, Charles, Anderson, Chelise, Key, Clinton, Lee, Youn Ok, Moloney, Mairead, Silver, Alexis, et al. (2007) 'Celebrity status', *Sociological Theory*, 25(4): 347–367.

Kwall, Roberta Rosenthal (1998) 'Fame', *Indiana Law Journal*, 73(1): 1–42.

Lacey, Robert (2003) *Monarch: The Life and Reign of Elizabeth II*. New York: Free Press.

Lamont, Michèle (1987) 'How to become a dominant French Philosopher: the case of Jacques Derrida', *American Journal of Sociology*, 93(3): 584–622.

—— (1995) 'Review of claims to fame: celebrity in contemporary America, by Joshua Gamson', *American Journal of Sociology*, 100(4): 1069–1071.

Lana, Renata (2002) 'Women and Foxite strategy in the Westminster election of 1784', *Eighteenth-Century Life*, 26(1): 46–69.

Lancaster, Elizabeth Lillian & Harvey, William (1869) *Geographical Fun: Being Humorous Outlines of Various Countries with an Introduction and Descriptive Lines. By 'Aleph'*. London: Hodder & Stoughton, 1869. Online: http://weddingphotography.com. ph/5284/12-illustrative-portraits-political-geography-europe/ (accessed 9 November 2011).

Landes, Joan B. (1988) *Women and the Public Sphere in the Age of the French Revolution*. Ithaca: Cornell University Press.

Lang, Kurt, & Lang, Gladys Engel (1956) 'The television personality in politics: some considerations', *Public Opinion Quarterly*, 20(1): 103–112.

—— (1988) 'Recognition and renown: the survival of artistic reputation', *American Journal of Sociology*, 94(1): 79–109.

Lanham, Richard (1997) 'The economics of attention', *Michigan Quarterly Review*, 36: 270–284.

—— (2001) 'Barbie and the teacher of righteousness: two lessons in the economics of attention', *Houston Law Review*, 38(2): 499–540.

—— (2006) *The Economics of Attention: Style and Substance in the Age of Information*. Chicago: University of Chicago Press.

Lanier, Henry Wysham (1930) *The First English Actresses, from the Initial Appearance of Women on the Stage in 1600 till 1700*. New York: Players.

Latour, Bruno (2004) 'Why has critique run out of steam? From matters of fact to matters of concern', *Critical Inquiry*, 30(2): 225–248.

Lawler, Peter A. (2010) 'Celebrity studies today', *Society*, 47(5): 419–423.

Le Bon, Gustave (2001 [1896]) *The Crowd*. Kitchener: Batoche Books.

Le Goff, Jacques (1988 [1964]) *Medieval Civilization 400–1500*. Oxford: Basil Blackwell.

Leach, William (1991) 'Brokers and the new corporate, industrial order', in W.R. Taylor (ed.), *Inventing Times Square*. New York: Russell Sage Foundation. pp. 99–117.

Learmonth, Michael (2006) 'The show's big winners', *Variety*, 8–14 May, 402: 98–99.

Leets, Laura, De Becker, Gavin, & Giles, Howard (1995) 'Fans: exploring expressed motivations for contacting celebrities', *Journal of Language & Social Psychology*, 14(1–2): 102–124.

Leslie, Larry Z. (2011) *Celebrity in the 21st Century: A Reference Handbook*. Santa Barbara: ABC-Clio.

Levin, Carole (2002) ' "We Princes, I tell you, are set on stages". Elizabeth I and dramatic self-representation', in M.W.-D.S.P. Cerasano (ed.), *Readings in Renaissance Women's*

Drama: Criticism, History, and Performance, 1594–1998. London: Routledge. pp. 113–124.

Levin, Jack, Mody-Desbareau, Amita, & Arluke, Arnold (1988) 'The gossip tabloid as agent of social control', *Journalism Quarterly*, 65(2): 514–517.

Levy, M.R. (1979) 'Watching TV news as para-social interaction', *Journal of Broadcasting* 23: 69–80.

Lewis, Lisa A. (ed.) (1992) *The Adoring Audience: Fan Culture and Popular Media*. London: Routledge.

Lilti, Antoine (2005) *Le monde des salons: Sociabilité et mondanité à Paris au XVIIIe siècle*. Paris: Fayard.

—— (2008) 'The writing of paranoia: Jean-Jacques Rousseau and the paradoxes of celebrity', *Representations*, 103(1): 53–83.

—— (2009) 'The kingdom of politesse: salons and the republic of letters in eighteenth-century Paris', *Republics of Letters: A Journal for the Study of Knowledge, Politics, & the Arts*, 1(1).

Lim, Gerrie (2005) *Idol to Icon: The Creation of Celebrity Brands*. London: Cyan Books.

Lind, Emma (2007) 'What about . . . (earnings of celebrities)', *Forbes Global*, 3(17): 52.

Linkman, Audrey (1993) *The Victorians: Photographic Portraits*. London: Tauris Parke Books.

Littler, Jo (2004a) 'Celebrity and "meritocracy"', *Soundings: A Journal of Politics & Culture*, 26: 118–130.

—— (2004b) 'Making fame ordinary: intimacy, reflexivity, and "keeping it real" ', *Mediactive*, 2: 8–25.

—— (2007) 'Celebrity CEOs and the cultural economy of tabloid intimacy', in S. Redmond & S. Holmes (eds), *Stardom and Celebrity: A Reader*. London: Sage. pp. 230–243.

—— (2008) ' "I feel your pain": cosmopolitan charity and the public fashioning of the celebrity soul', *Social Semiotics*, 18(2): 237–251.

—— (2011) 'Introduction: celebrity and the transnational', *Celebrity Studies*, 2(1): 1–5.

Loach, Jennifer (1994) 'The function of ceremonial in the reign of Henry VIII', *Past & Present*, 142: 43–68.

Loudon, J.B. (1961) 'Kinship and crisis in south Wales', *British Journal of Sociology*, 12(4): 333–350.

Loughlan, Patricia, McDonald, Barbara, & van Krieken, Robert (2010) *Celebrity and the Law*. Sydney: Federation Press.

Lowenthal, Leo (1944) 'Biographies in popular magazines', in P.F. Lazarsfeld & F.N. Stanton (eds), *Radio Research 1942–1943*. New York: Essential Books. pp. 507–548.

—— (1984a) 'Some thoughts on the 1937 edition of International Who's Who', in *Literature and Mass Culture*. New Brunswick: Transaction. pp. 237–240.

—— (1984b [1944]) 'The triumph of mass idols', in *Literature and Mass Culture*. New Brunswick: Transaction. pp. 203–235.

—— (1984c [1955]) 'The biographical fashion', in *Literature and Mass Culture*. New Brunswick: Transaction. pp. 189–202.

Lowenthal, Leo, & Fiske, Marjorie (1984) 'Eighteenth-century England: a case study', in *Literature and Mass Culture*. New Brunswick: Transaction. pp. 75–151.

Luckhurst, Mary, & Moody, Jane (eds) (2005) *Theatre and Celebrity in Britain, 1660–2000*. Basingstoke: Palgrave Macmillan.

Luhmann, Niklas (2000) *The Reality of the Mass Media* (K. Cross, trans.). Stanford: Stanford University Press.

Lukes, Steven (2005) *Power: A Radical View* (2nd edn). Houndmills: Palgrave Macmillan.

MacCaffrey, W.T. (1963) 'Elizabethan politics: the first decade, 1558–1568', *Past & Present*, 24: 25–42.

—— (1965) 'England: the crown and the new aristocracy, 1540–1600', *Past & Present*, 30: 52–64.

MacFarlane, Alan (1978) 'The origins of English individualism: some surprises', *Theory & Society*, 6: 255–277.

Macho, Thomas H. (1993) 'Von der Elite zur Prominenz: Zum Strukrurwandel politischer Herrschaft', *Merkur*, 47(9/10): 762–769.

Magubane, Zine (2008) 'The (product) red man's burden: charity, celebrity, and the contradictions of coevalness', *Journal of Pan-African Studies*, 2(6): 102.1–102.25.

Maguire, Nancy Klein 'The theatrical mask/masque of politics: the case of Charles I', *Journal of British Studies*, 28(1): 1–22.

Mah, Harold (2000) 'Phantasies of the public sphere: rethinking the habermas of historians', *Journal of Modern History*, 72(1): 153–182.

Mannheim, Karl (1952) 'On the nature of economic ambition and its significance for the social education of man', in *Essays on the Sociology of Knowledge*. New York: Oxford University Press. pp. 230–275.

Mansch, Larry D. (2005) *Abraham Lincoln, President-Elect: The Four Critical Months from Election to Inauguration*. Jefferson, NC: McFarland & Company.

Markovits, Andrei S. (2010) 'The global and the local in our contemporary sports cultures', *Society*, 47(6): 503–509.

Marks, Michael P., & Fischer, Zachary M. (2002) 'The King's new bodies: simulating consent in the age of celebrity', *New Political Science*, 24(3): 371–394.

Marsden, Jean I. (2006) *Fatal Desire: Women, Sexuality, and the English Stage, 1660–1720*. Ithaca: Cornell University Press.

Marsh, Christopher (2001) ' "Common prayer" in England 1560–1640: the view from the pew', *Past & Present*, 171: 66–94.

Marsh, David, Hart, Paul 't, & Tindall, Karen (2010) 'Celebrity politics: the politics of the late modernity?', *Political Studies Review*, 8(3): 322–340.

Marshall, P. David (1997) *Celebrity and Power: Fame in Contemporary Culture*. Minneapolis: University of Minnesota Press.

—— (2010a) 'The promotion and presentation of the self: celebrity as marker of presentational media', *Celebrity Studies*, 1(1): 35–48.

—— (2010b) 'The specular economy', *Society*, 47(6): 498–502.

Martin, John Jeffries (1997) 'Inventing sincerity, refashioning prudence: the discovery of the individual in Renaissance Europe', *American Historical Review*, 102(5): 1309–1342.

—— (2004) *Myths of Renaissance Individualism*. New York: Palgrave Macmillan.

Martin, Willis (2011) 'Constructing charisma: celebrity, fame, and power in nineteenth-century Europe', *European Journal of Cultural Studies*, 14(3): 373–374.

Marwick, Alice, & Boyd, Danah (2011) 'To see and be seen: celebrity practice on Twitter', *Convergence*, 17(2): 139–159.

Mathews, Oliver (1974) *The Album of Carte-de-Visite and Cabinet Portrait Photographs 1854–1914*. London: Reedminster Publications.

Mathieson, Thomas (1997) 'The viewer society: Michel Foucault's 'Panopticon' revisited', *Theoretical Criminology*, 1(2): 215–234.

Mathur, Lynette Knowles, Mathur, Ike, & Rangan, Nanda (1997) 'The wealth effects associated with a celebrity endorser: the Michael Jordan phenomenon', *Journal of Advertising Research*, 37(3): 67–73.

Mayer, Arno J. (1981) *The Persistence of the Old Regime: Europe to the Great War*. London: Croom Helm.

McCann, Graeme (1988) *Marilyn Monroe: The Body in the Library*. New Brunswick, NJ: Rutgers University Press.

McCannon, John (1997) 'Positive heroes at the Pole: celebrity status, socialist-realist ideals and the Soviet myth of the Arctic, 1932–39', *Russian Review*, 56(3): 346–365.

McCarthy, Patsy, & Hatcher, Caroline (2005) 'Branding Branson: a case study of celebrity entrepreneurship', *Australian Journal of Communication*, 32(3): 45–61.

McCauley, Elizabeth Anne (1985) *A.A.E. Disdéri and the Carte de Visite Portrait Photography*. New Haven: Yale University Press.

McCutcheon, L.E., Lange, R., & Houran, J. (2002) 'Evidence for non-pathological and pathological dimensions of celebrity worship', *British Journal of Psychology*, 93: 67–87.

McDayter, Ghislaine (2009) *Byromania and the Birth of Celebrity Culture*. New York: State University of New York.

McElroy, Ruth, & Williams, Rebecca (2011) 'Remembering ourselves, viewing the others: historical reality television and celebrity in the small nation', *Television & New Media*, 12(3): 187–206.

McLendon, Michael Locke (2009) 'Rousseau, amour propre, and intellectual celebrity', *Journal of Politics*, 71(2): 506–519.

McLuhan, Marshall (1962) *The Gutenberg Galaxy: The Making of Typographic Man*. London: Routledge & Kegan Paul.

McManus, Clare (2002) *Women on the Renaissance Stage: Anna of Denmark and Female Masquing in the Stuart Court (1590–1619)*. Manchester: Manchester University Press.

McNamara, Kim (2009) 'Publicising private lives: celebrities, image control and the reconfiguration of public space', *Social & Cultural Geography*, 10(1): 9–23.

McRobbie, Angela (2007) 'TOP GIRLS? Young women and the post-feminist sexual contract', *Cultural Studies*, 21(4–5): 718–737.

Meacham, Jon (1994) 'Gossip, politics, and power', *Washington Monthly* 2(6): 41–45.

Mead, George Herbert (1934) *Mind, Self and Society*. Chicago: University of Chicago Press.

Meindl, James R., Ehrlich, Sanford B., & Dukerich, Janet M. (1985) 'The romance of leadership', *Administrative Science Quarterly*, 30(1): 78–102.

Mennell, Stephen (1981) 'Montaigne, civilisation and 16th-century European society', in K. Cameron (ed.), *Montaigne and His Age*. Exeter: University of Exeter. pp. 69–85.

Merry, Sally E. (1984) 'Rethinking gossip and scandal', in D. Black (ed.), *Toward a General Theory of Social Control*, 2 vols. London: Academic Press.

Merton, Robert K. (1945) 'Sociology of knowledge', in G. Gurvitch & W.E. Moore (eds), *Twentieth Century Sociology*. New York: Philosophical Library.

——— (1963) 'The ambivalence of scientists', *Bulletin of the Johns Hopkins Hospital*, 112(2): 77–97.

——— (1965) *On The Shoulders of Giants: A Shandean Postscript*. New York: Free Press.

——— (1968) 'The Matthew effect in science', *Science*, 159(3810): 56–63.

——— (1971) *Mass Persuasion: The Social Psychology of a War Bond Drive*. Westport, Conn.: Greenwood Press.

——— (1988) 'The Matthew effect in science II', *Isis*, 79: 606–623.

Meyer, David S., & Gamson, Joshua (1995) 'The challenge of cultural elites: celebrities and social movements', *Sociological Inquiry*, 65(2): 181–206.

Meyers, Erin (2009) ' "Can you handle my truth?": authenticity and the celebrity star image', *Journal of Popular Culture*, 42(5): 890–907.

Meyrowitz, Joshue (1994) 'The life and death of media friends: new genres of intimacy and mourning', in S.J. Drucker & R.S. Cathcart (eds), *American Heroes in a Media Age.* Cresskill, NJ: Hampton Press. pp. 62–81.

Michels, Robert (1911) *Political Parties: A Sociological Study of the Oligarchical Tendencies of Modern Democracy.* London: Jarrold & Sons.

Michelson, Grant, & Mouly, V. Suchitra (2002) ' "You didn't hear it from us but . . .": towards an understanding of rumour and gossip in organisations', *Australian Journal of Management,* 27(1): 57–65.

Michelson, Grant, van Iterson, Ad, & Waddington, Kathryn (2010) 'Gossip in organizations: contexts, consequences, and controversies', *Group Organization & Management,* 35(4): 371–390.

Millar, John (1806) *The Origin of the Distinction of Ranks, or, An Inquiry into the Circumstances which give rise to Influence and Authority, in the Different Members of Society* (4th edn, corr., to which is prefixed, An account of the life and writings of the author / by John Craig. ed.). Edinburgh: W. Blackwood.

Mills, Colleen (2010) 'Experiencing gossip: the foundations for a theory of embedded organizational gossip', *Group Organization & Management,* 35(2): 213–240.

Mills, C. Wright (1957) *The Power Elite.* New York: Oxford University Press.

Milner Jr., Murray (1994) *Status and Sacredness: A General Theory of Status Relations and an Analysis of Indian Culture.* New York: Oxford University Press.

—— (2004) *Freaks, Geeks, and Cool Kids: American Teenagers, Schools, and the Culture of Consumption.* New York: Routledge.

—— (2005) 'Celebrity culture as a status system', *Hedgehog Review,* 7(1): 66–77.

—— (2010) 'Is celebrity a new kind of status system?', *Society,* 47(5): 379–387.

Missner, Marshall (1985) 'Why Einstein became famous in America', *Social Studies of Science,* 15(2): 267–291.

Moeran, Brian (2003) 'Celebrities and the name economy', *Research in Economic Anthropology,* 22: 299–321.

Mole, Tom (2007) *Byron's Romantic Celebrity: Industrial Culture and the Hermeneutic of Intimacy.* London: Palgrave Macmillan.

—— (2008) 'Lord Byron and the end of fame', *International Journal of Cultural Studies,* 11(3): 343–361.

—— (ed.) (2009) *Romanticism and Celebrity Culture 1750–1850.* Cambridge: Cambridge University Press.

Montaigne, Michel de (1958) *The Complete Essays of Montaigne, translated by Donald M. Frame.* Stanford: Stanford University Press.

Montrose, Louis (1996) *The Purpose of Playing: Shakespeare and the Cultural Politics of the Elizabethan Theatre.* Chicago: University of Chicago Press.

—— (2006) *The Subject of Elizabeth: Authority, Gender, and Representation.* Chicago: University of Chicago Press.

Moran, Joe (1998) 'Cultural studies and academic stardom', *International Journal of Cultural Studies,* 1(1): 67–82.

Morello, John A. (2001) *Selling the President, 1920: Albert D. Lasker, Advertising, and the Election of Warren G. Harding.* Westport: Praeger.

Morgan, Simon (2011a) 'Celebrity: academic "pseudo-event" or a useful concept for historians?', *Cultural & Social History,* 8(1): 95–114.

—— (2011b) 'Historicising celebrity', *Celebrity Studies,* 1(3): 366–368.

Morin, Edgar (2005 [1960]) *The Stars.* Minneapolis: University of Minnesota Press.

Morris, Colin (1987) *The Discovery of the Individual, 1050–1200*. Toronto: University of Toronto Press.

Mueller, Andrew (2001) 'Pro Bono', *The Weekend Australian*, 1 December.

Nalapat, Abilash, & Parker, Andrew (2005) 'Sport, celebrity and popular culture: Sachin Tendulkar, cricket and Indian nationalisms', *International Review for the Sociology of Sport*, 40(4): 433–446.

Nayar, Pramod K. (2008) *Seeing Stars: Spectacle, Society and Celebrity Culture*. New Delhi: Sage.

Needham, Catherine (2005) 'Brand leaders: Clinton, Blair and the limitations of the permanent campaign', *Political Studies*, 53(2): 343–361.

Neidhardt, Friedhelm (1995) 'Prominenz und Prestige. Steuerungsprobleme massenmedialer Öffentlichkeit', in *Berlin-Brandenburgische Akademie der Wissenschaften. Jahrbuch 1994*. Berlin. pp. 233–245.

Newbury, Michael (1994) 'Eaten alive: slavery and celebrity in antebellum America', *ELH*, 61(1): 159–187.

—— (2000) 'Celebrity watching', *American Literary History*, 12(1/2): 272–283.

Nickel, Patricia Mooney (2010) 'Philanthromentality: celebrity parables as technologies of transfer', *American Political Science Association Annual Meeting*, Washington, DC.

Nicol, Brian (2006) *Stalking*. London: Reaktion Books.

Nimmer, Melville B. (1954) 'The right of publicity', *Law and Contemporary Problems*, 19(2): 203–223.

Nolte, Kristine (2005) *Der Kampf um Aufmerksamkeit: Wie Medien, Wirtschaft und Politik um eine knappe Ressource ringen*. Frankfurt a.M.: Campus.

Nord, Walter (1973) 'Adam Smith and Contemporary Social Exchange Theory', *American Journal of Economics & Sociology*, 32(4): 421–436.

North, Adrian C., Bland, Victoria, & Ellis, Nicky (2005) 'Distinguishing heroes from celebrities', *British Journal of Psychology*, 96(1): 39–52.

Nussbaum, Felicity (2005) 'Actresses and the economics of celebrity, 1700–1800', in M. Luckhurst & J. Moody (eds), *Theatre and Celebrity in Britain, 1660–2000*. Basingstoke: Palgrave Macmillan. pp. 148–168.

Oestreich, Gerhard (1982) *Neostoicism and the Early Modern State*. Cambridge: Cambridge University Press.

Orgel, Stephen (1975) *The Illusion of Power: Political Theater in the English Renaissance*. Berkeley: University of California Press.

Orth, Maureen (2004) *The Importance of Being Famous: Behind the Scenes of the Celebrity-Industrial Complex*. New York: Henry Holt & Co.

Paine, Robert (1967) 'What is gossip about? An alternative hypothesis', *Man, New Series*, 2(2): 278–285.

Palmer, Gareth (2002) 'Big Brother: an experiment in governance', *Television & New Media*, 3(3): 295–310.

Pantti, Mervi, & Zoonen, Liesbet van (2006) 'Do crying citizens make good citizens?', *Social Semiotics*, 16(2): 205–224.

Parker, Geoffrey (2008) 'Crisis and catastrophe: the global crisis of the seventeenth century reconsidered', *American Historical Review*, 113(4): 1053–1079.

Parker, Harold T. (1971) 'The formation of Napoleon's personality', *French Historical Studies*, 7(1): 6–26.

Parnaby, P.F., & Sacco, V.F. (2004) 'Fame and strain: the contributions of Mertonian Deviance Theory to an understanding of the relationship between celebrity and deviant behavior', *Deviant Behavior*, 25: 1–26.

Parry-Giles, Trevor (2008) 'Fame, celebrity, and the legacy of John Adams', *Western Journal of Communication*, 72(1): 83–101.

Patterson, Lyman Ray (1968) *Copyright in Historical Perspective*. Nashville: Vanderbilt University Press.

Payne, Deborah C. (1995) 'Reified object or emergent professional? Retheorizing the restoration actress', in J.D. Canfield & D.C. Payne (eds), *Cultural Readings of Restoration and Eighteenth-Century English Theater*. Athens: University of Georgia. pp. 13–38.

Pearson, Roberta (1997) 'It's always 1895: Sherlock Holmes in cyberspace', in D. Cartmell, I.Q. Hunter, H. Kaye & I. Whelehan (eds), *Trash Aesthetics: Popular Culture and its Audience*. London: Pluto. pp. 143–161.

Pearson, Roberta E. (2002) 'Shakespeare's country: the national poet, English identity and the silent cinema', in A. Higson (ed.), *Young and Innocent? The Cinema in Britain 1896–1930*. Exeter: University of Exeter Press.

—— (2007) 'Bachies, Bardies, Trekkies, and Shelockians', in J. Gray, C. Sandvoss & C.L. Harrington (eds), *Fandom: Identities and Communities in a Mediated World*. New York: New York University Press. pp. 98–109.

Pels, Dick (2003a) 'Aesthetic representation and political style: re-balancing identity and difference in media democracy', in J. Corner & D. Pels (eds), *Media and the Restyling of Politics: Consumerism, Celebrity and Cynicism*. London: Sage. pp. 40–66.

—— (2003b) *De Geest van Pim: Het gedachtegoed van een politieke dandy*. Amsterdam: Anthos.

—— (2007) *De economie van de eer: een nieuwe visie op verdienste en beloning*. Amsterdam: Ambo.

—— (2011) *Het volk bestaatniet!* Amsterdam: De Bezige Bij.

Penfold, Ruth (2004) 'The star's image, victimization and celebrity culture', *Punishment & Society*, 6(3): 289–302.

Penfold-Mounce, Ruth (ed.) (2009) *Celebrity Culture and Crime: The Joy of Transgression*. New York: Palgrave Macmillan.

Perse, Elizabeth M., & Rubin, Rebecca B. (1989) 'Attribution in social and parasocial relationships', *Communication Research*, 16(1): 59–77.

Peters, B. (1996) *Prominenz. Eine soziologische Untersuchung ihrer Entstehung und Wirkung*. Opladen: Westdeutscher Verlag.

Peters, Ralph (2010) 'The riddle of charisma', *Society*, 47(6): 516–520.

Petersen, Anne Helen (2011a) 'The gossip industry: producing and distributing star images, celebrity gossip and entertainment news 1910–2010'. Unpublished PhD, University of Texas at Austin, Austin.

—— (2011b) 'Towards an industrial history of celebrity gossip: *The National Enquirer*, *People Magazine* and "personality journalism" in the 1970s', *Celebrity Studies*, 2(2): 131–149.

Piccirillo, M.S. (1986) 'On the authenticity of televisual experience: a critical exploration of para-social closure', *Critical Studies in Mass Communication*, 3(3): 337–355.

Plunkett, John (2003) *Queen Victoria: First Media Monarch*. Oxford: Oxford University Press.

Ponce de Leon, Charles L. (2002) *Self-Exposure: Human-Interest Journalism and the Emergence of Celebrity in America, 1890–1940*. Chapel Hill: University of North Carolina Press.

Ponte, Stefano, Richey, Lisa Ann, & Baab, Mike (2009) 'Bono's Product (RED) Initiative: corporate social responsibility that solves the problems of "distant others" ', *Third World Quarterly*, 30(2): 301–317.

Postle, Martin (2005a) 'The life and art of Joshua Reynolds', in M. Postle (ed.), *Joshua Reynolds: The Creation of Celebrity*. London: Tate Publishing. pp. 271–277.

—— (2005b) ' "The Modern Apelles": Joshua Reynolds and the creation of celebrity', in M. Postle (ed.), *Joshua Reynolds: The Creation of Celebrity*. London: Tate Publishing. pp. 17–33.

Postman, Neil (1985) *Amusing Ourselves to Death: Public Discourse in the Age of Show Business*. New York: Viking.

Poulantzas, Nicos (1975) *Classes in Contemporary Capitalism*. London: New Left Books.

Powell, Helen, & Prasad, Sylvie (2010) ' "As Seen on TV." The celebrity expert: how taste is shaped by lifestyle media', *Cultural Politics: An International Journal*, 6(1): 111–124.

Pringle, Hamish (2004) *Celebrity Sells*. Chichester: John Wiley & Sons.

Pritchard, Will (2000) 'Masks and faces: female legibility in the Restoration Era', *Eighteenth-Century Life*, 24(3): 31–52.

Pullar, Ellen (2010) ' "A new woman": the promotional persona of Anna Sten', *Celebrity Studies*, 1(3): 268–285.

Rader, Benjamin G. (1983) 'Compensatory sport heroes: Ruth, Grange and Dempsey', *Journal of Popular Culture*, 16(4): 11–22.

Rajagopal, Arvind (1999) 'Celebrity and the politics of charity: memories of a missionary departed', in A. Kear & D.L. Steinberg (eds), *Mourning Diana: Nation, Culture and the Performance of Grief*. London: Routledge. pp. 126–141.

Ranft, Annette L., Zinko, Robert, Ferris, Gerald R., & Buckley, M. Ronald (2006) 'Marketing the image of management: the costs and benefits of CEO reputation', *Organizational Dynamics*, 35(3): 279–290.

Ranum, Orest (1980) 'Courtesy, absolutism, and the rise of the French state, 1630–1660', *Journal of Modern History*, 52(3): 426–451.

Ratcliff, Marc J. (2004) 'Abraham Trembley's strategy of generosity and the scope of celebrity in the mid-eighteenth century', *Isis*, 95: 555–575.

Raymond, Joad (2004) 'Describing popularity in Early Modern England', *Huntington Library Quarterly*, 67(1): 101–120.

Redmond, Sean, & Holmes, Su (eds) (2007) *Stardom and Celebrity: A Reader*. London: Sage.

Rein, Irving J., Kotler, Philip, & Stoller, Martin R. (1997) *High Visibility: The Making and Marketing of Professionals into Celebrities*. Lincolnwood, Ill.: NTC Pub. Group.

Revel, Jacques (1997) 'The court', in P. Nora (ed.), *Realms of Memory: the Construction of the French Past. Vol. 2: Traditions*. New York: Columbia University Press. pp. 71–122.

Reyes, Oscar (2004) 'Cheriegate! Celebrity, scandal and political leadership', *Mediactive*, 2: 26–43.

Riall, Lucy (2007a) *Garibaldi: Invention of a Hero*. New Haven: Yale University Press.

—— (2007b) 'Garibaldi: the first celebrity', *History Today*, 57(8): 41–47.

Richards, Judith M. (1999) 'Love and a female monarch: the case of Elizabeth Tudor', *Journal of British Studies*, 38(2): 133–160.

Richey, Lisa Ann, & Ponte, Stefano (2008) 'Better (Red)™ than dead? Celebrities, consumption and international aid', *Third World Quarterly*, 29(4): 711–729.

Rindova, Violina P., Pollock, Timothy G, & Hayward, Mathew L.A. (2006) 'Celebrity firms: the social construction of market popularity', *Academy of Management Review*, 31(1): 50–71.

Rixon, Paul (2011) 'The role of the British popular press in re-imagining American television celebrities for the British audience: the 1950s to the 1960s', *Celebrity Studies*, 2(1): 44–55.

Roach, Joseph (2003) 'Celebrity erotics: Pepys, performance, and painted ladies', *The Yale Journal of Criticism*, 16(1): 211–230.

—— (2005) 'Public intimacy: the prior history of "it" ', in M. Luckhurst & J. Moody (eds), *Theatre and Celebrity in Britain, 1660–2000*. Basingstoke: Palgrave Macmillan. pp. 15–30.

Roberts, I.D. (2011) 'China's internet celebrity: Furong Jiejie', in L. Edwards & E. Jeffreys (eds), *Celebrity in China*. Hong Kong: Hong Kong University Press. pp. 217–236.

Roberts, Mary Louise (2010) 'Rethinking female celebrity: the ecccentric star of nineteenth-century France', in E. Berenson & E. Giloi (eds), *Constructing Charisma: Celebrity, Fame, and Power in Nineteenth-Century Europe*. New York: Berghahn. pp. 103–116.

Roberts, Penny (2007) 'The kingdom's two bodies', *French History*, 21(2): 147–164.

Rockwell, Donna, & Giles, David C. (2009) 'Being a celebrity: a phenomenology of fame', *Journal of Phenomenological Psychology*, 40(2): 178–210.

Rohrs, Emily R. (2007) *Queen Victoria: The Mother of Modern Celebrity*. Muncie, Ind.: Ball State University.

Rojek, Chris (2001) *Celebrity*. London: Reaktion Books.

—— (2005) 'Celebrity', in G. Ritzer (ed.), *Encylopedia of Social Theory*. London: Sage. pp. 83–87.

—— (2006) 'Sports celebrity and the civilizing process', *Sport in Society*, 9(4): 674–690.

Roll, Richard (1986) 'The hubris hypothesis of corporate takeovers', *Journal of Business*, 59(2): 197–216.

Rolph, David (2006) 'Dirty pictures: defamation, reputation and nudity', *Law Text Culture*, 19: 101–134.

Romel, Stephen (2011) 'It's a dog's life', *The Weekend Australian Review*, 26–27 February.

Rose, Jacqueline (1998) 'The Cult of Celebrity', *London Review of Books*, 20 August.

Rose, Nikolas (1996) *Inventing Our Selves: Psychology, Power and Personhood*. New York: Cambridge University Press.

—— (1999) *Powers of Freedom: Reframing Political Thought*. Cambridge: Cambridge University Press.

Rötzer, Florian, & Goldhaber, Michael H. (1998). The attention economy will change everything: an e-mail interview with Michael H. Goldhaber. Online: www.heise.de/tp/r4/artikel/1/1419/1.html (accessed 8 November 2008).

Rubin, Alan, & McHugh, M. (1987) 'Development of parasocial interaction relationships', *Journal of Broadcasting & Electronic Media* 31: 279–292.

Rubin, Alan, E. Perse, & Powell, R. (1987) 'Loneliness, parasocial interaction, and local television news viewing', *Human Communication Research* 12: 155–180.

Rubin, Alan M., & Rubin, Rebecca B. (1985) 'Interface of personal and mediated communication: a research agenda', *Critical Studies in Mass Communication*, 2(1): 36–53.

Rubin, Jerry (1976) *Growing (Up) at 37*. New York: M. Evans.

Samman, Emma, Auliffe, Eilish Mc, & MacLachlan, Malcolm (2009) 'The role of celebrity in endorsing poverty reduction through international aid', *International Journal of Nonprofit and Voluntary Sector Marketing*, 14: 137–148.

Samuelson, Paul (1966) 'Economics and the history of ideas', in J.E. Stiglitz (ed.), *The Collected Scientific Papers of Paul A. Samuelson* (Vol. II). Cambridge, Mass.: MIT Press. pp. 1499–1516.

Saul, Nigel (2011) 'Chivalry and the birth of celebrity', *History Today*, 61(6): 20.

Savage, Mike, & Williams, Karel (2008) 'Elites: remembered in capitalism and forgotten by social sciences', *Sociological Review*, 56(1): 1–24.

Sawelson-Gorse, Naomi (2000) 'On the hot seat: Mike Wallace interviews Marcel Duchamp', *Art History*, 23(1): 35–55.

Scaglione, Aldo (1991) *Knights at Court: Courtliness, Chivalry, and Courtesy From Ottonian Germany to the Italian Renaissance*. Berkeley: University of California Press.

Schelsky, Helmut (1983) 'Der "Begriff des Politischen" und die politische Erfahrung der Gegenwart. Ueberlegungen zur Aktualitaet von Carl Schmitt', *Der Staat*, 22(3): 321–345.

Schely-Newman, Esther (2004) 'Mock intimacy: strategies of engagement in Israeli gossip columns', *Discourse Studies*, 6(4): 471–488.

Schickel, Richard (1976) *Douglas Fairbanks: The First Celebrity*. London: Elm Tree Books.

—— (1985a) *Intimate Strangers: The Culture of Celebrity*. Garden City, NY: Doubleday.

—— (1985b) 'The rise and fall of Cafe Society', *Forbes*, 136 (28 October): 40–43.

—— (2010) 'I blog therefore I am', *Society*, 47(5).

Schwartz, Barry (1998) 'Postmodernity and historical reputation: Abraham Lincoln in late twentieth-century American memory', *Social Forces*, 77(1): 63–103.

Sconce, Jeffrey (2007) 'A vacancy at the Paris Hilton', in J. Gray, C. Sandvoss & C.L. Harrington (eds), *Fandom: Identities and Communities in a Mediated World*. New York: New York University Press. pp. 328–343.

Sennett, Richard (2002 [1977]) *The Fall of Public Man*. London: Penguin.

Sentilles, Renée M. (2003) *Performing Menken: Adah Isaacs Menken and the Birth of American Celebrity*. Cambridge: Cambridge University Press.

Service, Faith (1970) 'So you'd like to be a star?' in Martin Levin (ed.), *Hollywood and the Great Fan Magazines*. New York: Arbor House. pp. 142–143, 214–215.

Seymour, Bruce (1996) *Lola Montez: A Life*. New Haven: Yale University Press.

Sharpe, Kevin (2009) *Selling the Tudor Monarchy: Authority and Image in Sixteenth-Century England*. New Haven: Yale University Press.

Shaw, Lisa (2010) 'The celebritisation of Carmen Miranda in New York, 1939–41', *Celebrity Studies*, 1(3): 286–302.

Sher, Richard B. (2006) *The Enlightenment and the Book: Scottish Authors and their Publishers in Eighteenth-century Britain, Ireland, and America*. Chicago: University of Chicago Press.

Sheridan, Greg (2008) 'Politics of celebrity takes over', *The Australian*, 1 November.

Shovlin, John (2000) 'Toward a reinterpretation of revolutionary antinobilism: the political economy of honor in the old regime', *Journal of Modern History*, 72(1): 35–66.

Silverstone, Roger (1993) 'Television, ontological security and the transitional object', *Media, Culture & Society*, 15(4): 573–598.

Simmel, Georg (1957) 'Fashion', *American Journal of Sociology*, 62(6): 541–558.

—— (1971a) 'Freedom and the individual', in *Individuality and Social Forms*. Chicago: University of Chicago Pres. pp. 217–226.

—— (1971b) 'The nobility', in *Individuality and Social Forms*. Chicago: University of Chicago Press. pp. 199–213.

—— (1971c) 'The stranger', in *Individuality and Social Forms*. Chicago: University of Chicago Press. pp. 143–149.

—— (2007) 'Individualism', *Theory, Culture & Society*, 24(7/8): 66–71.

Simon, Herbert A (1971) 'Designing organizations for an information-rich world', in M. Greenberger (ed.), *Computers, Communication, and the Public Interest*. Baltimore: Johns Hopkins Press. pp. 37–52.

Simonson, Peter (2006) 'Celebrity, public image, and American political life: rereading Robert K. Merton's *Mass Persuasion*', *Political Communication*, 23(3): 271–284.

Singer, Sally (2002) 'Warrior One', *Vogue*, 1 October.

Skeggs, Beverley (2009) 'Moral Economy of person production: the class relations of self-performance on "reality" television', *Sociological Review*, 57(4): 626–644.

Smart, Barry (2005) *The Sport Star: Modern Sport and the Cultural Economy of Sporting Celebrity*. London: Sage.

Smith, Adam (1976 [1759]) *The Theory of Moral Sentiments*. Oxford: Oxford University Press.

Smith, Jay M. (1996) *The Culture of Merit: Nobility, Royal Service, and the Making of Absolute Monarchy in France, 1600–1789*. Ann Arbor: University of Michigan Press.

Smith, James W. (2005) *The Garibaldi Panorama*. New York: Dennis Powers Productions.

Smith, Philip (2000) 'Culture and charisma: outline of a theory', *Acta Sociologica*, 43: 101–111.

Spacks, Patricia Meyer (1985) *Gossip*. Chicago: University of Chicago Press.

Stacey, Jackie (1994) *Star Gazing: Hollywood Cinema and Female Spectatorship*. London: Routledge.

Stalpaert, Christel (2002) 'The entry of Charles-Alexandre de Lorraine into Brussels: monarchical discourse in public ceremonies and theatrical performances', *Eighteenth-Century Life*, 26(2): 69–82.

Sternberg, Ernest (1998) 'Phantasmagoric labor: the new economics of self-presentation', *Futures*, 30(1): 3–21.

Stevenson, Nick (2009) 'Talking to Bowie fans: masculinity, ambivalence and cultural citizenship', *European Journal of Cultural Studies*, 12(1): 79–98.

Stever, Gayle S. (2009) 'Parasocial and social interaction with celebrities: classification of media fans', *Journal of Media Psychology*, 14(3): 1–39.

—— (2011) 'Celebrity worship: critiquing a construct', *Journal of Applied Social Psychology*, 41(6): 1356–1370.

Stirling, Rebecca Birch (1956) 'Some psychological mechanisms operative in gossip', *Social Forces*, 34(3): 262–267.

Stone, Lawrence (1958) 'The inflation of honours 1558–1641', *Past & Present*, 14: 45–70.

—— (1964) 'The educational revolution in England, 1560–1640', *Past & Present*, 28: 41–80.

—— (1965) *Crisis of the Aristocracy, 1558–1641*. Oxford: Oxford University Press.

—— (1966) 'Social mobility in England, 1500–1700', *Past & Present*, 33: 16–55.

Stowe, David W. (1998) 'The politics of cafe society', *Journal of American History*, 84(4): 1384–1406.

Strate, Lance (1994) 'Heroes: a communication perspective', in S.J. Drucker & R.S. Cathcart (eds), *American Heroes in a Mediated Age*. Cresol, NJ: Hampton Press. pp. 15–23.

Street, John (2002) 'Bob, Bono and Tony: the celebrity as politician', *Media, Culture & Society*, 24(3): 433–441.

—— (2003) 'The celebrity politician: political style and popular culture', in J. Corner & D. Pels (eds), *Media and the Restyling of Politics: Consumerism, Celebrity and Cynicism*. London: Sage. pp. 85–98.

—— (2004) 'Celebrity politicians: popular culture and political representation', *British Journal of Politics & International Relations*, 6(4): 435–452.

—— (2007) 'Framing celebrity: new directions in celebrity culture', *British Politics*, 2(2): 289–290.

Swerdlow, Robert A. (1984) 'Star studded advertising: is it worth the effort?', *Journal of the Academy Of Marketing Science*, 12(3): 89–102.

Szakolczai, Árpád (2000) *Reflexive Historical Sociology*. London: Routledge.

Taylor, George (2000) *The French Revolution and the London Stage, 1789–1805*. Cambridge: Cambridge University Press.

Theodoropolou, Vivi (2007) 'The anti-fan with the fan: awe and envy in sport fandom', in J. Gray, C. Sandvoss & C. L. Harrington (eds), *Fandom: Identities and Communities in a Mediated World*. New York: New York University Press. pp. 316–327.

Thompson, John B. (1995) *The Media and Modernity: A Social Theory of the Media*. Cambridge: Polity.

Thomson, Peter (2005) 'Celebrity and rivalry: David [Garrick] and Goliath [Quin]', in M. Luckhurst & J. Moody (eds), *Theatre and Celebrity in Britain, 1660–2000*. Basingstoke: Palgrave Macmillan. pp. 127–147.

Thrall, A. Trevor, Lollio-Fakhreddine, Jaime, Berent, Jon, Donnelly, Lana, Herrin, Wes, Paquette, Zachary, et al. (2008) 'Star power: celebrity advocacy and the evolution of the public sphere', *International Journal of Press/Politics*, 13(4): 362–385.

Thrift, Nigel (2002) 'Performing cultures in the new economy', in P. Du Gay & M. Pryke (eds), *Cultural Economy: Cultural Analysis and Commercial Life*. London: Sage.

Tillyard, Stella (2005a) 'Celebrity in 18th-century London', *History Today*, 55(6): 20–27.

—— (2005b) ' "Paths of glory": fame and the public in eighteenth-century London', in M. Postle (ed.), *Joshua Reynolds: The Creation of Celebrity*. London: Tate Publishing. pp. 61–69.

Tolson, Andrew (2001) ' "Being yourself": the pursuit of authentic celebrity', *Discourse Studies*, 3(4): 443–457.

Tonello, Matteo & Rabimov, Stephan Rahim (2010) 'The 2010 Institutional Investment Report: trends in asset allocation and portfolio composition' (11 November), *The Conference Board Research Report, No. R-1468-10-RR, 2010*. Online: http://ssrn.com/abstract=1707512 (accessed 9 November 2011).

Tönnies, Ferdinand (2001 [1887]) *Community and Civil Cociety*. Cambridge: Cambridge University Press.

Trevor-Roper, Hugh (1967) *The Crisis of the Seventeenth Century: Religion, the Reformation and Social Change*. Indianapolis: Liberty Fund.

—— (1959) 'The general crisis of the seventeenth century', *Past & Present*, 16(1): 31–64.

Trotter, Wilfred (1921) *Instincts of the Herd in Peace and War*. London: Unwin.

Tsaliki, Liza, Frangonikolopoulos, Christos A., & Huliaras, Asteris (eds) (2011) *Transnational Celebrity Activism in Global Politics: Changing the World?* Bristol: Intellect.

Tulloch, John (2007) 'Fans of Chekhov: re-approaching "high culture"', in J. Gray, C. Sandvoss & C.L. Harrington (eds), *Fandom: Identities and Communities in a Mediated World*. New York: New York University Press. pp. 110–122.

Turner, Bryan S. (2003) 'Warrior charisma and the spiritualization of violence', *Body & Society*, 9(4): 93–108.

Turner, Graeme (2004) *Understanding Celebrity*. Thousand Oaks, CA: Sage Publications.

——— (2006) 'The mass production of celebrity: "celetoids", reality TV and the "demotic turn" ', *International Journal of Cultural Studies*, 9(2): 153–165.

——— (2007) 'The economy of celebrity', in S. Redmond & S. Holmes (eds), *Stardom and Celebrity: A Reader*. London: Sage. pp. 193–205.

——— (2010) 'Approaching celebrity studies', *Celebrity Studies*, 1(1): 11–20.

Turner, Graeme, Bonner, Frances, & Marshall, P. David (2000) 'Core territory: celebrities and the women's magazines', in *Fame Games: the Production of Celebrity in Australia*. Cambridge: Cambridge University Press. pp. 116–159.

Turner, Stephen (2003) 'Charisma reconsidered', *Journal of Classical Sociology*, 3: 5–26.

Twitchell, James B. (1996) *ADCULT USA: The Triumph of Advertising in American Culture*. New York: Columbia University Press.

——— (2004) *Branded Nation: The Marketing of Megachurch, College Inc., and Museum-world*. New York: Simon & Schuster.

Tye, L. (1998) *The Father of Spin: Edward L. Bernays and the Birth of Public Relations*. New York: Crown.

Tyler, Imogen (2007) 'From the me decade to the me millennium', *International Journal of Cultural Studies*, 10(3): 343–363.

van Iterson, Ad, & Clegg, Stewart R. (2008) 'The politics of gossip and denial in interorganizational relations', *Human Relations*, 61(8): 1117–1137.

van Iterson, Ad, Waddington, Kathryn, & Michelson, Grant (2010) 'Breaking the silence: the role of gossip in organizational culture', in N. Ashkanasy, C.P.M. Wilderom & M.F. Peterson (eds), *Handbook of Organizational Culture and Climate*, 2nd edn. London: Sage. pp. 375–392.

van Krieken, Robert (1999) 'The barbarism of civilization: cultural genocide and the "stolen generations"', *British Journal of Sociology*, 50(2): 297–315.

van Zoonen, Liesbet (2004) 'Imagining the fan democracy', *European Journal of Communication*, 19(1): 39–52.

——— (2005) *Entertaining the Citizen: When Politics and Popular Culture Converge*. Lanham: Rowman & Littlefield.

——— (2006) 'The personal, the political and the popular: a woman's guide to celebrity politics', *European Journal of Cultural Studies*, 9(3): 287–301.

Vande Berg, Leah R. (1998) 'The sports hero meets mediated celebrityhood', in L.A. Wenner (ed.), *Mediasport*. London: Routledge. pp. 134–153.

Vannini, Phillip (2004) 'The meanings of a star: interpreting pop music fans' reviews', *Symbolic Interaction*, 27(1): 47–69.

Vickery, A. (2011) 'Rogues gallery: paintings put first actresses in the spotlight', *The Guardian*, 14 October. Online: www.guardian.co.uk/artanddesign/2011/oct/14/paintings-first-actresses-national-portrait-gallery.

Virilio, Paul (2005) 'Democracy of emotion', *Cultural Politics*, 1(3): 339–352.

Vowinckel, Gerhard (1983) *Von politischen köpfen und schönen Seelen. Ein soziologischer Versuch über die Zivilisationsformen der Affekte und ihres Ausdrucks*. München: Juventa.

——— (1987) 'Command or refine? Cultural patterns of cognitively organizing emotions', *Theory, Culture & Society*, 4: 489–514.

Waddington, Kathryn, & Michelson, Grant (2010) *Gossip and Organizations*. London: Routledge.

Wade, James B., Porac, Joseph F., Pollock, Timothy G., & Graffin, Scott D. (2006) 'The burden of celebrity: the impact of CEO certification contests on CEO pay and performance', *Academy of Management Journal*, 49(4): 643–660.

——— (2008) 'Star CEOs: benefit or burden', *Oganizational Dynamics*, 37(2): 203–210.

Wall, David (2003) 'Policing Elvis: legal action and the shaping of post-mortem celebrity culture as contested space', *Entertainment Law*, 2(3): 35–69.

Wanko, Cheryl (1998) 'Three stories of celebrity: The Beggar's Opera "biographies" ', *Studies in English Literature, 1500–1900*, 38(3): 481–498.

—— (2003) *Roles of Authority. Thespian Biography and Celebrity in Eighteenth-Century Britain*. Lubbock: Texas Tech University Press.

—— (2009) 'Patron or patronised?: "fans" and the eighteenth-century English stage', in T. Mole (ed.), *Romanticism and Celebrity Culture, 1750–1850*. Cambridge: Cambridge University Press. pp. 209–226.

Ward, Ian (2001) 'Fairyland and its fairy kings and queens', *Journal of Historical Sociology*, 14(1): 1–20.

Warhol, Andy, & Colacello, B. (1979) *Andy Warhol's exposures*. London: Hutchinson.

Weber, Eugene (1976) *Peasants into Frenchmen: The Modernization of Rural France, 1870–1914*. Stanford: Stanford University Press.

Weber, Max (1930) *The Protestant Ethic and the Spirit of Capitalism*. London: George Allen & Unwin.

—— (1948) 'The meaning of discipline', in H.H. Gerth & C.W. Mills (eds), *From Max Weber: Essays in Sociology*. London: Routledge & Kegan Paul. pp. 253–264.

—— (1968) *On Charisma and Institution Building*. Chicago: University of Chicago Press.

—— (1978) *Economy and Society*. Berkeley: University of California Press.

Wee, Lionel, & Brooks, Ann (2010) 'Personal branding and the commodification of reflexivity', *Cultural Sociology*, 4(1): 45–62.

Weimann, Robert (1986) 'History and the issue of authority in representation: the Elizabethan theater and the Reformation', *New Literary History*, 17(3): 449–476.

Weiskel, Timothy C. (2005) 'From sidekick to sideshow—celebrity, entertainment, and the politics of distraction: why Americans are "sleepwalking toward the end of the earth', *American Behavioral Scientist*, 49(3): 393–409.

Welky, David (2008) *The Moguls and the Dictators: Hollywood and the Coming of World War II*. Baltimore: Johns Hopkins University Press.

Wendeborn, Gebhard Friedrich August (1791) *A View of England Towards the Close of the Eighteenth Century* (Vol. II). London: GGJ & J Robinson.

Wenzel, Harald (2000) 'Obertanen. Zur soziologischen Bedeutung von Prominenz', *Leviathan*, 28(4): 452–476.

Wert, Sarah R., & Salovey, Peter (2004) 'A social comparison account of gossip', *Review of General Psychology*, 8(2): 122–137.

West, Darrell M. (2005) 'American politics in the age of celebrity', *Hedgehog Review*, 7(1): 59–65.

West, Darrell M., & Orman, John M. (2003) *Celebrity Politics*. Upper Saddle River, NJ: Prentice Hall.

Whannel, Garry (2001) *Media Sport Stars Masculinities and Moralities*. London: Routledge.

—— (2010) 'News, celebrity, and vortextuality: a study of the media coverage of the Michael Jackson verdict', *Cultural Politics: An International Journal*, 6(1): 65–84.

Wheeler, Mark (2011) 'Celebrity diplomacy: United Nations' Goodwill Ambassadors and Messengers of Peace', *Celebrity Studies*, 2(1): 6–18.

Whigham, Frank (1983) 'Interpretation at court: courtesy and the performer–audience dialectic', *New Literary History*, 14(3): 623–639

Wickham, Chris (1998) 'Gossip and resistance among the medieval peasantry', *Past & Present*, 160(1): 3–24.

Williams, Penry (1963) 'The Tudor state', *Past & Present*, 25: 39–58.

—— (1979) *The Tudor Regime*. Oxford: Clarendon.

Wilson, Bee (2007) 'Boudoir politics: review of *Lola Montez: Her Life and Conquests*, by James Morton', *London Review of Books*, 29(11): 27–29.

Wilson, David Sloan, Wilczynski, Caolyn, Wells, Alexandra, & Weiser, Laura (2000) 'Gossip and other aspects of language as group-level adaptations', in C. Heyes & L. Huber (eds), *The Evolution of Cognition*. Cambridge, Mass.: MIT Press. pp. 347–365.

Wilson, Frank Percy (1955) 'The Elizabethan theatre', *Neophilologus*, 39(1): 40–58.

Wilson, Julie (2011) 'A new kind of star is born: Audrey Hepburn and the global governmentalisation of female stardom', *Celebrity Studies*, 2(1): 56–68.

Wilson, Julie A. (2010) 'Star testing: the emerging politics of celebrity gossip', *The Velvet Light Trap*, 65: 25–38.

Wilson, John Harold (1958) *All the King's Ladies: Actresses of the Restoration*. Chicago: University of Chicago Press.

Wilson, Sherryl (2003) *Oprah, Celebrity and Formations of Self*. Basingstoke: Palgrave Macmillan.

Wilson, Sarah (2008) 'Gossip girls', *Good Weekend*, 22 November: 28–34.

Wise, J. Macgregor (2002) 'Mapping the culture of control: seeing through The Truman Show', *Television & New Media*, 3(1): 29–47.

Wise, Sue (1984) 'Sexing Elvis', *Women's Studies International Forum*, 7(1): 13–17.

Wittrock, Bjorn (1998) 'Early modernities: varieties and transitions', *Daedalus*, 127(3): 19.

Wood, Helen, & Skeggs, Beverley (2004) 'Notes on ethical scenarios of self on British reality TV', *Feminist Media Studies*, 4(2): 205–208.

Young, Michael (1959 [1958]) *The Rise of the Meritocracy: The New Elite of our Social Revolution*. New York: Random House.

Young, Toby (2008) 'Lulled by the celebritariat', *Prospect Magazine*, 20 November.

Yrjölä, Riina (2009) 'The invisible violence of celebrity humanitarianism: soft images and hard words in the making and unmaking of Africa', *World Political Science Review*, 5(1): 1–22.

Zafirau, Stephen (2008) 'Reputation work in selling film and television: life in the Hollywood talent industry', *Qualitative Sociology*, 31: 99–127.

Zalmanovich, Tal (2009) 'Woman Pioneer of Empire': the making of a female colonial celebrity', *Postcolonial Studies*, 12(2): 193–210.

Zapparoni, Rosina (2004) 'Propertising identity: understanding the United States right of publicity and its implications: some lessons for Australia', *Melbourne University Law Review*, 28(3): 690–723.

Zuckerman, Harriet (1977) *Scientific Elite: Nobel Laureates in the United States*. New York: Free Press.

Index

Note: page numbers in **bold** refer to tables; page numbers in *italics* refer to figures.

academia, celebrity and peer recognition in 50–1, 54–5, 142–3
accounting, as sector of celebrity production 52
actresses: fan imitation of 92–3; relationship with audiences 34–6; self-promotion of 48, 51
Adams, John 38, 57, 65
Agassi, Andre 52
Albert, Prince 44, 112
Alexander the Great 5, 15–16
All American Girl 64–5
Angelyne 133
Annan, Kofi 113
anti-war movement 109–10
appearance sector 52
Apple 115, 122, 129
aristocracy: and actors 34, 36; and celebrity 3–4, 8, 16, 57, 62; de-militarization of 18–19; modern popularity of 80; personal service by 30; sincerity and rationality of 28–9; visibility of 71; and Whig party 38, 103
Armour, P.D. 121
attention: and business elite 125; in celebrity society 4, 11; as coordination device 56; falseness of 6; as income 60; public figures' claims to 7, 57; and relation of figure and ground 58–9; scarcity of 55, 58; self-accumulating nature of *see* attention-capital, accumulation of
attention-capital: and academia 60, 142; accumulation of 10, 57, 59–61, 135, 138; in celebrity production 56–7; increasing value of 135; management of 13; property rights to 75–6, 79–80; transformation of 5; Winchell's role in 12

attention economy 56, 58, 140
authenticity: in Boorstin's analysis 6; in court society 21, 28–9; and performance 97
authority, different forms of 69–70
authors: as celebrities 37; self-promotion of 39

Barnum, P.T. 11, 42, 46, 89, 106
Barry, Elizabeth 35–6
Barrymore, Ethyl 107–8
Bay City Rollers 86
Beckham, David 113–14
Bernays, Edward L. 12, 108, 147n6
Bernhardt, Sarah 47–8, 70
best-sellers 6
Betty, William 42–4
Big Brother 72, 145n6
biographies 35, 70, 84, 100, 128
Black, Rebecca 133
Boccaccio 25
Bono (Paul Hewson) 40, 67, 99, 113–15
Boorstin, Daniel, definition of celebrity 2, 6, 55, 58
Bourdieu, Pierre 60, 66, 89, 135, 152
bourgeoisie: in French salons 23–4; incorporation into nobility 30; and literacy 31; public sphere of 32; rationality of 19, 28; takeover of court society 3
Brady, Mathew 42
branding: and celebrity CEOs 119; and celebrity firms 129; earnings of 53; increasing importance of 135; of self 73
Branson, Richard 122, 126, 129
Brown, Jerry 112
Buffalo Bill 11, 47
businessmen, as celebrities 119, 121, 126–7

café society 12, 62–3
Cage, John 59
Çağri, Mahir 132
Campbell, Naomi 77
capital: celebrity as 4–5; cultural 8, 66; and
    meritocracy 17; social 66, 84; symbolic
    8, 19
capitalism: consumer 64, 68;
    corporatization of 120; and court society
    17; evolution of 120–2; ongoing
    critiques of 127; post-Fordist 125, 143;
    and status 67
Carnegie, Andrew 119–20
Caroline of Monaco 78–80
Carson, Johnny 76
cartes-de-visite 41–2, 105
Catholic Church 17–18, 71, 102
CCP (Chinese Communist Party) 136–7
celebrification: of academia 60; of CEOs
    124, 127; of environmentalism 115; of
    politics 101, 140–1; use of term 5
celebrities: definition of 58; and aspiration
    126; as 'attention-traps', 59–60, 74, 135;
    as commodities 54; of consumption and
    production 100; dead 53, 76; earnings of
    53–4; endorsing political candidates
    12–13, 107–9, 143; as icons 90; legal
    status of 67, 75; military 137; as
    'ordinary folk', 10, 17, 91, 111; political
    causes of 55, 112–15; and power elites
    62, 66, 127; as representatives 115–16;
    and social networks 82; social status of
    125; surveillance of 71
celebrity: definitions of 10; as 'bread and
    circuses', 74; and charisma 69–70;
    cross-over between fields 53, 109–10;
    de Girardin's use of concept 48;
    economics of 11, 58; evolution of 36–7,
    39; and inequality 139–42; literature on
    10–12; and mass communication 5,
    30–1, 63–4, 68; and narrative 97;
    negative connotations of 5–6; origin of
    term 15–16; power relations of 2, 8, 73;
    and recognition 8–9; significance of
    1–2; social pedagogy of 83–4; and status
    66–8; surplus value of 4, 7, 10;
    transitory nature of 131–2; triadic logic
    of 56
celebrity culture: elite origins of 24; use of
    concept 2, 138–9
celebrity diplomacy 112, 114–15
celebrity–fan relationship: idealized nature
    of 94; and identity 82, 92; illusion of
    familiarity in 36, 47; and ownership of

attention-capital 76; panopticism and
    synopticism in 68; pathological aspects
    93; and photography 41; and politician–
    citizen relationship 141;
    psychodynamics of 85–7; and real-life
    relationships 85–6, 95–6
celebrity from below 70
celebrity function 8, 56, 73
celebrity gossip: becoming more critical
    91–2; columns 48, 62–3; magazines 80;
    safety of 88–90; and social norms 8, 72,
    83, 90–1; specificity of 12
celebrity identity: artificiality of 89;
    constitution of 50; legal regulation of
    75–6, 80; and political activity 111; and
    products 54, 58; property rights in 78;
    and social function 61; types of 70
celebrity images 41–2, 93
celebrity literacy 141
celebrity philanthropy 112, 115
celebrity production: and CEOs 119;
    competition in 65; democratization of
    16, 36–8, 46; Diana's role in 4;
    economic value of 52–3;
    industrialization of 12, 40–2, 48–50; and
    Internet celetoids 133; logic of *see*
    celebrity function; and politics 106;
    spread of 136; sub-industries of 52
celebrity rationality 22, 24, 141, 143
celebrity sectors 50–1, 54, 109
celebrity service 52
celebrity society: background of concept
    2–4; basic principles of 39; in China
    136–7; and commodification 74; critique
    of 138–9, 141; future of 13–14;
    globalization of 135–6; industrialization
    of 40; leveraging of established celebrity
    in 135; and modernity 11; political
    implications of 143–4; status and
    charisma in 66
celebrity-watching 88–9, 96
celetoids 133, 136
CEOs: appointment of 122–4; as
    aspirational figures 124–7; business
    leadership of 127; as celebrities 13; as
    corporate symbols 119, 125; private
    lives of 122; virtual 128–9
Chaplin, Charlie 107
charisma: and authority 69–70; of CEOs
    122–4; in politics 116–17; Weber on
    68–9
Charles I 34
Charles II 11, 15, 34, 36–7
Charney, Dov 126, 129

China: celebrity production in 136; state-sponsored celebrities in 127–8, 137
Cibber, Colley 36
citation, academic 51, 60, 142
Clinton, Bill: allure of 70; association with celebrities 109; as celebrity 98, 112; and intimacy 46
coaching, as sector of celebrity production 52
Cody, William *see* Buffalo Bill
communication: mass *see* mass media; modes of 11, 17, 30; as sector of celebrity production 52
communities: imagined *see* imagined community; virtual 82, 138
confidence, breach of 77
Coolidge, Calvin 108, 113, 147n7
copyright 37
court self 22
court society: and celebrity society 3, 11, 22, 86; competition in 22; and education 19; evolution of 16–19; persistence of 24, 29; power relations in 19–22; and salons 23; and state-formation 17–18
Cromwell, Oliver 37, 69
cultural governance 141
cultural pessimism 2, 138, 141
culture, commodification of 74
Cyrus, Miley 65

Dante 25, 31
Davis, Moll 34–5
democracy: and celebrity 8, 13, 109, 115–16; framing of authority under 99, 105–6; and individualism 29; reduction of participation in 116–17
democratization, and celebrity 12, 16
Diana, Princess of Wales: as celebrity 4–5; emotional resonance of 1; marketing of 104; as 'Queen of Hearts', 45; and Elizabeth I 102
Dietrich, Marlene 78
discipline 21–2, 24, 26–8, 50
Dolly sisters 108
Douglas, Michael 79
Duchamp, Marcel 58–60
Duchess of Devonshire 12, 38, 103
Durkheim, Emile 90, 135

eccentricity 47–8, 122
Einstein, Albert: as celebrity 7; posthumous earnings of 53
Elizabeth I: as celebrity 11–12, 102; performative power of 18, 20–1; as

'Queen of Hearts', 45; theatre under 20, 33–4
Emerson, Ralph Waldo 16
emotional labour 73
emotions, management of 20–1, 29
endorsements: as sector of celebrity production 52; Tiger Woods's earnings from 54
English Restoration, theatre in 34–6
Enron 131
entertainment, as sector of celebrity production 50–2
entrepreneurs: as celebrities 13, 127–8; public relations of 119–22; workers as 126
environmentalism 112, 115
etiquette 20, 22, 86
European Court of Human Rights 78–9
everyday life, commodification of 16
exhibitionary complex 71
experts: in celebrity production 12; critique of 117; relationship with public 51
expression, freedom of 76–7, 79–80

Facebook 134–5
Fairbanks, Douglas 107–8, 112
Fairy Queen 45, 102
fame, modernization of 16
fandom 85–6, 92–6
fan fiction 94
fashion, and celebrities 24, 93
favouritism 22
Felix, Rachel 77–8
femininity: media images of 84, 93; and private life 35
film: importance of stars in 57–8, 93; politicians on 106; and sports stars 49
film stars, and politics 107
firms: as celebrities 129–31; internal structure of 124–5; mergers and acquisitions 125
Forbes magazine 53, 136
Foucault, Michel 12, 60, 70, 74–5, 135
Fox, Charles 103
France, privacy law in 77–8
Franklin, Benjamin 7, 38, 103
Frederick, Pauline 108
French Enlightenment 24
French Revolution 29
French salons 23–4, 135
Freud, Sigmund 72, 86–7, 108
Fry, Stephen 55, 134, 151
Furong Jiejie 136

Garibaldi, Giuseppe 11–12, 46–7, 70, 104–5
Garland, Judy 95–6
Garrick, David 36–7, 43–4
gaze: centripetal 12, 72, 139–40, 143; sovereign 65
Geldof, Bob 98–9, 113–14
gemeinschaft and *gesellschaft* 81
gender: and celebrity 64, 70, 72–3; and sport stars 83
Germany: political celebrity in 64, 106; privacy law in 78–80
Girardin, Delphine de 48, 63
Gish, Lillian 107–8
globalization 51, 83, 135–6, 138
Golub, Harvey 123
Gordon, Jeff 73
Gordy, Berry 48–9
gossip: about celebrities *see* celebrity gossip; and empowerment 91; as para-social relationship 85; social function of 12, 67, 87–8
Guerre, Martin 28
Guevara, Che 70, 105
Gutenberg galaxy 81, 138
Gwynn, Nell 15, 34–5

Habermas, Jürgen 17, 32–3, 60
habitus 3, 22, 72
Haider, Jörg 117
Harding, Warren 67, 107–8, 113, 147n5
Harding–Coolidge Theatrical League 107–8
heat magazine 41, 89
Henry VIII: as celebrity 11–12, 102; performative power of 18
Hepburn: Audrey 112; Katherine 93
heroes: and celebrities 5–7, 47, 98, 138, 142; compensatory 49
Hilton, Paris: attention-gathering strategies of 59–60; as meta-celebrity 135; as negative example 1, 7–8, 142; as potential spokesperson 113; and Obama campaign 5–6, 98–9
Hitler, Adolf 100, 102, 116
Honneth, Axel 9
honour, Weber's definition of 66
Hsu, Dee 134
Human Rights Act 1998 (UK) 77

Iacocca, Lee 124
identity: communal 26–7; social 20, 90, 127 *see also* self-formation
I-ideal, Freudian *87*

image-management 12
imagined community: and celebrity 8; in mass communication era 81–2
impostors 28
individualism: historical emergence of 25–7, 29; increasing value of 16; and media narrative 110; and printing 31
individuality: as business asset 124; pseudo- 74; social production of 17
information: and attention 55; circulation of 6, 68
information industry 124
information societies 55, 58, 138
Internet: and celebrity 13, 39, 132, 134; fandom on 93; and public sphere 17
intimacy: long-distance *see* long-distance intimacy; mediated 84; public 33, 35
investors, institutional 122, **123**
Italy, origins of individualism in 25–6

Jackson, Michael 1, 53, 61
Javacheff, Christo and Jeanne-Claude 59
Jewel, John 15, 145n1
Jobs, Steve 129
Johnson, Jack 114
Johnson, Samuel 7, 37–8
Jolie, Angelina 99, 113–14
Jolson, Al 67, 107–8, 147n7
Jordan, Michael 7, 54, 83
the Josephine machine 11, 40, 50

Kardashian, Kim 134–5
Kaye, Danny 112
Kennedy, John F. 108

Lady Gaga 47, 133–4
Laemmle, Carl 6
Lamartine, Alphonse de 139
Langtry, Lillie 42, 48
Lasker, Albert 12–13, 107–8, 147n4
law, as sector of celebrity production 52
Lawrence, Florence 6
leader-celebrities: attention focused on 56–7, 110; authority of 100–1, 115–16; examples of 105–6; mobilization of popularity 117–18
leadership, romance of 124–5
Lely, Peter 37
Lennon, John: emotional resonance of 1; murder of 94, 96; posthumous earnings of 53; right to privacy of 77
Lincoln, Abraham: photography of 42, 67; use of public relations 7; and P. T. Barnum 46, 106

Lipsius, Justus 27–8
Liszt, Franz 42, 48, 59, 69–70, 139
long-distance intimacy: and celebrity 8,
  12; and fictional characters 85–6; in
  mass media 83–4; politics as 111
Louis XIV: appearance of 21; and
  expansion of nobility 30; performative
  power of 18, 102
Luther, Martin 28, 31

Madonna 8, 48
Major, John 112
management, celebrity in 13
Mao Zedong 127, 136–7
masculinity: media images of 84; and
  sports celebrity 52
mass communication *see* mass media
mass media: and attention-capital 80; in
  China 136; commercialization of 117;
  competition for attention in 132–3; and
  corporate organization 124–5;
  development of 8, 11, 39, 58, 70;
  dramatic narratives in 129–30;
  effect on political movements 104,
  109–11; images of business elite
  in 120; and individualism 16;
  'personalities' in *see* media
  personalities; and the public sphere
  17; and synopticism 71
Matthew effect 54–7, 70, 142, 146n6
Mazzini, Giuseppe 46, 104–5
McCain, John 5, 12, 98–9, 106
McDonald, Ronald 13, 129
media *see* mass media
media personalities 83, 85
Menken, Adah 48
meritocracy: and capitalism 121; and
  celebrity 4, 17; and individualism 29;
  and inequality 141–2; and modernity 25;
  and status systems 67
meta-branding 135
meta-celebrities 135
Mills, C. Wright 12, 62–6
misappropriation 76
Mitterand, François 78
modernity: and celebrity society 11; date
  of emergence 58; identification of 16;
  and tradition 24–5
monarchs: as actors 102; bodies of 30;
  relationship with court society 19–20;
  visibility of 20–1, 71
monarchy: absolute 17–18, 33–4, 82, 118;
  as celebrity 44–5; English presentation
  of 45

Monroe, Marilyn: associations with
  Kennedy 108; posthumous earnings of
  53; rights of publicity 76; Warhol's
  portraits of 58
Montez, Lola 11, 47–8, 70
Morgan, J.P. 100, 119–20
Mosley, Max 79
Motown 48

name economy 53
Napoleon I 43–4, 69–70, 102
Napoleon III 78
Nasser, Jacques 123
nationalism 83
nation-states, formation of 106
neoliberalism: and personal responsibility
  75, 92; and reality TV 72–3
Neo-Stoicism 27–8, 30
News of the World 79
newspapers: in industrial era 40; tabloid 90
Nike 54, 119, 129, 131
nobility *see* aristocracy
novelty 7, 25–6, 130

Obama, Barack: association with
  celebrities 109; attacked as celebrity
  5–6, 12, 98, 106; celebrity type of 112;
  projected image of 101; Twitter
  followers of 134
ordinariness, and celebrity *see* celebrities,
  as 'ordinary folk'

Paganini, Nicolò 42, 59, 70
Paine, Thomas 45
Palin, Sarah 12, 61, 99, 103, 112
panopticism 70, 72–4
panoramas 105
Pepys, Samuel 37
performativity 16, 18, 24, 28, 111
Perot, Ross 112
Perry, Katy 133–4
Petrarch 25–6, 28
philanthropy 112–13, 120–1
phone-hacking scandal 79
photography: introduction of 41–2;
  regulation of 78–9
Pickford, Mary 107–8, 112
Pitt, Brad 114
PLA (People's Liberation Army) 137
politicians: as celebrities 99–103, 110–12,
  111, 143; as 'real men', 106–7
politics: aesthetic dimensions of 111; and
  celebrity logic 45, 98, 103–4, 109;
  complexity reduction in 117–18;

environmental 113–14; importance of sector 51; personality in 44, 116–17, 139–41, 143; theatrical representation of 101

portraiture: and celebrity 37–8; and individualism 26; modern 58; under Elizabeth I 20–1

post-industrial society 55, 58

power: and attention 71–2; Foucault's analysis of 70–1; panoptic and synoptic 12; representation of 101–2; third face of 73

Presley, Elvis 53, 76, 94–5, 97

prestige, projection of 66

printing: impact of 30–2; liberalisation of 36–7; and public sphere 17

prisons 71

privacy, regulation of 75, 77–9

private life: in bourgeois society 3, 32; of celebrities 10, 37, 75–7, 79; in court society 20, 22; of firms 130; police regulation of 27

productivity, increasing 124–7

prostitution 64, 78

Protestantism: and celebrity 97; and modern social relations 3, 26; and printing 31; and theatre 33

pseudo-events 2, 6, 139

publicity: and consumer capitalism 63–4; experts in 12; right to 67, 76; as sector of celebrity production 52

public opinion: manipulation of 6; and promoting virtue 65–6

public relations: Boorstin's critique of 2, 7; and changing the conversation 120; evolution of 38–9; experts in 12

public sphere: and celebrity 8–10, 16; democratization of 47; evolution of 17, 32; and theatre 33, 36; in United States 63; women in 103

Queen of Hearts 45

radio, mediated intimacy in 83–4

rags-to-riches narrative 126, 128

reading clubs 24, 32, 37

Reagan, Ronald 99, 101, 108, 112

reality TV 72, 84–5, 114, 135

recognition: distribution of 29; self-accumulating character of 57; social theory of 8–10; universal 82, 115

Reformation 26, 31

religion, celebrity as replacement for 68, 96–7

representation: and reality 143; as sector of celebrity production 52

reputation, in court society 21–2

Reynolds, Joshua 11, 37–8

risk-capital 56

Rockefeller, John D. 119–21

Rousseau, Jean-Jacques: as celebrity 4–5, 13, 38; depicted with Franklin and Voltaire 103

Rubin, Jerry 109–10

Russel, Lillian 107–8

Ruth, Babe 7, 49

Sachs, Jeffrey 114

sacredness 68

Sanders, Colonel 13, 128–9

Schmidt, Steven 98

scholarship *see* academia

Schwarzenegger, Arnold 99, 101, 108–9, 112

secondary attachment 94

self: as commodity 103; enterprising 75, 126; presentation of *see* self-presentation; private and public 3, 97; technologies of the 74–5

self-confidence, and recognition 9

self-discipline *see* discipline

self-display *see* self-presentation

self-evaluation, and evaluation of celebrities 72

self-formation: and celebrity 5, 73, 95–6, 143–4; Chinese narratives of 127; and cultural governance 141; and fandom 92–4; and generalised other 91; and virtual characters 12, 96; in the workplace 73

self-observation, in court society 21, 24

self-presentation: of artists 59; conscious organization of 28, 39, 46; of Elizabeth I 20; of film fans 93; of heroes 7; in job market 73; of politicians 101; and the theatre 33

self-representation 50, 93

sexual ambiguity 43–4

Shakespeare, William 7, 28, 31, 34–5, 95

Sherlockians 94–5

Shooting the Past 1

Siddons, Sarah 35, 43

simulacra 47, 83, 133

Sinatra, Frank 53, 108

sincerity 28–9, 89, 99

soccer 51–2

social media 13, 134, 140

social mobility 4, 16–17, 25, 126

social networks 8, 20, 61, 81–2, 86–7
social order, maintaining 27, 33–4, 65
social technology 24
social worlds, real and artificial 84
society: celebritization of 5, 15, 138; weak
   and strong ties in 82
solidarity, social 9, 68
Southwest Airlines 130–1
Spears, Britney 53, 90, 98–9, 134
sport, importance of sector 51
sports stars: early examples of 49; growth
   in importance of 50–2; and identity
   formation 83
Stalin, Josef 102, 116
stalking 82, 85, 93
Stanley, Henry Morton 70
star system 36, 65, 139–41
Star Trek 94–5
'Star Wars kid' 147–8n2
state-formation 8, 17, 139
status, Weber's definition of 66
status systems 66–8
Stephanie of Monaco 78
Sting (Gordon Sumner) 114
subjectivity 3, 8, 72, 75
Sugar, Alan 126
surveillance 12, 71–2, 74, 77
Symbionese Liberation Army 147n8
symmetrical esteem 9
synopticism 71–4, 143

talents, parable of 146n6
television: mediated intimacy in 83–4;
   panopticism and synopticism in 72; and
   public discourse 74; reality *see* reality
   TV
televisual experience 85
theatre: and celebrity 11, 57; elite embrace
   of 32–4; in industrial era 40; and
   political power 101–2; women in 34–6
theatre states 18
Thomas, Dave 128
Thumb, General Tom 46, 67, 106
transparency 29
Trump, Donald 50, 126
Twitter 93, 134–5

United Kingdom, privacy law in 77
United Nations 112–13

United States: celebrity production in 46;
   industrialization of 40
universities: and celebrity 51; performance
   measurement of 142 (*see also* academia)
urbanization 16–17, 26, 40

Victoria, Queen: as celebrity 12, 106;
   philanthropy of 112–13; photography of
   42; public support for 44–5; and P. T.
   Barnum 46
VLC (virtual leader construct) 128–9

Wang Shi 127–8
Warhol, Andy 13, 53, 58–60, 132
Washington, George 38, 69
Watson, Emma 114
Weber, Max: on charisma 117; on
   evolution of social relations 3, 26; as
   object of publication 60, 135; on status
   and charisma 66–9
Wedgewood, Josiah 103
Welch, Jack 122–3, 126
Whig party 38, 103
White, Pearl 107–8
Whitfield, Lynn 50
Wilders, Geert 117
Wilhelm II of Germany 99–100, 106
Winchell, Walter 12, 63
Winfrey, Oprah: Book Club 6, 114;
   earnings of 53; importance of 50;
   leveraging own celebrity 135; and
   Australia 58; and confessional TV 145n6
women: achieving celebrity status 47; as
   actresses 11, 34–5; and Charles Fox's
   campaign 103; as film viewers 93; in
   French salons 23; images of 64–5; in
   politics 103–4; social roles of 92
Woods, Tiger 54, 83, 114
workplace: identity in 72–3, 82; inspiration
   in 124

x-factor 73, 126, 141

Yahoo! 130
Yao Chen 134
YouTube 132–3, 135

Zeta-Jones, Catherine 79
Žižek, Slavoj 135